Trave ~~~~
Mama

Mothers, Mothering, and Travel

edited by Charlotte Beyer, Janet MacLennan,
Dorsía Smith Silva, and Marjorie Tesser

DEMETER

Travellin' Mama
Mothers, Mothering, and Travel
Edited by Charlotte Beyer, Janet MacLennan, Dorsía Smith Silva,
and Marjorie Tesser

Copyright © 2019 Demeter Press

Demeter Press
140 Holland Street West
P. O. Box 13022
Bradford, ON L3Z 2Y5
Tel: (905) 775-9089
Email: info@demeterpress.org
Website: www.demeterpress.org

Demeter Press logo based on the sculpture "Demeter" by Maria-Luise Bodirsky www.keramik-atelier.bodirsky.de

Printed and Bound in Canada

Front cover image: Grandfailure (istockphoto).
Front cover artwork: Michelle Pirovich
Typesetting: Michelle Pirovich

Library and Archives Canada Cataloguing in Publication
Title: Travellin' mama : mothers, mothering, and travel
Editors: Marjorie Tesser, Dorsía Smith Silva, Janet MacLennan, Charlotte Beyer.
Names: Tesser, Marjorie, editor. | Silva, Dorsía Smith, editor. | MacLennan, Janet, editor. | Beyer, Charlotte, 1965- editor.
Description: Includes bibliographical references.
Identifiers: Canadiana 20190050330 | ISBN 9781772581799 (softcover)
Subjects: LCSH: Mothers—Travel. | LCSH: Women travelers. | LCSH: Motherhood. | LCSH: Travel.
Classification: LCC G156.5.W66 T73 2019 | DDC 910.85/2—dc23

MIX
Paper from
responsible sources
FSC
www.fsc.org
FSC® C004071

This book is dedicated to Holly Anderson,
one of the book's contributors,
who passed away due to illnesses caused
by her volunteer service at the
9/11 Ground Zero World Trade Center site.

Acknowledgments

Grateful thanks to Andrea O'Reilly, editor-in-chief at Demeter Press, for her continued support and encouragement throughout the length of this book project. The entire editorial team at Demeter also receive our heartfelt thanks for their assistance with the manuscript and preparation of this book for publication.

We are deeply thankful to the contributors of *Travellin' Mama*. Your work has not only shaped this book but has added diverse scholarly and creative voices to the essential conversations about maternal travel that are long overdue. Together, we have undertaken a journey of discovery into the many creative, affective, psychological, social, ethical, literary, postcolonial, and legal aspects of motherhood and travel.

Lastly, we thank our family and friends for their love, support, and encouragement.

Contents

Chapter 20

Chapter 21

Notes on the Contributors

Into the World around Us and into the World Within

Charlotte Beyer, Janet MacLennan, Dorsía Smith Silva, and Marjorie Tesser

*I soon realized that no journey carries one far unless,
as it extends into the world around us, it goes an equal
distance into the world within— (Lillian Smith, 194)*

Imagining Maternal Travel

The author Pamela Michael says this of her experience of travelling with her adult son: "we are never more nakedly ourselves than when removed from routine and familiar comforts" (50). Travel has the capacity to allow us to perceive ourselves and the world afresh. However, when confronted with cultural narratives concerning travel, mothers are frequently missing or omitted. In their volume *A Mother's World: Journeys of the Heart* (1998), Marybeth Bond and Pamela Michael question this silence surrounding representations of maternal travel and inquire, "*Don't women with children travel?*" (xv). Referring to the proliferation of books and other materials on the topic of travel, Bond and Michael point out that few of these writings focus specifically on mothers travelling with or without their children, or performing in caring roles. They conclude that "This omission—this whole over-looked, rich realm of travel experience—implies that having children and journeying (beyond traditional vacations) are incompatible" (Bond and Michael, xvi). The ability of travel to confront us with our innermost complexities and, at the same time, to place mothering in a whole new light is a central dimension of our book, *Travellin' Mama: Mothers, Mothering, and Travel.*

Organized around a number of thematic sections, this book explores compelling and resonant ideas governing the representation of maternal travel, such as adventure, relocation, identity, discovery, work, culture, and exigency. These broad themes serve to encapsulate the compelling experiences, representations, and issues treated in the various creative and scholarly contributions this book contains. *Travellin' Mama: Mothers, Mothering, and Travel* hopes to appeal to a wide and mixed audience, as it incorporates creative responses, autoethnography, and scholarly analyses, among others—all centred on the overarching theme of motherhood and travel. Therefore, for the purposes of this book, we treat the term "travel" as inclusive and as encompassing a range of historical, social, cultural, postcolonial, and geographical circumstances, including forms of forced travel and travel compelled by various economic circumstances. The word "travel" broadly means to journey (Oxford Living Dictionaries), and it is in this wider and inclusive sense that we use the term in this book. Our primary concern as editors is to enable the stories, reflections, and studies of maternal travel to be told rather than to seek to limit or exclude certain types of investigations from consideration. The subject of the representation of maternal travel is still growing, expanding, and in process. New perspectives are continually emerging, as historical travel narratives by women continue to be uncovered and forms of forced travel are further investigated. With this book, we hope to contribute in important ways to this growing body of creative and critical work on motherhood studies in general and maternal travel in particular.

Mothers and Travel: Context, History, and the Tradition

The image of the travelling mother disrupts traditional cultural perceptions of travel and the location of motherhood. Li Miao Lovett, one of the contributors to this book, explores this contradiction in her piece "Waterfalls in the Dark." She explains how, on the one hand, mothers may yearn to explore farther horizons because "the wilderness tests our boundaries ... we really don't know what is beyond that glowing lantern in a deserted parking lot." On the other hand, Lovett argues, mothers may recoil from travel, feeling that their primary responsibility lies in nurturing and looking after others in a domestic setting. This impulse towards maternal stasis, she states, must be resisted: "I must not be the only mom who wants to reclaim my earlier self sooner than retirement, when it might be too late, and all we want to do is keep the empty nest warm and stocked with food to entice our grown children back home." Such contradictions reflect the continued reluctance in our culture to relinquish the long-lasting popular association of mothers with the private and domestic sphere—a sphere largely incompatible with activities requiring agency and self-determination, such as travel. The critic Kristi Siegel comments on the omission of representations of maternal travel in popular culture and asks us to consider "the vast number of women's journeys that have never been written —journeys of flight, exile, expatriation, homelessness; journeys by women without the means to document their travel; and journeys whose records have been lost or ignored" ("Intersections," 2). The act of unearthing such "lost or ignored" stories and records of travel, both forced and by choice, and of giving voice to overlooked or marginalized depictions of maternal travel are key aims of this book, while recognizing that much more work, including academic scholarship, is required on the topic of motherhood and travel.

In their volume of travel writing by various international authors, Bond and Michael explore the subject's multifaceted aspects. Their work seeks to connect motherhood and travel and to demonstrate that these are not mutually exclusive but rather they are both essential to knowing and sharing our world. However, as they state, "being a mother can render a woman invisible in society, can limit her career choices and advancement, and even diminish her own sense of herself. Nowhere is this more apparent than in the realm of travel literature" (xv). The different texts in *Travellin' Mama* investigate these and other issues by foregrounding the impossible contradictions within patriarchy's constructions and expectations of mothers, and by celebrating the strategies that mothers devise, individually or collectively, to break free from such restrictions mentally, psychologically, physically, and creatively. Our book explores creative, reflective, and scholarly investigations of maternal travel in all its complexity while acknowledging that mothers frequently travel in difficult and/or traumatic circumstances. Mothers often endure forced travel, as in the case of refugee mothers or asylum-seeking mothers. A number of socioeconomic conditions affect travel by both limiting it and forcing it, in the case, for example, of migrant worker mothers or mothers travelling in order to access abortion. A number of chapters in this book address various forms of forced maternal travel, both in historical and present-day cultural contexts. These investigations into forced maternal travel, together with the impact of a range of socioeconomic factors on maternal travel, form part of emerging academic fields of enquiry. Coupled with the use of feminist, postcolonial, inter-disciplinary, and/or autoethnographic critical approaches, *Travellin' Mama* uncovers new and important academic and creative areas for further exploration.

The contradictions inherent in maternal travel are exacerbated by myriad factors— social, cultural, and religious. Cultural narratives contribute to creating certain ideas and representations, including of mothers and the types of narratives and roles they appear in. For example, fairy tales often use plots centred on a heroic individual going into the world on a dangerous and exciting adventure, thereby gaining a sense of self-identity, accomplishment, and self-determination (see also Canepa 117-19). Fairy tales featuring such individuation motifs include Jack and the Beanstalk, Little Red Riding Hood, and Hansel and Gretel, but they do not tend to depict mothers travelling or engaging actively with mobility. Such traditional plotlines serve to underline the perception that mothers are characters left behind at home when children and menfolk go out into the world. However, the works in this book move beyond such prescribed narratives and depictions; this book aims instead to present motherhood and travel as intrinsically connected while striving to exemplify the complexities of maternal travel. Siegel observes the significant role that travel writing plays: "Travel writing shapes and influences the way we understand the world" ("Intersections" 11). It is crucial, now and in the future, that mothers who travel are regarded as part of this understanding. Achieving this aim begins by reimagining our cultural narratives and representations of travel and the women who undertake it.

Within historical traditions, depictions of mothers travelling have often been fraught with omissions, silences, and even taboos. These issues are closely connected to the ways in which travel by women, especially maternal travel, has been perceived historically. Siegel explains that "prior to the enlightenment, the meaning of the word *travel* was closer to the Old French word *traveiller* which meant 'to labor,' and this original sense of the word reflected the arduous nature early journeys often entailed" ("Women's Travel" 57). Siegel discusses "the rhetoric of peril," which historically underpinned the prohibition against women travelling, and asks, "is the belief that women are too weak to travel alone (or unescorted) socially constructed or biologically determined?" ("Women's Travel" 61). She demonstrates how from the eighteenth century onwards, women's bodies began to be regarded as pathological, resulting in domestic sphere confinement. She argues that "it was not only proper for a woman to stick to home and hearth but also a matter of safety: a woman's inherently diseased body required the care of her husband and the constant surveillance of (male) physicians" ("Women's Travel" 61). Such assumptions contributed to the broadly held cultural view that it would not be safe for women to travel, especially unaccompanied or without a chaperone.

These prohibitive views put severe restrictions on female mobility well into the twentieth century. At this point, discursive and social attempts at controlling and limiting female mobility rested on motherhood, the pregnant female body, and medicalization. In the twentieth century, the pathologization of the pregnant female body required constant medical surveillance as well as the prohibition for pregnant women to travel, especially abroad. Conforming to female expectations meant obeying her doctor, remaining at home. and not travelling anywhere (Siegel, "Women's Travel" 62-63). These constraints on female mobility, especially maternal travel, are evident in mid-twentieth century narratives celebrating male freedom, self-determination, and travel, such as Jack Kerouac's novel *On the Road* (1957). Commenting on Kerouac's novel, and the role and representation of women within it, Siegel argues that "women function as objects of conquests, rather than as mobile subjects" ("Intersections" 4). Mothers in *On the Road* are presented mainly as carers providing a nurturing and secure hinterland for tired hipsters taking refuge from their lives of excess on the road or as "love them and leave them" figures whose role it is to stay back and wait for their lovers to return (or not) from their road adventures. Bond and Michael argue that "most women in travel literature 'leave behind' motherhood, children, and family ties when they travel" ("Introduction" xvi). However, the contributors in this book reject the restrictive image of the fixed and static mother as well as the passive and obedient mother. Instead, they explore the personal qualities and attributes of mothers in travel literature, such as agency, self-determination, and autonomy. Importantly, being a travelling mother can lead to the formation of new female friendships, closer relationships between mothers and daughters, and new alliances forged between women—a powerful act of solidarity and sisterhood (Bond and Michael, xvi). Such expressions and representations of female solidarity are important dimensions conveyed in the creative and scholarly pieces in our book.

Motherhood and Travel: Contrasting Contemporary Perspectives

The phrase "travellin' mama" originally derives from the blues singer Mississippi Joe Calicott's song "Travellin' Mama Blues" from 1930, but it has also served to inspire women writing in the contemporary period about their experiences of motherhood and travel. The blogosphere— an easily accessible and diverse contemporary online media—provides a useful format for mothers to explore their travelling experiences. Mothers have used this relatively new form to write back to traditional travel narratives that have excluded them for a variety of reasons; they have embraced the possibility of reaching out and communicating with wider audiences. The following presents a snapshot of a few contemporary motherhood and travel blogs and web-based content that contextualize the ways in which motherhood and travel are discussed and represented in contemporary popular culture. These texts serve as illustrations of the myriad ways in which mothers reflect on and depict their experiences of both travelling and mothering.[1]

Nancy Harper, an Ontario-based self-proclaimed "travel junkie," is a prominent example of how a mother can build an ongoing narrative and context around her experiences as a travelling mother. Her book and accompanying travel blog, both called *Travellin' Mama*, aim to inspire mothers to challenge and break from the norms and expectations seeking to define them. In her description of her book on the blog, Harper dedicates the book to "every North American mom who dares forge her own way—when all around her are the suburban ideals of keeping up and conforming—there are a zillion others who will consistently say: 'I'd love to do this or that but I can't because of the kids.'" For Harper, a mother travelling with her children is a way of demonstrating the values of nonconformity and of being another kind of mother—not a "soccer mom" but a mother capable of "ditching the routine and tossing out the play-by-the-rules parenting playbook," as she puts it in the press release for her book. For Harper, her depiction of motherhood and travel is a narrative-in-progress; it is a constantly developing and changeable mode of being rather than a linear and predictable process.

In her article "On Motherhood and Travel," Kate Mason, founder of the communications consultancy Hedgehog + Fox, writes of her experiences of maternal travel through different stages of motherhood and starting with very early pregnancy. She states that "the first time I travelled as a mother, it was a secret." Travelling as a mother and being separated from her child is difficult and is fraught with feelings of ambivalence. As Mason states, "I have loved being away, and yet feel a simultaneous compulsion to return." She concludes that her outlook on travel has changed now that she is a mother, pinpointing an ambivalence which many mothers who travel for professional reasons will recognize. Another blog author, Katrina Woznicki, describes the sense of emotional ambivalence and toil of travelling as a mother when she leaves behind her tween daughter. In her blog post titled "On Motherhood and Travel," Woznicki assesses the importance of independence versus her need to be there for her daughter through all of her everyday experiences during her years of growing up. She explains her continuing desire to travel and her ongoing attempt to reconcile this need with her mothering: "I have this constant tug to keep going, to see places where I know no one, to get on a train, a boat, a plane and go forward.... Wanderlust and motherhood are a tricky mix. I'm not sure I'm doing a great job at either, yet I swing back and forth between the two, perhaps one inspiring the other." Sherry Ott uses her blog to share fascinating photography and travel writing in a unique way that appeals to a contemporary audience. However, in one of her reflective blogposts, she poignantly discusses her decision not to be a mother, the importance of children in her extended family, and the priority she places on her ability to travel unimpeded. Ott describes the divide she perceives between motherhood on the one hand and travel and self-determination on the other. For her, it is a clear choice between the two rather than a case of uniting both identities and lives. She describes motherhood as a "foreign concept." She explains how she has arrived at being the person she is now and how she chose not to be a mother—for her, travel means refusing to be somebody's mother. Ott suggests that her own childless travelling life could be perceived as a kind of journey along the "less travelled" path to echo Robert Frost, and she concludes her essay with "sometimes it leaves me a bit baffled, wondering how in the world I have ended up on the small path that I am on and not on the interstate of motherhood and familydom. I guess I just figure that someone has to take the path less travelled." Ott's essay exemplifies the choice some women feel they have to make—between travelling and having children of their own.

The blogposts examined here tend to treat maternal travel as a matter of choice or as part of a job and career, even a marketing ploy. However, there are myriad circumstances, some of which are documented in this book, in which travel is not a choice made by mothers as consumers or customers but rather one enforced by difficult, dangerous, and traumatic circumstances. Maternal travel and mobility may be fraught with danger or condemnation; it is influenced by intersecting categories of oppression, such as race/ethnicity, religion, class, sexuality, and age, which has been the case historically as well as culturally, as Siegel demonstrates: "Historically, travel writing participated in the colonial realm by disseminating the goals of Empire: stories of 'faraway lands' were crucial in establishing the unequal, unjust, and exploitative relations of colonial rule" (1). Siegel's observation calls attention to the complex issues surrounding colonialism and imperialism, which travel writing has frequently interrogated and problematised. Portrayals of maternal travel can also be used to highlight problems of access and inequality in our society, disparities that mean that travelling as a mother can be complicated and fraught with practical difficulty when society fails to be inclusive. The scholar Honor Nicholls investigates the issues encountered by mothers who travel with disabled children: "Mothers had to manage travel often on their own, which sometimes placed them, and the child, at physical risk. Social travel for the child and mother was avoided. Contact with family and friends by mothers, and vice versa, are consequently reduced, adding to the isolation of mothers" (301).

When motherhood and travel are combined in such circumstances, navigating the practicalities of travel can literally seem to be like "going between worlds," to echo the phrase from Nicholls' article. It follows that this "going between worlds" is far from straightforward. Rather, travelling as a mother and mothering while travelling can make profound demands on the individual woman—demands that go far beyond traditional representations of travel—and can open up spaces for unheard stories of maternal travel; stories that certainly need to be told.

Maternal Travel and Global Perspectives

Central aspects of examining maternal travel include the economic factors driving travel, forced travel, migration, and flight from persecution and war. Depictions of such maternal travel are crucial to gaining a complex understanding of the pressures brought to bear on mothers; they have the capacity to challenge and transform debates around motherhood and mobility. In her book *The Global Politics of Contemporary Travel Writing* (2006), the critic Debbie Lisle refers to the "transformative potential" of travel writing (xi). She furthermore argues that "travel writing has the potential to re-imagine the world in ways that do not simply regurgitate the status quo or repeat a nostalgic longing for Empire" (xi). *Mothers, Mothering, and Globalization* (2017), edited by Dorsía Smith Silva, Laila Malik, and Abigail L. Palko, explores how mothers must navigate through a climate in which they travel as a result of global forces and social problems. In this regard, travellin' mamas may become transnational mothers who may mother "at a distance"—"an arrangement of motherhood that has evolved in direct response to a situation where a large number of immigrant others find themselves geographically separated from their children over long periods of time" (Firth and Lavery 89). Although it is largely due to the demands that increased labour needs place upon the recruitment of women, this arrangement has complex implications. One significant aspect is that transnational motherhood challenges the conceptualization that mothering is strictly linked to the biological mother: "The idea of biological mothers raising their own children is widely held but it is also widely broken at both ends of the class spectrum. Wealthy elites have always relied on others—nannies, governesses, and boarding schools—to raise their children, while poor families often rely on kin and 'other mothers'" (Hondagneu-Sotelo and Avila 557). In this extended kin network of "othermothers,"[2] the definition and relationship between mothers and children are expanded to include nonbiological mothers and women who become mothers through their emotional attachments and responsibilities as caretakers.

Another important consideration when studying the subject of motherhood and travel is that transnational mothers may have greater access to financial means and, therefore, can send remittances back to their homeland. In doing so, their children usually have better opportunities to receive schooling, basic goods, shelter, clothing, and medical services. At the same time, however, transnational mothers and their children may experience social and emotional hardships. Since they are geographically separated from their children, transnational mothers may worry about their children's emotional and physical care when left in the hands of family members or "other mothers." As Melanie Nicholson states in her study on transnational migrant women, "transnational mothers are living a particularly difficult form of shared mothering, a form dictated by their arduous journeys, their long separations from their children, and their relegation to the lowest rungs of the economic and social ladder" (14). In addition, they may experience guilt that they had to leave their children behind and feel pressure that they are mothering at a distance—a form of mothering that is complicated by the oppressive patriarchal constructions that so-called good mothers take care of their own biological children's emotional and physical needs. For the children of transnational mothers, tensions may arise from being separated from their mothers, particularly regarding depriving them from "that primary maternal-child bond" (Levitt 76). While these children acknowledge the receipt of goods and opportunities from their transnational mother's hard work and sacrifice, they often miss their mothers and may experience loss, guilt, anger, and depression.

The good mommy versus bad mommy dialogue may also occur when mothers occasionally travel for business purposes. According to psychologist Laura Kastner, "problems arise" when "Mom talks about feeling guilty" (qtd. in Weed). "As much as we would like to believe that gender roles have changed quite a bit in our society," explains Patricia Stevens, president of the International Association of Marriage and Family Counselors, "moms still spend more time with their kids than dads and can feel very guilty and conflicted about being away for business and leaving their spouse in charge" (qtd. in Koss-Feder 43). Conflicts may also arise because mothers who travel still feel the weight of completing household duties and managing the emotional labour for the household while travelling. In *The Managed Heart: Commercialization of Human Feeling* (1983), Arlie Russell Hochschild coins the term "emotional labour" as work done (mostly by women) in the service industry to make clients feel cared for. Genna Hartley succinctly summarizes the idea in "Women Aren't Nags—We're Just Fed Up" as women being "the manager of the household," which "was a lot of thankless work." And all of which, more importantly, can direct women like Amy Kossoff Smith, the founder of a parenting website, to leave "a printed itinerary of all the carpools, sports practices, and games, baby-sitter hours and anything else her husband might need" when she travels (qtd. in Weed). Similarly, a woman named Lauren Fix "used to store premade meals in the freezer and refrigerator for her children and husband" when she travelled for business engagements (qtd. in Weed).

This tension for mothers who travel can also lead to liminality, argues Christena Nippert-Eng, a sociologist at the Illinois Institute of Technology in Chicago, who has experienced "business-trip angst" when she leaves her two children. "Being a liminal is a state of being betwixt and between," says Nippert-Eng (qtd. in Koss-Feder 42). For working mothers who travel they may be between home and work: "They're not a home at home, surrounded by their families, nor are they fully embedded in the normal workplace" (Nippert-Eng qtd. in Koss-Feder 42). Moreover, Nippert-Eng finds that travelling mothers may feel liminality because they are "sitting on a plane" and "feeling extracted from that I'm going to bed when my family's coming home from school" (qtd. in Koss-Feder 42-43). Given the context in which travelling mothers may be caught in the binds of feeling "neither here nor there," we must examine the ways in which travelling mothers feel empowered and reject the emotional burdens within certain paradigms of mothering and motherhood. In doing so, travelling mothers can travel for business with or without their children and feel a sense of agency that their narratives will represent strong empowered mothers, who, in turn, will engender strong empowered children.

Overview of *Travellin' Mama*

Travellin' Mama is divided into interrelated thematic sections. Each explores and examines central themes and ideas in relation to motherhood and travel, and mix scholarly essays with creative and reflective writing. As editors, we made the decision to avoid being overly prescriptive in terms of the connections and links between the different sections and the individual works; rather, we trust the reader to make their own connections through active engagement in the reading process. Scholarly essays are interwoven with creative or reflective pieces to provide a structural underpinning for the reader's engagement with the book's nonlinear and multifaceted exploration of maternal travel. Rather than presenting a series of disparate moments, these diverse representations of motherhood and travel contribute to creating a more expansive and complex idea of motherhood and travel. In other words, each text in this book is like a piece in a quilt— together, they make sense because they form part of a larger creation. And what binds them together is their focus on motherhood and travel.

The book is interdisciplinary in its approach, as it uses perspectives from a variety of academic fields and types of investigation engaging with maternal travel. These range from children's literature, migration, and anthropology to poetry, history, autobiographical writing, food studies, contemporary Irish abortion travel, and mountain climbing. Through this approach and thematic organization, *Travellin' Mama* confidently assumes that creative writing itself is a form of academic inquiry that uses linguistic expression and exploration as a means of research (see also Skains). The loosely associative and suggestive linking of creative, reflective, and scholarly pieces demonstrates a crucial point that this book makes: the significance of the personal voice and perspective in both scholarship and creative writing is experiential, and, therefore, important and valuable rather than anecdotal and trivial. Contributors using autoethnographic methods demonstrate how analysis and reflection involving the writing subject in a personal way can help create new ways of describing and understanding motherhood and travel, posing fascinating questions and challenges for maternal scholarship. In the context of using autoethnography in her research into the journey of becoming a mother, Brooke Haugh defines autoethnography as "hybrid in character because it blends an individual's personal story with his or her scholarly story." She establishes that "the purpose of analytic research is not just to provide an insiders' perspective or evoke an emotional response but also to gain insight into a broader set of social phenomena" (Haugh 2016). Interestingly, Haugh uses the word "journey" to describe her own lived process of becoming a mother and learning how to breastfeed her baby, which echoes the symbolic aspects of travel and inner journeying central to the maternal experience and creates a conceptual link between autoethnography and travel.

Involving the self through autoethnographic approaches reflects the notion of venturing "into the world within us." The phrase suggests that maternal travel is as much as a reflective process of inward journeying as it is an outward physical travelling of the body. Therefore, the different sections in this book mix creative and autoethnographic work with academic essays to demonstrate that not only can these distinct and different modes of exploration stand alongside one another, but they can also enhance and strengthen the book's examination of maternal travel. This particular scholarly approach allows the book to use creative and imaginative represent-ations of dimensions of maternal travel to generate suggestive links and associations to academic and scholarly discussions, thus enabling processes of research and reflection to be understood in new and complex ways. As we shall see, the different sections in the book initiate conversations and speak to each other; they connect, echo, or expand on ideas and themes, thereby creating a fuller and more complex picture of maternal travel through their different approaches and perspectives. This complex approach, in turn, is crucial to reimagining our cultural narratives and representations of travel and the mothers who undertake it.

The opening section in *Travellin' Mama* explores the topic of relocation, tackling increasingly pertinent topics in relation to maternal travel, such as immigration and the problems of assimilation. Mothers may travel not temporarily but actually relocate, so as to escape hardship or to obtain economic or educational advantages. In doing so, they are often subject to difficult events and circumstances. They may have to migrate without other family members or without adequate preparation or resources, and those relocating can encounter hardship and danger. Upon arrival, they may have to deal with the judgments or prejudices of officials and residents in their new location. In some ways, relocation journeys can be understood as analogous to the "journey" of mothering. Each experience requires ingenuity, vigilance, and continual adaptation to novel circumstances; each is sometimes monitored and subject to exigencies and rules beyond one's control. Kimmika Williams-Witherspoon depicts, in poetry, an entrance interview with an immigration officer in "Day 2: 22 January 2106, Immigration: London." In this short conversation poem, the attitudes and prejudices of the officer and the ambivalent, fearful feelings of the mother who accompanies her exchange student son are implicit. Williams-Witherspoon's evocative poem demonstrates the difficulties travelling mothers encounter in navigating immigration laws and regulations and dealing with the individuals who enforce those laws. In "Travelling the Same Road: The Parallel Journeys of Motherhood and Migration," Karem Roitman investigates how both motherhood and migration disrupt doxic knowledge—internalized structures of belief systems—by presenting the individual with new experiences that challenge habitual patterns. Both motherhood and migration require adaptations, which affect the individual's conception of self and others. The author asserts that those undergoing both states simultaneously may experience greater vulnerability and require additional support.

The next section of *Travellin' Mama* explores adventure and presents a series of creative and imaginative engagements with maternal travel. Some mothers who travel seek encounters with different worlds. Through travel, they go through physically demanding and unforeseen experiences, encounters with other civilizations and cultures, and a freedom from the everyday routines of their normal lives. Mothers who travel with children are required to modify their own activities in fulfilling their concomitant role as nurturer-guardian to mitigate or moderate the impact of the stresses of travel on their children's routines and safety. However, they also model for their children the concept that motherhood need not require relinquishing adventure and that childhood, too, does not disqualify one from such opportunities. As we shall see, mothers and children participate in a shared set of rich experiences to the ultimate benefit of each.

In her creative prose piece "Travelling Light," Nicola Waldron details the challenges of lengthy transatlantic air travel with a lively fourteen-month-old with specificity and humour. Handling plane delays as well as interactions with other passengers and crew, controlling a restless child, managing trips to the lavatory, and breastfeeding are some of the issues Waldron discusses. The piece articulates the practical logistics of travelling with a very young child with both hilarity and truth.

Li Miao Lovett's "Waterfalls in the Dark" focuses on the author's life-changing experiences hiking the Appalachian Trail as a young solo traveller, and contrasts them with her later trip to Yosemite with her young son. Her earlier trip combined moments of wonder with those of danger and discomfort; it tested her and led her to surmount insecurities and fears. In contrast, as she describes, her travel with her child was much more circumscribed.

"Annapurna Epiphany" by Dena Moes recounts the author's yearlong journey through India and Nepal with her family. This work of creative prose depicts a five-day trek the family experienced, hiking to elevations of up to ten thousand feet. Moes describes the mountain setting intimately, and she details the advantages of travel for mother and children alike—expansive vistas, cross-cultural encounters, and learning opportunities—and the challenges—infection, altitude sickness, and balky teenagers. An unplanned solo moment for the author leads to a personal epiphany before she reconnects with her family, who are safe and happily engaged.

Jane Frank's poem "Long Haul Flight After a Visit to the Dali Museum" combines evocative imagery with a meditation on travel as an opportunity for both observation ("(o)utside") and reflection and reconciliation of competing exigencies and concerns ("inside"). In her poem "Mexican Restaurants in Deutschland," Vanessa Couto Johnson highlights the feeling of discovery in travel—the almost giddy pleasure of odd juxtapositions and random connections—and the sheer joy of experience outside one's usual realm. Katharyn Howd Machan's poem, "As I Travel to Key West," reflects on the freedom of a middle-aged woman traveller journeying alone, without children. She employs the metaphor of comfortable and festive attire to evoke the feelings of expansiveness and self-sufficiency that travel engenders.

The next section about identity explores themes and ideas connecting selfhood and travel. In literature, the "hero's journey" is one in which she strikes out alone and, in doing so, becomes an agent for change and ultimately achieves his destiny. The hero's journey for mothers may be undertaken with or without their children. Mothers who travel with their families forge change not only in their own lives but also in their children's. Mothers who travel without their families may bear them emotionally and experience feelings of guilt, loss, or liminality. Travel of any kind provides the opportunity of learning about and defining oneself in the process of encountering the other.

Critics have rarely concerned themselves with the topic of motherhood and travel in children's literature. Charlotte Beyer's essay, "'No Ship Is Going to Sink with My Family on It': Motherhood and Travel in Jackie French's Children's Novel *How the Finnegans Saved the Ship*" seeks to redress this absence. Her essay examines the portrayal of mothers and travel in Australian author Jackie French's 2001 children's novel *How the Finnegans Saved the Ship*. Jackie French is a widely known children's author and was the 2014-2015 Australian Children's Laureate. Examining French's depiction of an Irish family led by the formidable mother, Mrs Finnegan, and their voyage to Australia in 1913 to start a new life, Beyer argues that children's literature plays an important role in portraying and shaping but also transforming our understanding of both maternal identities and travel.

Melanie Duckworth's essay "'Everyone Wants to Escape from Their Own Lives Sometimes, Don't They?': Motherhood, the Train to Edinburgh, and the work of Kathleen Jamie" interweaves a scholarly consideration of Kathleen Jamie's poetry and prose with a reflection on the author's own journeys through England and Scotland with her two small children. The author's travels with her own children are limited, which impacts her professionally, and when undertaken, her travels are circumscribed by her children's needs and wants. Jamie's travel was done without children, as detailed in her books, but the poet also claims childbirth and childrearing as subject matter in her poetry and essays, and recognizes motherhood's kinship with the natural world. Thus, even when escape is physical, mothering appears in Jamie's observations and work.

The next section in *Travellin' Mama* is about discovery and explores how in travel, mothers not only encounter personal change but may also experience vicariously the lives and journeys of others. Reconstructing and replicating journeys of one's forebears can provide insight into the influences of history and geography on past privations and migrations; these can also affect subsequent generations. Viewing different countries first hand provides an intimacy of experience that secondary exposure lacks.

Titled "Voices from the Oublie: Ghostings of Dutch and Portuguese Colonization" May Joseph's excerpt is part travel memoir, part maritime sea log, and part autoethnography. It is a journey of personal excavations of the author's grandmothers and great-grandmothers based on rumour, confessions, and the colonial archives of the Dutch East India Company at The Hague, Netherlands. Following their ghosts, the author has created site-specific performances along the Dutch and Portuguese sea routes of the sixteenth century that transformed the Malabar Coast as a form of purging the violence of the past. What began as a historical excursion into the archaeological past of the Malabar region of South India morphed into a project in montage history, multiple moments mapping a particular region's fractured social imaginary through the self-ethnography of one woman traveller.

The poem "Twilight" by C.M. Clark considers the more sobering side of travel and reveals the ways travel confronts us with the extreme conditions existing in the world, such as having to undertake an arduous journey, impelled by the urgency of a child's hunger. "Pomegranates in Tehran" is a short prose poem by Laura Foley about the contradictions and unsettling juxtapositions evident in a trip to Iran, where the official politics are subverted by the hospitality and welcome of local individuals.

In the next section on work, mothers who participate in volunteer work, research and fieldwork, and creative work away from their home base explore the interplay of the roles of worker, traveller, and parent. Although the multiple requirements can create frustration and a feeling of being torn, these travellin' mamas mediate and negotiate between competing interests to accommodate work, children, and their own personal encounters with the remote location.

Anne Hamilton volunteered overseas in Bangladesh when she was single and childless; she continued to do so upon having her son. In "'Was It Not Lucky That the Boy Was with His Mother?': A Travellin' Mama in Bangladesh," she considers divergent attitudes in Bangladesh and her own country concerning childlessness and mothering as well as travel with and without children. Hamilton discusses issues that arise in travel with a five-year-old: explanations of cultural differences, maintenance and making exceptions of routines, safety issues, and cross-cultural communication and educational opportunities.

In "Negotiating Fieldwork and Mothering," Angela Castañeda uses autoethnography to examine the intersections between fieldwork and mothering. The piece reflects on the ways in which travelling with her children affects her work as an anthropologist. Her visible identity as a mother contributes to rapport building with the subjects of her research but also makes her the subject of ethnocentrism or cultural judgment. Castañeda describes the varied results of travelling with and without her children for work, and examines her intersecting identities as a mother-researcher.

The late poet, photographer, and lyricist Holly Anderson made journal entries during travels taken when her daughter was just shy of two years old, which are published here as "Ink Black Sky Bright White Page." The family had recently suffered a catastrophic death, and the working vacations Anderson, her musician husband, and their daughter took provided a needed respite from grief. Although her baby was an intrepid traveller, braving mosquito-ridden beaches and loud nightclubs alike, the author wrestled with her dual roles: "hourly skirmishes that involve motherprotector vs. writerpoet whatever I was/ am trying to regain become be creator but mother isn't always producer in the same way someone without child(ren) might be can be."

The penultimate section in the book is about culture, and it looks at how for mothers, observing and participating in the interplay of culture are some of the rewards of travel and how travelling with children provides additional depth to that exploration. Children allow one to bypass strangeness by enacting a commonality between the traveller and the visited. Accordingly, children can serve as bridges to communication with the visited culture. Traditional practices from other cultures that have been recently adopted in the West, such as "baby wearing," can be observed in original lands and can enhance a sense shared experience. Another universality that is culturally individuated is food. Eating and food practices may be explored for cultural norms, assumptions, and procedures, which provide opportunities for dialogue and insight.

In "Attached Bodies: Movement, Babywearing, and the Travelling Mother," an essay that is simultaneously academic and creative nonfiction, Maria Lombard examines the textiles of movement and travel for women who mother. The piece is about wraps for baby wearing—a historical textile made modern in the West. Baby wearing is an ancient practice of motherhood; the mother carries the infant in a cloth on the front or back of her own body. As a conceptual fourth trimester of pregnancy, baby wearing is an external womb, allowing the child to be visible, audible, and interactive, but still attached. Lombard also considers how the complexity of baby wearing in the modern world means different things in the Global South than it does for Western women. In the Global South, baby wearing is functional for carrying water, working in fields, and walking long distances.

Lynn Mastellotto's "A Taste of the Good Life: Expatriate Mothers on Food and Identity" examines two relocation memoirs that focus on family life through an expatriate lens: *French Children Don't Throw Food* (2013) by Pamela Druckerman, an American journalist in Paris; and *The Lost Art of Feeding Kids: What Italy Taught Me About Why Children Need Real Food* (2014) by Jeannie Marshall, a Canadian writer in Rome. Mastellotto argues that the authors, in their depiction of the central role culinary attitudes and practices play in raising children in France and Italy, reveal the importance of eating real food in a processed world. Mastellotto further argues that the writers' culinary adventures serve to illustrate the mobilization of food through a local-global nexus of food practices, which offers the possibility for multiple identifications and dialogical identities to emerge through engaging with cultural difference. Mastellotto thus shows that relocation memoirs are situated at the intersection of life writing and travel writing, and that they form a distinct subgenre of travel writing concerned with the everyday experiences of foreigners who become settlers abroad through voluntary migration.

The closing part of the book is about exigency and how it spurs travel; travel, at times, can also be subject to exigency. When a vital resource is prohibited locally but available elsewhere, or when a natural disaster impacts a home, travel is compelled by urgent necessity, and the need to travel at a time of stress provides additional privations. Abortion limitations may be seen as part of a societal fabric of limiting women's choices and activities regarding sexuality and procreation that has continued to the present day, whereas in the travel diaries of nineteenth-century women, normal processes of female sexuality and maturity are solely conveyed implicitly, as a result of cultural norms.

In "From the Backstreet to Britain: Women and Abortion Travel in Irish History," Cara Delay offers a complex and comparative analysis of Irish abortion history. Having been illegal in Ireland in almost all cases, a 2018 referendum saw the Irish people vote in favour of offering pregnancy terminations. Up until that point, abortion in mainland Britain had been relatively accessible for Irish women. The advent of social media helped publicize Irish women's abortion journeys and has brought much-needed attention to a serious healthcare crisis. Most analyses of Irish abortion travel centre on the experiences of women who have embarked on cross-border voyages since decriminalization in Britain in 1967. Based on an analysis of archival materials, memoirs, and first-hand accounts, this chapter sheds light on the migrations—near and far, past and present—that Irish women have undertaken to end unwanted pregnancies across generations.

Even with the dangers of nineteenth-century wagon travel—including confrontations with Native Americans, sickness, wagon accidents, stampedes, or even erroneously-charted trails—nearly half a million people risked and sacrificed much to settle in the American West. Forging everyday life along the lengthy journey were mothers, who cooked, washed, nursed, healed, and mourned. Many of these mothers wrote of their travel experience in diaries and journals. The diaries, however, were only semiprivate, which inhibited mothers from directly revealing details considered taboo in the 1800s, especially matters of sexuality. Monica Reyes's "Sins of Omission: Unpacking the Rhetoric of Sexuality within Nineteenth-Century American Mothers' Travel Diaries" explores the writing choices of American travelling mothers and aims to reveal the purposeful, intentional, and rhetorical omissions and edits commonly found in mothers' travel-diaries concerning sex, menstruation, pregnancy and birth. The travel diaries of Susan Shelby Magoffin (1846) and Amelia Stewart Knight (1853) provide a window into the enigmatic worlds of motherhood, travel writing, and sexuality. In "When Monsters Move the Mother in You," Janet MacLennan details two migrations, one desired and one imposed. She contrasts her experiences travelling as an individual with her different mindset when travelling as a mother. Having relocated to Puerto Rico from Canada, she found that the birth of her son led her to experience her chosen home in new ways. The impact of a natural disaster—on her as an individual and as a parent—is considered.

Conclusion

Exploring the diverse histories, stories, communities, and voices of mothers who travel requires reflecting on the many current debates on motherhood and the processes necessary for rewriting motherhood and thereby envisioning empowered mothers. The creative texts, scholarly essays, and autoethnography in *Travellin' Mama: Mothers, Mothering, and Travel* extend the narratives on mothers who travel, by choice, force or circumstance, and explore their identities without conforming to specific mothering practices and models. The radical and challenging nature of such representations is evident from the various contributions in this book. It is difficult to overstate the life-changing, knowledge-enhancing or cathartic impact of reading about mothers and their travelling, whether the travel is forced or is by choice.

Endnotes

1 Motherhood and travel are also used as a commercial marketing tool to sell super-robust iPhone cases, as can be seen in a recent blog post on the website Walking on Travels. In the article, "Weathering the Elements of Motherhood and Travel with Tech21 iPhone Cases," Keryn Means extolls the virtues of a particularly sturdy iPhone case, which, she explains, is ideally suited for mothers who travel and generally lead physically active lives.

2 For discussions on "othermothers", women who raise children that are not biologically their own, see Sharon Abbey and Andrea O'Reilly, Simone A. James Alexander, Charlotte Beyer, Susan E. Chase and Mary F. Rogers, and Patricia Hill Collins.

Works Cited

Abbey, Sharon, and Andrea O'Reilly, editors. A *Redefining Motherhood: Changing Identities and Patterns.* Second Story, 1998.

Alexander, Simone A. James. *Mother Imagery in the Novels of Afro-Caribbean Women.* University of Missouri Press, 2001.

Beyer, Charlotte. "'My Mama Had a Story': Mothers and Inter-generational Relations in Andrea Levy's Fiction." In *Reading/*

Speaking/Writing the Mother Text: Essays on Caribbean Women's Writing, edited by Cristina Herrera and Paula Sanmartin. Demeter Press, 2015, pp. 121-142.

Bond, Marybeth and Pamela Michael. "Introduction." *A Mother's World: Journeys of the Heart*, edited by Marybeth Bond and Pamela Michael. Travelers Tales, 1998, pp. xv-xviii.

Canepa, Nancy. "Trickster heroes in 'The Boy Steals the Ogre's Treasure'". The Cambridge Companion to Fairy Tales, edited by Maria Tatar. Cambridge University Press, 2015, pp. 117-134.

Chase, Susan E., and Mary F. Rogers. *Mothers and Children: Feminist Analyses and Personal Narratives.* Rutgers University Press, 2001.

Collins, Patricia Hill. *Black Feminist Thought: Knowledge, Consciousness, and the Politics of Empowerment.* Routledge, 1991.

"Travel." *English Oxford Living Dictionaries,* https://en.oxford dictionaries.com/definition/travel. Accessed 24 Jan. 2018.

Firth, Claire H., and Jane E. Lavery. "Transnational motherhood in Brazilian community in South-eastern Massachusetts." *Immigration: Views and Reflections—Histories, Identities and Keys of Social Intervention,* edited by Rosa Santibáñez and Concepción Maiztegui Oñate, University of Deusto, 2006, pp. 89-119.

Harper, Nancy. *Travellin' Mama,* http://travellinmama.blogspot.co.uk/. Accessed 24 Jan. 2018.

Haugh, Brooke. "Becoming a Mother and Learning to Breastfeed: An Emergent Autoethnography." *The Journal of Perinatal Education*, vol. 25, no. 1, 2016. https://www.ncbi.nlm.nih.gov/pmc/articles/ PMC4719102/. Accessed 8 Sept. 2018.

Lisle, Debbie. *The Global Politics of Contemporary Travel Writing.* Cambridge University Press, 2006.

Hartley, Gemma. "Women Aren't Nags—We're Just Fed Up." *Harper's Bazaar,* 27 Sept. 2017, www.harpersbazzar.com/culture/features/ a12063822/emotional-labor-gender-equality/. Accessed 8 Feb. 2018.

Hochschild, Arlie Russell. *The Managed Heart: Commercialization of Human Feeling.* University of California Press, 1983.

Hondagneu-Sotelo, Pierrette, and Ernestine Avila. "'I'm Here, but I'm There'": The Meanings of Latina Transnational Motherhood." *Gender and Society*, vol. 11, no. 5, 1997, pp. 548-71.

Smith Silva, Dorsía, Laila Malik, and Abigail L. Palko, editors. *Mothers, Mothering, and Globalization.* Demeter, 2017.

Koss-Feder, Laura. "Road Rules." *Working Mother,* Mar. 2001, pp. 41-45.

Levitt, Peggy. *The Transnational Villagers.* University of California Press, 2001.

Mason, Kate. "On Motherhood and Travel." *Future Travel*, 19 January 2016. https://futuretravel.today/on-motherhood-and-travel-2401c07ad58c. Accessed 24 Jan. 2018.

Means, Keryn. "Weathering the Elements of Motherhood and Travel with Tech21 Iphone Cases." *Walking on Travels*, 24 Apr. 2017, https://walkingontravels.com/tech21iphonecasestravel/. Accessed 24 January 2018.

Michael, Pamela, "Apron Strings," *Travelers' Tales Food: A Taste of the Road.* Excerpt in *A Mother's World: Journeys of the Heart*, edited by Marybeth Bond and Pamela Michael. Travelers Tales, 1998, p. 50.

Nicholl, Honor. "'Going Between Worlds': Travelling With Children With Complex Needs." *Journal of Child Health Care,* vol.19, no.3, 2015, pp. 293-303.

Nicholson, Melanie. "Without Their Children. Rethinking Motherhood among Transnational Migrant Women." *Social Text*, vol. 24, no. 3, 2006, pp. 13-33.

Ott, Sheryl. "Travel vs Motherhood." *Ott's World*, 8 July 2008. https://www.ottsworld.com/blogs/travel-vs-motherhood. Accessed 24 Jan. 2018.

Siegel, Kristi. "Intersections: Women's Travel and Theory." *Gender, Genre, and Identity in Women's Travel Writing*, edited by Kristi Siegel, Peter Lang, pp.1-14.

Siegel, Kristi. "Women's Travel and the Rhetorics of Peril: It Is Suicide to Be Abroad." *Gender, Genre, and Identity in Women's Travel Writing*, edited by Kristi Siegel, Peter Lang, 2004, pp. 55-72.

Smith, Lilian "Prologue." *A Lilian Smith Reader,* edited by Margaret Rose Gladney and Lisa Hodgens. University of Georgia Press, 2016, pp.191-194.

Skains, R. Lyle "Creative Practice as Research: Discourse on Methodology." Media Practice and Education, vol. 19, issue 1, 2018, pp.82-97.

Weed, Julie. "When Moms Travels for Work." *The New York Times*, 16 Apr. 2012, www.nytimes.com/2012/04/17/business/for-mom-business-trips-call-for-emotional-and-digital-logistics.html. Accessed 8 Feb. 2018.

Woznicki, Katrina. "On Motherhood and Travel." *Katrina Woznicki*, 7 Mar. 2017, http://katrinawoznicki.com/on-motherhood-and-travel/. Accessed 24 Jan. 2018.

RELOCATION

Chapter 1

Day 2: 22 January 2016
Immigration: London

Kimmika Williams-Witherspoon

And you are?

His mother

And he is?

My son...

And why is he here?

With me...

Will he be joining the Study Abroad?

No...

Well,

What will he be doing during the day?

He's going to be an exchange student

Where?

St Ignatius College...

in Enfield.

In Enfield?

Yes...Enfield.

How do you spell that?

Ignatius—

I. G. N. A. T. I. O. U. S.

And where is the paperwork for that?

I don't have any...

"Paperwork."

So, what you just thought you'd come over here and see what happens?

No ... I've been

Communicating

Emailing back and forth—

Talking with the headmaster

Six months.

And, he couldn't stay with anyone

While you were here?

NO

No?

No...

No ... Alright then ... next?

Chapter 2

Travelling the Same Road: The Parallel Journeys of Motherhood and Migration

Karem Roitman

Mothers and migrants are both travellers. Their journeys of migration and motherhood, I propose, both disrupt doxic knowledge—the structures we internalize and naturalize to guide our understanding of reality and our actions, what Bourdieu has termed our habitus: "a system of durable, transposable dispositions, structured structures predisposed towards acting as structuring structures" (Gledhill 136). Both the motherhood and the migration journey present women with new experiences that prevent them from indulging in normal patterns of behaviour—experiences that require a new language and narrative and that force women to reconceptualize themselves and others. Salman Akhtar notes the need to explore the "third individuation" of migrants (qtd. in Ainslie et al.), and although rarely theorized in the same way, a similar exploration of the individuation of mothers is needed, even more so of migrant mothers. Migrant mothers are very much in the crux of change; they are vulnerable and need support and understanding.

Motherhood and migration are physical, psychological, and social journeys—journeys into new identities, new spaces, and new knowledge. Physically, migration means leaving behind the familiar for a new land, where light reflects differently, where the smells of childhood vanish, and where migrants are immersed in indecipherable noises through which they struggle to communicate. Mothering is also a move into a new physical reality. At the micro level, stem cells from the child cross the placenta and invade the woman, literally making her into a new person. Her brain also undergoes significant changes as synaptic pruning fine tunes its social coding skills. At the macro level, mothers are immersed in new smells, sounds, and schedules that transform senses and perceptions. Forming a new being in one's body, having a new psyche emerge from ours, and learning to love a person who reflects us and is entirely dependent on us are also psychological journeys that necessitate change and growth. Motherhood might cause us to reflect on our own life path, on the values and beliefs we have unwittingly absorbed, and the longings that are unexpectedly gaping. These are similar to the concerns and reflections that culture shock can bring upon a migrant: longing for the comfort and familiarity of the motherland while becoming aware of naturalized values, hidden wounds, and unfulfilled needs. Finally, both migration and mother-hood are social processes; they can be pathways to a new community but may also result in isolation. New mothers in the UK often find themselves alone with their child for most of the day. Even if not alone, many may be unable to translate and share their experiences and feelings with those who surround them. Similarly, immigration is often characterised by periods of isolation due to linguistic and cultural barriers.

To support the mental and social wellbeing of immigrant mothers, their experiences need to be understood—to study where migration and motherhood run in parallel, where they overlap, and how they build on each other. As primary agents of socialization, mothers' experiences will affect their offspring and, in aggregate, the nature of society's fabric. Previous research on migrant mothers has concen-trated on their prenatal, birth, and postnatal care (see, for example, the meta-reviews by Benza and Liamputtong, and Higginbottom et al.). I would like to engage with how migration shapes the identities and experiences of women during motherhood. Although migration has been extensively researched sociologically, less attention has been given to it as a psychological experience (Ainslie et al.). The dynamics between migration and motherhood require further study. Western understandings of motherhood, moreover, have been framed by psychoanalytic assumptions of the mother-child dyad (Chodorow and Bowlby), and research has concentrated on the pathological. Although much ground has been covered by feminist scholars deconstructing and exploring the "distinctions between motherhood as institution, mothering as an experience, and motherhood as an identity" (Davis), migrant mothers provide further insights for this critical project by highlighting cultural biases. There is, therefore, much to be gained by turning our attention to the journey of migrant mothers who are "twice burdened," or as Margarita Melville notes, "twice a minority" (qtd. in Liamputtong 195).

I started this research, unknowingly, as a migrant mother myself. As a participant observer in both the world of migrants and the world of mothers, I started to reflect on the overlap between the two, wondering if their confluence is additive. In attempting to make objective the effects and implications of my own migrant and mothering background, as well as the academic preconceptions I have acquired, I followed Bourdieu in the "objectivation of the subject of objectivation"—a daily exercise of awareness, engagement, and separation (Bourdieu 282). There were numerous obstacles to overcome in my research. First, motherhood is utterly exhausting. Seeking to relate rationally to physical and visceral experiences is almost impossible in the throes of sleep starvation. This is why I did not conduct this research until my second child was three; this delay, however, implies my own separation from the intense period of transitioning into motherhood. I am also not a recent migrant. I note these two points to highlight that motherhood and migration are affected by time—the mother of a six-week-old is not the same mother when her second child is five years old. In the same way, a new migrant is in a different space from someone who has mastered the local tongue and built a network over decades. The exhaustive nature of motherhood also implies that my research population will be self-selecting. Mothers with limited social support, those who have not chosen, or are unable, to use childcare, and those not fluent in the local tongue are less likely to be accessible to researchers, which presents a bias.

I met mothers through a plethora of networks—such as neighbourhood and baby/toddler groups, social media baby and parenting groups, local children's centres, home-schooling networks, and parks—and I used a snowballing technique to gather participants. Beyond participant observation, I conducted brief interviews with nine women and in-depth interviews with four. Finding child-friendly interview spaces was another challenge. Most often conversations were built over many meetings, and stories were whispered quickly in between pushing children on swings, distributing snacks, and preventing falls. Obtaining data from mothers with whom I had developed an emotional bond implied a possible interviewer effect, even while it made the data richer. To address this, I asked parenting groups in Oxford to put out a call for research volunteers. La Leche League and Baby Café Oxford accepted, and I was able to send out my questionnaire to fifteen migrant mothers (whom I had not previously met), out of whom four replied. Triangulating questionnaire responses with responses gathered through interviews validated the patterns I had inferred—first through personal experience, then via anthropological research, and, lastly, through interviews. Two provisos must be noted. The parenting networks I used to gather questionnaires attracted mothers who breastfeed and often, though not always, those who identify with attachment parenting. Further research is needed to tease out whether these parenting styles affect the mothers' experience, or to what extent migrant mothers' home cultures overlap with this parenting strategy, which led them to join these communities. The variety of mothering subcultures may interact differently with the tensions of migration, necessitating further research. Second, I would note that none of the women interviewed had suffered severe trauma before or during the migration process. The women interviewed were all between twenty-five and forty-five years of age, university educated, and had chosen to stay at home at some point during their mothering career. Further research needs to nuance the class dimension of migrant mothers' identity (Phoenix). It is important to highlight that my main purpose in this chapter is to provide a space for the voices of migrant mothers in order to point to the various paths that need further research rather than to provide definitive findings. Finally, the confidentiality of all participants was protected via the use of pseudonyms.

Parallels between Motherhood and Migration: Vulnerability, Ambivalence, and Isolation

This chapter weaves through and explores three parallels I noted between migration and motherhood: vulnerability, ambivalence, and isolation. It is important to note that the experiences of my interviewees may not be different from those of other non-migrant mothers and that the dynamics of migration can be felt even by those who move within a country. Therefore, there are processes that might be known to non-migrant mothers but are more intense for migrant mothers, and, therefore, clearer.

To start with, international migrants are generally extremely vulnerable. For example, migrants depend on others to translate signs and information until they can speak the language; they are vulnerable to mockery or to being isolated for their cultural traits, and they are vulnerable to poverty. These vulnerabilities overlap with the vulnerability of motherhood. The physical nature of motherhood can make a woman physically vulnerable, while the undervalued and unremunerated nature of mothers' work makes all mothers, to some extent, financially and emotionally vulnerable. For migrant mothers, this vulnerability can be exacerbated by linguistic and cultural isolation, which can make them feel trapped and insecure.

One of my interviewees, Marie, discussed the vulnerability of motherhood in terms of freedom and drew an interesting parallel to the process of migration. She discussed her fear of feeling trapped behind boundaries and of being limited by bureaucratic paperwork she could not obtain; she compared this to the limits imposed by motherhood:

> You know when you ... migrate you have this amazing feeling, with a passport and a visa. You can move. Wherever I have travelled the most important thing for me was to feel free. I could always leave! ... [When I had a baby], it was like my passport was taken from me. I can't leave. I physically couldn't for a long time, but even with an older kid, well you can't just leave him. And no, I don't want to, but ... well it is just the option is gone and it is ... suffocating.

Another respondent, Linda, discussed her vulnerability in terms of financial security:

I migrated as a child and I guess ever since then I have been looking for security. Certainty. When you navigate a culture better than your parents, you feel they cannot protect you. So I made myself feel secure [with] a job ... and then I had a baby. Suddenly I could barely get up. I stopped working and became financially dependent on someone else. It is terrifying. All my security is gone. I am protected only by being a mother . . . and it is a [paradox because] nothing makes you more vulnerable.

In her research on Thai mothers in Australia, Pranee Liamputtong found women unable to leave unhappy marriages because they did not want to lose their children and were financially dependent on their partner. For migrant mothers, leaving a marriage is complicated by the geographical distance of their support networks, which increases their vulnerability to abuse.

A third source of vulnerability discussed by an interviewee was the body. Linda, who is Latin American mother, discussed how one of the attractions of immigrating to Europe was feeling physically safer: "It is so nice to just walk down the street and not worry about someone grabbing you. I know it can still happen here, but it is very rare compared to my country ... here I felt less 'a body' for a long time. I was me, people ... related to my ideas, rather than to my body."

However, for Linda, the embodied process of motherhood meant a vulnerable reconnection to being a body: "Suddenly I was a body again—pregnancy is all about the body. And during the birth and after my body was taken over—by the baby, by the doctors, by the follow up check-ups, by nurses touching my breasts to try to help me breastfeed. I felt taken over again ... No one wants to hear your ideas ... You are all body."

Ainslie et al. remind us that researchers cannot fully understand the psychological experience of migrants without considering how ethnicity and race affect their journey. Race and ethnicity also overlap with motherhood, which is inherently embodied. In interracial partnerships, the mothering experience entails coming to terms with internalized racial narratives and identities. Linda discussed this process as she worked through her relationship with her light-skinned daughter:

> I love my daughter…. When she was born, I was struck by her white skin on my chest … And now people ask me if I am her nanny. I still catch myself watching her in surprise sometimes. Because she is mine but looks so different from me because I grew up in a context where her skin was considered more beautiful than mine, and yet I made her. Having her, loving her as she loves me, has also been a process of learning to love me, and realizing I didn't before.

Linda's experiences with her daughter are a microcosm of the larger process of women reframing their relationship with their body through motherhood. For migrant mothers, the experienced is layered, as they are simultaneously vulnerable to multiple national and local narratives of women, motherhood, and the body.

How can a mother verbalize what she feels at seeing the being she produced, her own flesh, embody racial structures from which she suffered and from which her child will likely benefit? How can any mother translate her learning to nurture and sustain into words? How can a new mother ask for help when she does not know the words for the experiences that scare or hurt her? The struggle to find the language to translate impressions into words is another challenge mothers and migrants have in common, and which overlap in migrant mothers. Another mother said the following: "There are some things that just don't translate. I remember during the birth wanting to SCREAM in my language, but I couldn't because it felt strange in an English-speaking space. And I didn't feel I could scream in English! So I just laboured quietly, but I wanted to scream!" Rudolph Loewenstein classically argued that "language is the vehicle through which [our memories] are externalized and objectified … concretized through articulation, they come to occupy a different place in our intrapsychic lives" (qtd. in Ainslie et al.). Pregnancy, birth, and mothering are indescribably intense experiences. How do migrant mothers process and share these in a foreign tongue? How can they externalize their feelings and concretize memories and experiences in order to process them? Do they need to discuss their struggles in their native tongue in order for the cathartic power of language to be fulfilled? J. Amati

Mehler further asks the following: "How are conscious, unconscious and preconscious levels between the thing represented and the word representation linked and articulated when the 'words' are brought into play in more than one language?" (qtd. in Ainslie et al. 668). How are migrant mothers processing their experiences when sharing these in one language for their partners and doctors, for example, and in a different one with distant family or fellow migrants?

Interviewees who found difficulties communicating their activities and feelings felt increasingly isolated and vulnerable. They might have also lacked the cultural language to understand and explain their experiences if they were unable to discuss these with older women who could locate them in broader cultural patterns. An interviewee named Lisa said the following:

> I hold my baby and joke with him in [my language], and I feel transported to my childhood and I feel connected to this part of me that has been somehow dormant when I was living, working, in English. And I want to share this with my husband too, of course, but how? There are jokes, there are, I don't know, flavours to life that don't translate…. It makes me both happy to have it with my children and deeply sad and lonely that I cannot share it beyond them. This is probably why I feel so refreshed and fulfilled when I am around other [language] speakers. All those bits of me can be alive again.

Ralph R. Greenson, looking at bilingual parents, argues that "speaking in one's mother tongue may allow one to connect more immediately and directly with the emotions that surround childhood memories and experiences" (qtd. in Ainslie et al. 668). This connection may be one of the tools through which cultural roots are passed and nurtured, and why some migrant mothers felt a strong need to speak to their children in their native tongue. Lisa had this to say: "We had discussed bringing up the children bilingual. But once our daughter was born, there was no question, I just had to speak to her in my language. It felt wrong, unnatural to do anything different. When I tried to speak in English, I felt untrue, unable to connect, as though I was acting like a mother rather than being her mother."

Mothers particularly noted the struggles of speaking to their children in their native language when they lacked a community of the same tongue. Some discussed tensions when speaking among non-migrants, and different strategies to cope with these tensions. A woman named Rosa said, "My in-laws get upset when they cannot understand what I am saying. My husband gets paranoid and accuses me of making him feel left out. But it is not about them; it is about my ability to mother, to connect with my child. I feel torn between pleasing them and being a good mother." And another interviewee, Sofia, said, "I try not to speak [language] to my child when we are out [to avoid tensions]... I am lucky that I can "mother" my baby in both languages." Interestingly, the language struggles were present even in mothers' whose first language was English but who were not from the UK. For example, Tania noted her "inability to fully grasp the secret code and to teach this code to her children."

Beyond its psychodynamic uses, language is enmeshed in cultural signs and symbolism that an migrant mother must translate for herself, her child, and others. Migrant mothers are linguistically straddling two cultures, as they simultaneously translate for their children and those around them. The role of translator places them in a liminal space, where they are never immersed in any one reality; they must always be ready to translate, with each language pulling to its own distinct emotional realm. In this liminal space, they may be able to experience two means of understanding, or they may remain unable to integrate fully into either version. For some, as for Tania above, this liminality brings up the possibility of worrying gaps not just with their partners but also with their children in the future: Nastia said the following: "I speak to my children in [my native language] ... and worry about possible culture/language gap I could have with [them, as they] are being brought up in the UK ... language (also books, songs, foods, etc.) is such a big part of who we are." Mothers wanted their children to be fluent in the national code so they could succeed in their home, while also wanting them to maintain their own native language (when this was not English) and links to their mother's land and culture. A desire to walk in both lands as well as an ambivalence about which land was best was evident in discussions about the spheres beyond language. Although both motherhood and immigration can provide new opportunities, status, and membership, both also entail significant losses that must be acknowledged and mourned. In this respect, the experience of migrants has been more commonly acknowledged than that of mothers. Popular discourse might take note of migrants' gratitude for their new home but also understand that they may miss what they have left behind and that they may struggle to relate to their new culture. Far less is the sadness mothers may feel for what they have lost by entering motherhood discussed in any media. Leon Ginberg and Rebeca Grinberg note the complex mourning migrants undergo in response to the "loss of contextual continuity"—the loss of the familiar background that makes us feel at ease (Ainslie et al. 666). Migrant mothers also mourn the context lost. Tania related her elation at spending some time with a childhood friend: "Even my husband and my children, they could see me, for once, as me, because I was in context. I am never in context here … I have perpetual homesickness, sadness, which I fear I burden my children with."

Migrant mothers mourn the loss of ideals—the ideal of the new country and its promises (Tummala-Narra 168) but also the ideal of motherhood and its rosy glow. Both migrants and mothers mourn freedom lost—whether it be moving confidently through familiar spaces or being able to act on a whim without thinking of a child. Both mourn the past, such as the country, family, and culture left behind. Particularly, migrant mothers may mourn the identity they built before children, as Sofia said, "[I] am not the same person. Having children does make you lose your identity a little. You are not you, but someone's mum. Especially when you practice gentle attachment parenting you don't really know where your baby ends and you start." Nastia also added that, "My personal needs and wants have moved to the background. I have very little time and energy for myself. [My] circle of casual friends has changed. My interests have changed." The other side of mourning what was and what could have been is disillusionment with what is. Is this it? Is this what we sacrificed for? Is the terrible journey worth the price? Ambivalence towards the current state, the new country, and motherhood is seldom stated for fear of derision or for of being condemned as ungrateful or for failing at motherhood. There is a bit of ambivalence in Marie's comments above about feeling suffocated, and her subsequent fear of mentioning this by quickly clarifying that she does not want to leave. Similarly, Tania noted, "In many ways I am glad [my children] are here rather than in the horrifying hellhole devoid of culture [I grew up in] … but I miss family and worry that I can never fit in and cannot teach my children to fit in either." Part of mourning might be nostalgia and regret, and some idealization of what was left behind, as indicated by Sofia: "The culture of my childhood is long gone, and I do look at it with a bit of nostalgia.... Sometimes when I visit 'home,' I have a feeling that life in my old hometown seems so much simpler and less stressful, and maybe if I had not ever left..."

Part of the wish to go back is a wish to return to the motherland and to the mother. Nancy Chodorow has indicated the complex relationship of a woman to her own mother as she herself experiences motherhood, and she begins to identify as both the mother and the child. Motherhood is often a period of reassessing and reconnecting with one's own mother—reassessing her mothering against the new mother's own efforts, confronting emotional injuries, reattaching ourselves in new shared experiences. Thus mothers might mourn what they lacked when they were mothered. Sofia said the following:

> My journey through motherhood has made me remember certain things from my own upbringing. But sadly, not the nice things. I suddenly remembered how I missed my dad when he had to leave to work abroad for a long period of time and how my mum would get frustrated and angry with me and shout sometimes. I must have been only three or four years old then?

Integration of the old, the mothering received, and the new, the mothering one wishes to give, are needed to complete the process of mourning for past failings and present disillusionment—to complete individuation. Interviewees discussed being drawn anew to their mother and a longing for connection, even while reflecting on ways they were insufficiently mothered. As an interviewee named Stella stated, "Since becoming a mother I have grown a little closer with my own mum, [even as] I have been questioning her about my own upbringing and the choices she and my dad have made." Migrant mothers, however, may find it harder to access this process: "Physical and psychological separation from one's mother is intensified both for migrant and second-generation women in their own formation of maternal identity" (Tummala-Narra 170). This was echoed by Rosa: "I have found it hard being so far from my mother ... We do send loads of pictures and videos, but she feels like she is missing things. Part of me

KAREM ROITMAN

is glad to be separate so I can do things my way without comments.... But when [my son] is sick or moving into a new stage, her advice would be nice to have immediately." Again, in Rosa's words, there is ambivalence: an appreciation for the space gained to mother with one's own values, but also a longing for the comfort and support of one's mother close by. Tania noted the importance of her grandmother's clock as a symbolic connection to her home: "I have accepted I will never feel at home again ... except when my grandmother's clock chimes ... it soothes me so deeply."

Mothers also spoke of the strength, physical and emotional, they had found in their migration and mothering. Thus, although they were aware of what they had lost in the journey of migrant mothering, the mothers also discussed what they had gained, which added another layer of complexity to their ambivalence, Nastia indicated: "[As a migrant mother] in my view, my experiences are richer ... deeper [and] wider ... wider because I am passing on my knowledge of the three cultures to my children and not just one, and deeper because the nature of my native cultures." Another interviewee, Dina, said the following: "To me, migration was not traumatic, since I came here freely travelling rather than intending to migrate ... and staying here has given me an advantage as a mother as I am removed from the bad influence [and pressure] from my family. I have been able to be the mother I want to be."

Some of the gains from immigration and mothering, however, must be paid for in loneliness. Starting their career as mothers abroad, migrant mothers are particularly vulnerable to loneliness and isolation. Although all role transitions disrupt existing social networks and put individuals at risk of loneliness (Red Cross), migrant mothers are distinct in that they must transition twice, sometimes within a short span of time. Migrant mothers are likely to have lost deep, inter-generational, familial, and communal networks needed to support their transition into motherhood. Moreover, the embodied and gendered nature of mothering will expose them to new aspects of the culture they have immigrated into, resulting in new culture shocks and the need to navigate further acculturation. Thus, it is not surprising that isolation and loneliness were common themes in interviews. When asked how migration affected her experience of mothering, Tania's first reflection was "lack of support": "Here I have

52

no parents, siblings, aunts ... and blood matters. I have come to realize [as a mother] that blood matters. You cannot make family."

Interviewees often discussed how the loneliness of motherhood might have been assuaged by family. One interviewee, Arianne, noted the importance of the networks left behind: "I am sure motherhood can be lonely anywhere. But I just kept thinking of my aunties. If I had had my baby at home, they would have been ... making me soup, taking turns to hold the baby, telling me stories about [my cousins].... Here, once my husband left for work, I was alone for hours." Several interviewees found the networks they had built before motherhood, through work or hobbies, insufficient support once they became mothers, as noted by Tania above. Concentrating on the lack of understanding of what motherhood entails, Marie related that "when I told a friend I used to work with how tired I was, she kindly suggested I just leave the baby for a few days and come stay with her ... she was just clueless. I was too, until I had a baby."

Building new networks is always challenging, and in seeking a new group of "mummy friends," migrant mothers face the added hurdles of language and culture. Marie said the following: "I lived here for ten years before I had a baby. I had a job and friends. But once you have a baby ... all your friends are at work. Your job is gone.... It was like being new again. I felt lost ... I would go to baby classes to try and meet others and realized I didn't know a single nursery rhyme in English." Learning the new culture of motherhood and seeking to enter the local community of mothers force migrants to relive the stress of migration—the loss of networks, the cultural and linguistic isolation, and the struggle to establish new connections. The barriers appear double because one is not just another new mother but also a foreigner, as Sofia highlighted: "I always found I need to make myself more 'British' to fit in. What I mean is that you are not honest about your mothering experiences.... [At] baby groups, I found that mothers go there in groups, and being a new mom, [it] is hard to fit in and [make] friends—harder if you are foreign and already lack in self-confidence." Mothering, furthermore, can bring with it new culture shocks, as local gender roles and values are crystalized through the parenting process. Even for those who feel settled in their new country, motherhood can be destabilizing and isolating; they once again feel foreign and misunderstood, unable to relate to the local. Marie offered the following:

I thought I felt at home here, until I had my children.... I was asked to choose to let my baby cry so my husband would not feel abandoned. In my culture, you don't let children cry, but my mother-in-law was shocked that I was not "putting my husband first".... When my husband did anything, he would always tell me that he was helping me.

Looking specifically at the cultural norms of parenting and their effects on migrant mothers, Pratyusha Tummala-Narra notes that in the West, great emphasis is placed on a mother's ability to help her children become autonomous and independent. Sociologically, this independence is sought to ensure mothers can re-enter the market as economic agents. Childhood independence is not, however, a global value, and can therefore create tensions, as "the mother ... struggles with culturally divergent values of parenting and with her disconnection to either her parental figures or cultural representations" (Tummala-Narra 172). In other words, the mother's taken-for-granted values of parenting, childhood, and gender are disturbed when they do not fit neatly within the prevalent cultural norms of her new home, which often leads to loneliness and isolation. This struggle was exemplified among some of Tummala-Narra's Indian-American patients who hesitated to share with others that their infants and toddlers slept with them at night, a custom vilified in the Western context (173). Likewise, Liamputtong describes the tension in Thai-Australian families as mothers feeling torn between their doxic values and the cultural expectations of their Australian husbands. My interviewees shared similar experiences of finding themselves at odds with the parenting and mothering values held by friends and partners. Linda had this to say: "I didn't realize how antichildren this culture was until I had one. Here ... kids go to nurseries, and outside the house, you just don't see kids.... And [people in the new country] were always asking 'is she a good baby?' meaning does she sleep well on her own all night, which she never did. It made me very lonely." Similarly, Sofia said the following:

I believe in different upbringing values and sometimes those clash with my English mummy friends. I often feel inferior and that I have to prove that what am doing is right. I feel that having no relatives who can support me in what [I] am doing,

I constantly need to justify my actions…. I feel a strong pressure to go out with friends, and I simply don't want to…. I feel a little isolated sometimes.

In short, the loneliness of motherhood is amplified by the lack of familial networks, especially when confronting new cultural voids with those regarded as intimate, such as close friends and partners.

When asked which she thought was harder, migrating or mothering, Sofia succinctly summarized the parallels between the two, as she noted the cost of isolation and the inherent mourning and vulnerability of both processes:

If you take into account that [they were] your well thought through decisions, then I would say both are as hard as each other. You take that step into the unknown, hoping it will turn out fine…. However, when you emigrate and start a life in a different country it usually takes a few years to settle, fit in. By then you have a job, a purpose, and you live your life like one of them. [However], it is much harder to be a mother. After you fall pregnant you suddenly realize that this blessing will stay with you forever! There is a settling period, figuring out what you are doing, what language does your baby speak and what is your purpose in life. But then this does not stop! [But] … neither of these things have to be hard if you have someone to share your experiences with.

Motherhood is inherently a process of migration: a new label, "mother", is handed out like a passport into an unknown space where the consistency of time is altered from minutes to the cries of a child, where we must learn a new language to communicate with ones who do not speak, and where we inhabit areas at once crowded and lonely. Motherhood is also a journey to recreate a woman, as her identity is consumed, physically and metaphorically, by the desperate needs of a child and by a capitalist system that nullifies her once she exits the monetary economy.

Crossing national boundaries can sharpen the internal journey of motherhood and that can exacerbate the tensions inherent in migrating. Implicit cultural expectations of a woman as a mother, wife, and homemaker often emerge only once her babe is in arms—when women are particularly psychologically and physically vulnerable. Migrant women often face these expectations without a cultural or social support network. A migrant woman's body is grounded in the state through medical encroachment on her pregnancy and birth, yet she remains a link to the home country even while she is the child's root in the new land.

Works Cited

Ainslie, Ricardo C., et al. "Contemporary Psychoanalytics Views on the Experience of Immigration." *Psychoanalytic Psychology*, vol. 30, no. 4, 2013, pp. 663-679.

Benza, Sandra, and Pranee Liamputtong. "Pregnancy, Childbirth and Motherhood: A Meta-synthesis of the Lived Experiences of Immigrant Women." *Midwifery*, vol. 30, no.6, 2014, pp. 575-584.

Bourdieu, Pierre. *Outline of a Theory of Practice.* Translated by Richard Nice. Cambridge University Press, 1977.

Bowlby, John. *Attachment and Loss, Vol. 1: Attachment.* Hogarth Press and the Institute of Psycho-Analysis, 1969.

Chodorow, Nancy. "The Psychodynamics of the Family." *Psychoanalysis and Woman: A Reader,* edited by Shelley Saguaro, New York University Press, 2000, pp. 108-127.

Davis, Angela. "I Want Them to Learn about Israel and the Holidays: Jewish Israeli Mothers in Early-Twenty-First-Century Britain." *Religion and Gender*, vol. 6, no.1, 2016, pp. 80–94.

Espin, Olivia M. *Women Crossing Boundaries: A Psychology of Immigration and Transformations of Sexuality.* Routledge, 1999.

Gledhill, John. *Power & Its Disguises: Anthropological Perspectives on Politics, Anthropology, Culture, and Society.* Pluto, 1994.

Grinberg, Leon, and Rebeca Grinberg. "A Psychoanalytic Study of Migration: Its Normal and Pathological Aspects." *Journal of the American Psychoanalytic Association*, vol. 32, no. 1, 1984, pp. 13-38.

Higginbottom, Gina, et al. "Immigrant Women's Experience of Maternity Services in Canada: A Meta-ethnography." *Midwifery*, vol. 30, no. 5, 2014, pp. 544-559.

Liamputtong, Pranee. "Motherhood and the Challenge of Immigrant Mothers: A Personal Reflection." *Families in Society*, vol. 82, no.2, 2000, pp. 295-301.

Loewenstein, Rudolph. "Some Remarks on the Role of Speech in Psychoanalytic Technique." *The International Journal of Psychoanalysis*, vol. 37, 1956, pp.460-468.

Phoenix, Anne. "Narrow Definitions of Culture: The Case of Early Motherhood." *Enterprising Women: Ethnicity, Economy and Gender Relations*, edited by Sallie Westwood and Parminde Bhachu, Routledge, 1998, pp. 121-139.

Red Cross "Trapped in a Bubble." *British Red Cross*, 2016, https://www.redcross.org.uk/about-us/what-we-do/action-on-loneliness. Accessed 28 Jan. 2019.

Tummala-Narra, Pratyusha. "Mothering in a Foreign Land." *The American Journal of Psychoanalysis*, vol. 64, no. 2, 2004, pp. 167-181.

ADVENTURE

Chapter 3

Travelling Light

Nicola Waldron

Hypothesis

In a passenger jet crossing the Atlantic, a mother travelling with a young child new to advancing unaided through space on hands and knees will manifest signs of rapid ego deterioration.

Collateral subjects in the closed site will demonstrate a variety of stress responses, as stimulated by the introduction of the id-dominant pair (child and mother) into a presumed—or hoped—controlled environment. These mature individuals will develop coping strategies designed to create and confirm their distance from the infantile-maternal realm. Chief among these strategies: disappearing into movies or literature containing, but not limited to, political intrigue, adult humour, nonprocreational sex, and barbarism.

An increase in the airline's sales of sedative items may, with some confidence, be predicted.

Materials

- One fourteen-month-old boy, possessing winning smile and impressive verbal and social skills: adored first child of previously infertile couple. Newly crawling. Ear infection. Oncoming gastrointestinal distress.

- One forty-year-old mother, severely sleep deprived, lactating: British native and long-time resident of United States, married to child's American father (absent from experiment).

- One transatlantic jet plane (as in "leaving on …", as in airborne holding pen).
- Three hundred to four hundred additional human subjects (diverse range).
- Diapers/wipes/changeofclothes/hat/socks/toys/books/breastpads/burpcloths/liquidantibiotic/liquidTylenol/handsanitizer/scented diaperdisposalbags/blankets/pillows/phone/passports/pictures of Daddy.

Experiment

Place mother and child on round trip flight between Chicago, the family's recently adopted home, and London Heathrow. Seal entranceways. Observe.

Purpose

To examine the dark reaches of human sanity.

To please Grandma.

Variables

Everything.

*

Phase One—OUTBOUND

7 hours, 40 minutes … or about the time it takes to watch a season of *Parenthood*, if not the entire oeuvre of *Dora the Explorer*. ¡Vámonos! A cinch, surely, compared with the picaresque adventures of my youth, those sleepless summers spent at the mercy of Italian train schedules and testosterone-oozing *ragazzi*, or a month-long bus tour across the Union in my twenties, insufficiently supplied with funds and survival skills. Also: the early days of motherhood. That mildewed daze.

It was February, off-season, so I figured we might benefit from shorter lines and possibly even an empty seat over which to drape ourselves and the many items of unpleasant-to-all baby paraphernalia I'd schlepped along—not to mention cheaper fares. My husband, father to the little chimp, wouldn't be joining us; we'd just moved to Chicago in order that he might progress in his academic career (my own, in education, having been curtailed, partly by choice, in the hopes I might write while enjoying our long-awaited infant son). Just the two of us then on our big adventure to visit "Gran'ma in England."

I booked a night flight. Surely our offspring would sleep for the duration, thereby saving me the agony of his frustrated twistings and turnings as our fellow passengers tried to steal a few hours rest. (Never was I fool enough to imagine that I might be allowed that blessed luxury.) On our return to Chicago, we'd arrive halfway through the snowy night, able to sneak in and tumble directly between the blissful covers...

It was a plan.

Flying, especially to the uninitiated, acts as a stimulant, the effects on a small child being comparable, perhaps, only to those of Adderall or cocaine on a full-size counterpart. On the outward leg of the journey, my son sprawled across my increasingly deadened thighs and turned—true to the Guthrie lyric his dad and I had sung him so often, "around and around and around and around"—refusing to surrender to the glorious nothingness of sleep and shut his lovely, cerulean eyes. His ear infection ("bulging," the doctor called it the day before we left) chose to coincide exactly with the moment of our departure, too late to exchange the tickets. That and a nasty bout of gut-scouring rotavirus. In my attempts to travel light, I'd packed exactly the number of Pampers Size 2 sufficient for a child with a normal schedule of exemplary bowel movements. No more, no less.

Ah, but how I kept my cool, gliding between seat and lavatory pod. (Wasn't I the initiator of the *true* mile-high club: changing diapers at turbulent elevations, clinging simultaneously to child and wipes, standing my heroic ground, thighs turned out in a determined plié, pressed against sink and door, while singing "Ay-yay-yippee" as if I'd dreamed of yodeling that melody all my life?). Watch me now and marvel as I relieve my own, much pressed-upon bladder and, reaching over my baby's fevered head, depress with a spare finger first hot then cold tap, managing somehow soap, somehow hand towel, washing off the impious germs, this hand then that, child lodged on expert hip.

Smiling all the while.

Forget, of course, eating. For while my globe-trotting companions munched on their chicken tikka masala dinners and mini ice cream bars, I worked to extract, separately, discreetly, my boobs from beneath three layers of thermal underwear, where I found my nipples crushed flat by my child's not inconsiderable weight—that compression increased by the tightened extender-seatbelt, an object the flight attendant had dandled before me on boarding like something I should know how to use. The elegant African Madonna who sat at the other end of our row managed to feed her little daughter, when she woke sweetly murmuring, at a geniously Mannerist angle from her ample bosom, while my pasty equipment, sucked flat as Lenten pancakes, refused to oblige.

We shared a wistful smile.

In front of my child's lovely head, a movie screen. With Oscar season approaching, the offerings were enticing: a choice between *Million Dollar Baby* (ours had come, courtesy of IVF, at a cost of a mere twenty thousand dollars, give or take) and *Eternal Sunshine of the Spotless Mind.* I watched as my fellow fliers drank in this artsy fare. It had been a long time since I'd enjoyed a film from beginning to end, the opportunity of movie-going being to parenthood as quaffing wine is to breast milk, as pulped carrot is to a sickly stomach, as lovemaking is to mastitis. Jim and I had managed one trip to the theatre since the arrival of our firstborn, when we'd been treated to *A Series of Unfortunate Events* while the NICU nurses who'd encouraged the trip, provided (I borrow here their words) "the most expensive babysitting service in the world." My milk, before the second act was through, had leaked two great, amorphous lakes across the front of my gauzy designer blouse.

Needless to say, when my son and I landed at Heathrow and Grandma appeared at the meeting point, face shining, then led us away in the direction of her Toyota, my brain was as fresh and yeasty as an airline breakfast roll. Her grandson, inevitably, nodded off in the car, lulled by the soothing roar of British motorway traffic, so that he'd wake later in the stilly English night, first puking, and then eager for mommy cabaret.

I wish I could tell you about the visit. Here is what I remember, or rather, what I learned (for I had much to learn):

- Introduce at your peril a crawling child into a house embellished with low-level candles burning.

- Do not underestimate the deprivations to joy afforded by the frightening depletion of your child's weight as lost through the body's various efforts to expel a nasty invasive germ. (I managed the multiple episodes of vomiting rather well, I thought, avoiding contamination of my mother's carpets *and* soft furnishings, an effort which kept me on my un-pedicured toes.)

Cultural side trips and matinees in the sparkling capital? Shopping? Those glorious hill walks of old? As new parents, we learn nothing if not how to handle disappointment. ("We'll try again when he's a bit older.")

But *Noddy* was on TV, so all was well. Oh yes, make way for Noddy. Shout a big HOORAY.

Phase Two—RETURN

8 hours, 55 minutes (the wind not, as the blessing has it, ever at our backs).

Naturally our departure was delayed, and we had to sit strapped to our seats on the runway. My little boy was now mostly recovered and ready for some full-throttle, postviral playtime. I'd stuffed my bags with Grandma's many donations: a fluffy hand puppet bunny that sprang out of its green felt lettuce patch; a jolly, squeaking bee; a sackful of interactive books—*Where's Spot? Pat the Bunny. Dear Zoo.* But what Young Sir wanted, more than any manipulation of defective, saliva-soaked tabs or peeking behind torn flaps, was to join the passengers up ahead in Club Class; there where the blue curtain beckoned. (What was behind it?) As soon as we finally got up in the air and the seatbelt sign flashed off, I freed the two of us from marsupial union, and—faster than those cushy customers could knock back their preflight champagne—he found his way forward. He'd learned by then a delightful scoot that had rubbed a hole in one leg of his overalls, and up the aisle he propelled himself on that excited, dominant knee.

"Wait ... we're not supposed..."

Half a swollen foot squeezed into each of my now Lilliputian-tight Danskos, I wrestled myself upright and clomped into the halcyon regions after my lightning charge—"Sorry, sorry"—grabbing him from behind by the scruff of his Grandma-knitted sweater and hauling him back to his starting place by the bulkhead—that haven of extra legroom situated with thoughtful proximity beside the (come-one, come-all) toilet pods. Oh, but it was a game! And off he went again. Only seven hours to go.

Those Club-Classers pulled in their sleep-socked feet; they peered over the lenses of their Prada collection reading glasses. I avoided the steward's gaze, and standing my son up on his slippered feet, I gripped his eager fingers from above so we might turn back to walk the aisles of coach class together, a staggering, adventuring pair. In the mirror of the cramped bathroom, where we stopped for frequent breaks, my eyes glowed scarlet, my hair mocked me, a static phantom of its former glory days. Then came the turbulence of a snowstorm over the Atlantic as the plane lunged into the moistureless Midwestern winter.

"PLEASE RETURN TO YOUR SEATS."

And I buckled us back together.

He wriggled; I reviewed the safety card. "*EXIT.* Can you see one? Look! The lady is jumping on the slide." I shared a nervous smile with the other mom at the far end of our row, a beauty from Nigeria on this occasion, travelling—like me—alone with her baby. Who was fast asleep.

Notes

1. The crawling child headed without apology for the boundary: he tugged back the curtain.

2. The appearance of the child's face, bright and expectant at this or that knee or elbow nudged into openness the stoniest of strangers, broke open (who knew!) the mother.

3. Passengers and crewmembers alike squatted down to whisper to the mother how seeing her with her sweet child made them long for home.

4. The child from Nigeria, her skin dark as roasted coffee beans, reached, mid-flight, across the seats for the boy's hand. The boy, milky white, arched his body and stretched to catch her fingers.

5. When the children connected hands, they laughed. Their mothers laughed.

6. Their mothers held them, as long as they could, aloft.

7. The boy, afterwards, slumbered on his mother's lap, balletic hands poised, eyes gently fluttering: travelling, *where?* the mother wondered. She watched him for many minutes: the way a heron watches, at dusk, the incoming ripples of a lake.

8. Somewhere over Greenland, the mother carried her son to the thick ledge of the emergency door. Through a window dressed in crystals, they watched the mountains play shadow games on the valleys below; a bronzed waterway carving its way through ice.

9. He sat, looking down on that mystical landscape, a contented prince.

10. Which made her, standing there, a queen.

Chapter 4

Waterfalls in the Dark

Li Miao Lovett

We're standing in the middle of a deserted parking lot, a few miles past the Yosemite National Park entrance. It's early spring, and the air is filled with the scent of pine, cedar, and damp asphalt. I try to coax my four-year-old out of his car seat. Alex is wide eyed and squirrelly after a four-hour drive on winding roads through rain that stabbed relentlessly at the pale light until it, too, disappeared with all that was familiar. He takes my friend's lantern; the glow is soothing in the coal black darkness. But he refuses to get out of the car.

At the outer edge of the national park, we are utterly alone except for the halo of lantern light in a vast fortress of granite rock and pine. My trusty Corolla—a grandma car enduring many a trip to the desert and high Sierras—has delivered us to this ominous place. It's hard to imagine that hours earlier we might have encountered an intrepid hiker or two, dishevelled and pumped with endorphins in the wake of a rainstorm. Now that night has fallen, we have every right, two women and a young child, to run screaming from the first blip of movement or noise that might disturb this dark forest.

My friend is itching for a short hike to the falls, but Alex will have none of it. We've driven through heavy rain all the way from San Francisco to Yosemite, and he doesn't care to hunt for waterfalls at night. It's only six o'clock, and the temperature is forty degrees, dropping as we speak. He clings to the lantern, the only ray of sanity amid the adults who must have lost their minds.

"Come on lamb, it'll be okay. We're just going on a short walk." My words make no sense to Alex. He looks to my friend, who is waiting patiently as she zips up her jacket and adjusts her boots, and then towards me, looking for a reassuring cue to unfreeze his instinctual panic. I understand his fear; I've felt it myself, at times facing it head on. For my son, this isn't about walking on lit coals, or any other scheme to overcome one's fears. His eyes say it: *Don't take away my fear; it's all I have.* Now I am the frozen one, caught between a mother's instincts to protect and my own desires. Beyond the dark cavern of this paved lot, soils will yield under my foot to shake off the stupor from the drive. That's what my body craves. The walk to the falls beckons me with its mysteries. And for a mom who has sought refuge in the woods, these pines are inviting in the pitch black of night, when the hum of nearby cars reminds us of civilization. But the will of a four-year-old is immense. It swallows my own, and I surrender to the safety of the car, to my maternal self.

I love being a mother, but I miss this part of my life in the age BCE—Before Children Emerged. Growing up in San Francisco's Chinatown, I was a cautious kid who waited until I was a young adult to take risks in nature and in life. But motherhood compels me to look left-right-left a second time before crossing the street. It also restrains me from crossing the boundaries of domestic life much nowadays. Someday I may take Alex to those places where I backpacked in my single days. I'm wistful for the freedom of sleeping under the stars, and frankly, the ability to pack up and take off when I sorely need to break away from the stresses of life.

Ten years earlier, I'd landed at the southern end of the Appalachian Trail, on a similarly dark night, but one that was filled with stars and devoid of company. It must have been past midnight when my driver dropped me off at the trailhead in Springer Mountain, Georgia. I stood there for a few minutes to compose myself, and then heaved on my backpack to search for the trail with my flashlight. Suddenly, a flutter of tiny red lights. Were they fellow hikers approaching or axe murderers in the night? I braced, ready to dive into the bushes. And then, to my amazement, I saw the cluster of lightning bugs with their glow playing off the glass surface of a trail sign. That was my introduction to the South. In the quiet of darkness, I hiked at least an hour until I found a place to unroll my sleeping bag. I'd located my trail home for the night, the first of many nights to come on that 600-mile journey. I hiked alone for most of those two months, relying on what I could carry on my back and the occasional company of strangers for sustenance.

In my culture, you're not really considered an adult until you have children. I defied my roots—I needed to enter adulthood on my own terms by encountering the unknown. Those forays into the wilderness allowed me to untether myself from my parents' hopes and fears. In my twenties, I'd lived through their disappointment that I would not become a doctor, lawyer, or engineer—the only professions that bring prestige to a Chinese immigrant family. It didn't matter that over the next several years, I would check off a few key markers of maturity, including a professional job and owning my own house at thirty. I became a college counsellor who worked with students, many of Asian descent, who struggled to find their path amid the blur of demands, expectations, and dangled rewards. I had stood for my convictions, but now my own path seemed to be a long train ride to retirement—with pleasant scenery along the way. I needed more. Those one hundred things to do before dying, that book I wanted to write, the gospel songs left unsung. They were the waterfalls in the darkness.

During the summer of 2001, my long-distance hike in the Appalachians did more than slake my thirst for adventure. To claim a stake in an unconventional life, I needed to go down a wilderness path that, if not exactly untrodden, was pretty sinuous and gruelling. I was about to give up a tenure-track position and lifetime security to pursue my creative passions. Giving up my identity as a good daughter—the Chinese kind who got straight A's and attended a college my folks could brag about—was as easy as getting some teeth pulled without Novocain. On the heels of change, insecurities and obsessive thoughts surrounded me and wouldn't let me go, much like the horsefly that encircled me for half an hour on the Appalachian Trail in Tennessee. I had to wrestle with my demons far away from the chatter of civilization.

As a long-distance hiker, I explored the boundaries of true adulthood, finding solace through Mary Oliver's poetry, through silence, and the distraction of sore feet challenged by these ancient mountains. *You do not have to be good. You do not have to walk on your knees for a hundred miles through the desert, repenting.* That final word changes everything. While huffing up and down the hills of Appalachia, I must have recited the lines in "Wild Geese" a hundred times and then a hundred more. It would be another six years before my son's birth, but in retrospect, this was a huge chasm between the Age of Searching and the Epoch of Settling Down.

Our first night in Yosemite, my son insists on going straight to the motel. Because of the rain, we had scaled the trip back from camping out. With this last concession, I'm resigned to a Disneyland experience in John Muir's haunting grounds. My craving for wilderness lingers, but the feeling is overshadowed by this mother's protective instinct. When you make a certain choice that leaves you wanting, a kind of confirmation bias sets in, perhaps to melt away that ambivalence. Yes, there could be axe murderers or falling branches weaponized by the storm. Dangers lurk in these woods. A dark, chilly parking lot is much scarier than Daddy playing monster or the "gobble-ins" in Alex's imagination.

The real bears are nowhere to be seen, but the fake ones are no better. At the motel, their images are everywhere, splashed across gift shop racks, carvings on hollow tree trunks, and signs admonishing us not to feed the bears. I want to tell him that you could chase a black bear away and that little insects are much peskier than a furry Chewbacca in the woods. I merely tell Alex that the bears are sleeping, night or day.

The first time I encountered bears on the Appalachian Trail was after one of the worst nights on my journey. I'd hiked until dusk, after circling the periphery of Brushy Mountain in Virginia on the ninth week of my trek. At an outcropping with gorgeous views of the Blue Ridge Mountains, I made camp. For my tent, I used a plastic tarp, a mere eight ounces that freed up weight in my forty-five-pound backpack for the essentials. The tarp was actually a large tube suspended by cords, which I tied at one end to a scraggly tree. It didn't occur to me that the ashen grey branches without any leaves would spell trouble. As I was tidying up my camp, the snag came down and tumbled onto my makeshift tent leaving an orange heap of plastic. A dead tree and lifeless tent—this was an omen of things to come. That evening, millipedes pooped in my food bag. I encountered a curious skunk that paid a visit during dinner, a house call without any spraying. I felt a burst of simple pleasure in this brief encounter by moonlight and went back to chewing my pasta alfredo.

This was the best part of the evening. The worst was the unwanted guests in my pop-up tent: no-see-ums that penetrated my mosquito netting and nipped at my face throughout the night with pin pricks. I swiped at them, but true to their name, these buggers were nearly invisible. The next morning, I railed silently against the deceptions of nature, a beautiful campsite where agents of torture lurked in the night. Wearily, I pulled together my belongings and got back on the trail. A half hour later, I caught sight of two junior bears about a hundred yards ahead of me on the trail. In my zombie state, I was grateful to be in the presence of living creatures. Black bears are generally shy, and no mother was in sight. Reading *A Walk in the Woods* before my trip, I'd startled at the tale of the hikers mauled by black bears. But this was an anomaly, and it wasn't going to stop me from going. Perhaps those other bears were starving during a bad berry year. Maybe they'd been provoked or disturbed from their slumber. I'd be upset too.

My encounters in the wild have helped me to combat primal fears around the things we think will bite, hurt, or kill us. The wilderness tests our boundaries because we really don't know what is beyond that glowing lantern in a deserted parking lot. When we encounter our limits, it's actually a step towards freedom from the delusion that we can do it all or do it alone. On blazing hot days in the Appalachians or on tortuous climbs in the Mojave Desert, I've learned to accept the help of strangers and comrades. The wilderness forces us to accept our place in the grand scheme of things, and when the ego quiets down, we can pause and appreciate the silence. The unexpected turns and the disasters that become fodder for stories, these are the parts of outdoor travel that have kept me limber in mind and body. Ordinary life, especially in the city, is noisy and demanding. I must not be the only mom who wants to reclaim my earlier self sooner than retirement, when it might be too late, when all we will want to do is keep the empty nest warm and stocked with food to entice our grown children back home.

The next day on our Yosemite trip, Alex finds his stride on the trail to Mirror Lake. No crowds, just a valley of rocks big and small and puddles to skip around. He asks about the bears, but they are inconsequential at the moment. He moves through space fearlessly, at one point running up a giant slab of granite with a vertical drop off. That's the signal for Mom to use her outside voice and hustle him down. Yet I'm heartened that he takes to the rocks so naturally that he skips ahead of us with boundless energy like the fresh snowmelt tumbling down Tenaya Creek. He is reserved around other young children; to him, they are hungry animals waiting to pounce when they spot a desirable toy, an empty swing. But on this day, he is completely at home in a landscape shaped by great movements of water, wind, and rock.

I had few opportunities for such fearlessness growing up. Vacations took us to casino country, where my parents and I whizzed past the spectacular scenery of the Golden State with the windows rolled up. At home, my only outdoor experiences were the city's playgrounds, where I kept away from the fireman poles, the dark chambers of wooden climbing structures, and the old men who played mahjong while sitting on concrete benches. I only knew urban places filled with concrete—well contoured and predictable. My routes of travel were well defined. Each morning and afternoon, I passed the same houses and shops along the ten blocks to and from school. By the time I was thirteen, when I lived with my mother's relatives, I was emboldened to explore the streets of San Francisco on foot and by bus. My mom joined my dad in our house in the suburbs, but I would stay to finish eighth grade surrounded by aunts and uncles newly arrived from Taiwan. They hated the quiet streets devoid of nightlife; they missed their friends, and they found fault with me, a prepubescent niece in their midst. This propelled me to take the first steps towards independence. I did not rebel like other young adolescents, as I still had too much of the Chinese daughter and Catholic upbringing in me. Instead, I combed the streets on my own after school—staying out as late as possible to explore the perimeters of North Beach and downtown San Francisco and wending my way among the tourists, business suits, and homeless folks.

Nowadays, I feel the tug between the life of independence I once had and the duties attendant to raising a kid in a culture where child-rearing doesn't get a lot of support. Becoming a parent in my late thirties—geriatric in medical terms—I had a chance to find my footing and be an adult on my own terms. I get to engage Alex in ways that my parents never did. I could never imagine having played with my own mother as Alex plays with me, whether it's pickup basketball in our backyard or a round of kiddie Monopoly that he usually wins. Since our Yosemite trip, we've gone camping a few times and explored trails around the San Francisco Bay Area. But these are infrequent, and I admit that there's a firewall I keep between family travel and my pilgrimages in the outdoors. As the years scroll by, I'm aware that the time we spend with our children goes all too quickly. Our routines become well-etched grooves, and it appeals to the middle-aged parts of me that like the world to be predictable and comfortable. But this Epoch of Settling Down must lead to more than the Path of Going Downhill with senility and death waiting. I want to explode those age-old myths.

Growing up as a latchkey kid has its perks later in life. It has made me fearless as a solo traveller, able to sleep in the woods amid screeching owls, backpacking strangers, and the occasional mouse in the Appalachian Trail shelters. For now, my own mountaineering adventures seem like a film reel, packed away in the attic. As my son grows older, I hope he will share the same zest for exploring wild places—if only in broad daylight, not a deserted lot on the way to promised waterfalls. Someday I imagine finding places off the beaten path with my son and seeing him off on his own adventures with a wistful hug.

On our road trip to Yosemite, we spent only two hours hiking, which barely scratched an itch for exploring wild places. I suppose I've just scratched the surface of motherhood, which has its share of adventure. It's a long and winding road, and you never know what might be around the corner—a black bear or the dance of fireflies to light the way.

Chapter 5

Annapurna Epiphany

Dena Moes

"Annapurna Peak is 26,500 feet," my fourteen-year-old daughter Bella read from the guidebook, as the car bumped along. "Everest is 29,000 feet; so really, it is almost as tall as Everest. It is the tenth highest mountain in the world." She put the book on her lap and smiled at me, impressed. My family was midway through our yearlong sojourn through India and Nepal. We had walked the sacred *ghats* of Varanasi, prayed under the tree where the Buddha attained enlightenment, canoed in the backwaters of Kerala, and celebrated Holi in Rajasthan. We had ridden buses, trains, rickshaws, and camels. The last place we had been was Boudanath, near Kathmandu. My husband Adam and I spent two weeks there studying Buddhist philosophy with a Tibetan *Rinpoche*. Bella took Buddhist seminars and also volunteered at a school and an orphanage. Our ten-year-old Sophia had studied Tibetan painting in an art studio facing the pillar of Buddhist pilgrimage, the Great *Stupa*. Now we were on our way to the trailhead for a five-day trek on the Poon Hill Circuit. For this, we had a temporary fifth family member, a strapping young guide named Isur. Our route would take us along a ridge of mountains, in view of the massive glacial peaks, without going above ten thousand feet in elevation. This made the trek suitable for beginners and families; we were both.

"This day will be easy for the first three hours; then, we will climb four thousand stone stairs to get to our lodging," Isur explained.

Months of lemon pancakes for breakfast, sweet cups of chai throughout the day, and no regular exercise had softened me considerably. I asked, "How are we going to make it up four thousand stone steps?"

Isur ignored the question, so Adam answered instead. "One at a time."

*

The modern world slipped away in fragments. First, we walked along a dirt road, jeeps and trucks passing us every so often. Even then, the green, lush landscape called to me. The soft hillsides, verdant glens, and blossoming rhododendron trees hummed seductive ballads as I walked. After two hours, the road ended. Now we were on a rocky, uphill trail, the primordial mountain byway. People and their pack animals had traversed these trails since at least 550 BC. High peaks played peek-a-boo with strands of fog above us. Butterflies and bubbling creeks gave the scenery a tropical feel. Wobbling steel suspension bridges spanned roaring rivers. These terrified Sophia, who crossed them with her eyes squeezed shut. Every hour or so, we passed a village with subsistence farms on tiny terraced plateaus, stone houses, healthy-looking chickens and dogs, ruddy-cheeked children, and anything we could want for sale: soda, Snickers, Pringles, chai.

The trail was full with other hikers from all over the world. Sherpas passed them, heavy gear and supplies in baskets tied to their heads. Ancient local women trotted the steep trails in plastic flip-flops and saris, dusting us with their speed and grace. Once in a while, the tinkling of bells warned us to step aside and let the donkey trains loaded with food and supplies go by.

Sophia complained, "Mom, all the hikers have walking sticks but us." She was right. To a person, every foreign hiker had a high-tech trekking pole in hand.

"Sorry, I didn't get the memo about trekking poles," I said, tripping over a rock. A walking stick would come in handy. We rounded a bend, and a Nepali family sat by the trail, brightly painted sticks of bamboo in their hands.

"Walking sticks, Madam?"

"How much?"

"One hundred rupees each [one dollar]."

"Fine, we will take four. Pick yours first, Sophia."

We got our sticks just in time to face the four-thousand-step ascent. Throughout the five days, Adam, Bella, and I relied heavily on those sticks to assist us along the rocky trails. Sophia, however, only used hers when she was tired. Then she would put it between her legs like a

Harry Potter *quidditch* broomstick, get a burst of energy, and go running up the trail ahead of everyone.

*

The night before the Poon Hill ascent, I didn't sleep well. Perhaps it was the altitude, but I tossed and turned, anxious I would miss the 4:30 a.m. wake-up. I didn't. Up and out of bed in the freezing cold, I woke up the girls. Bella looked at the clock and yelled at me for not waking her up at four on the dot, so we could go at the exact time as the German family we met the day before. I woke up Adam, and he sat up groaning, his face green. He had been sick since yesterday, when he chugged the raw yak milk that a farmer offered him. Note to self: don't drink a stranger's raw yak milk out of a dirty bucket.

We bundled up and were on the trail by 4:40 a.m. We went without Adam or we would miss the sunrise. The trail was already packed with trekkers. It was pitch black; our headlamps gave us thin circles of light. The trail was steep steps, straight up. I hurried to keep up with Isur and the girls, and stay ahead of a wolf pack of hikers behind me. I was so strained and out of oxygen that when I tried to speak my words sounded as though I had a mouth full of pebbles. We made it to the top just as the sun was beginning to rise, gasping for breath. Isur fetched us hot chocolate and coffee from the stall on the summit.

The peaks, Annapurna and Dhaulagiri, soared above the clouds, looking like they were floating in the ether, untethered to the earth. The Poon Hill summit was a multinational madhouse of cheers and the wrangling of tripods and massive cameras with lenses like long tongues reaching out to lick the view. Most of these people had come all the way to Nepal just for this sunrise. The mountain peaks turned bright pink and then appeared to be lined with golden fire.

At breakfast back at the lodge, Adam moaned and belched and made sad faces. I choked on my eggs trying stifle the "I told you so" that rang through my head. Adam went back to bed; Isur went to find him medicine, and I watched as within an hour, every last one of the hundreds of hikers cleared out. The bustling village was deserted, and I had the view of the peaks, clouds forming and dancing around them, all to myself. Bella stomped around, positively livid that her new German friends had left while she was stuck here alone again.

"It figures when I finally meet some kids my age, after months with no friends, Dad has to do this."

"You're right, Bella. I am sorry you have learned the truth: Dad got sick just to torture you."

After a two hour nap, Adam got up, took the Flagyl Isur found at the village pharmacy, and announced he was feeling better. I could hardly walk with my muscle fatigue, but out into the Himalayan sunshine we marched. Sophia placed her stick between her legs like a broomstick and zoomed off along the trail. Bella glowered at me and walked along, head hanging. Adam went silently, bearing the sickness he'd brought on himself with dignity. I let them all get ahead of me, and as I walked along, it suddenly hit me that I was not responsible for anyone's happiness but my own. As the mom, I thought, I am always trying to fix everything for everyone. I can't do it anymore; what experiences they have are up to them. I just need to look at myself now; where am I at. What am I bringing to this?

Sore and exhausted, that's where I was at. To keep going forward, I attended to the placement of every footstep along the treacherous trail. I leaned heavily on the red and yellow bamboo staff. Step, step, stick. Step, step, stick. In rhythm with my clumsy footfalls, *pat, pat, pat,* cold raindrops began to fall. The Himalayan sun had just been beating down from a bright blue sky. I was so groggy that at first I thought I was imagining it when the eerie twilight fell. I looked up to see that the mountains had vanished behind a wall of black clouds. Thunder boomed, and streaks of lightening licked the foothills behind us.

"Girls!" I called out. "Put on your rain ponchos."

Isur stopped to tell us there was a teahouse an hour's walk ahead. "I'm gonna sprint there with your pack of gear," he said. "Just stay on the trail," he called back, as he took off running. "I'm going with him!" announced Bella, breaking into a run before I could respond. Sophia was at her heels, her long legs and blond ponytail disappearing around a bend. I took off my daypack with a groan and fished out my rain poncho. I thought Adam was still standing beside me. But when I looked up, he was gone too.

"Wait,'" I said to no one. "I think we should stay together."

Rain dripped into my eyes and soaked through my sneakers. Every moment I dawdled, the distance between my family and me grew larger. So I plodded on. After twenty minutes of walking, the rain turned to thick snow. A blanket of silence fell, broken only by an occasional rumble of thunder. My wet feet were cold, even as I sweated with exertion. My thighs felt hammered by the meat pounder of over-ambitious trekking; each step was an excruciating choice to keep going. The landscape was blurred by thick white flurries, many of them lodged in my eyelashes. I could see just a few feet in front of me, and I wondered if I had wandered off the trail. I thought about my children, running on the narrow path in slippery snow to an unknown destination, with a man we had only met two days ago. In other words, I started to worry.

I heard myself panting—a mix of fear and the strain of not quite enough oxygen at ten thousand feet. While I caught my breath, I looked this way and that, willing someone to appear and escort me to shelter. A handsome Nepali youth in a colourful wool cap was my first choice. But a sturdy grandmother in a sari, a wizened shepherd with his goats—anyone would be fine. No one came. *That's okay,* I told myself. *You're fine. Keep going.* As I made slow, sloshing progress on the trail, my mind skimmed through an encyclopedia of emotional states, feelings storming through me in rapid succession and then falling away.

First, was my automatic whiny California-girl response: *Shit, I don't want a storm on my trek. Now I can't even see the beautiful mountains. We were supposed to have perfect weather. Maybe we should have done this next week.*

Then, fear and blame. *I am sure this is dangerous and I should be alarmed. I can see the headlines now; "The Terrible Fate of a California Family Caught in a Himalayan Blizzard." Whose idea was this? Oh yeah, mine.*

Maternal fear. *My girls! How could I have let them run ahead? What if something happens to them? I can't even see them; I have to just trust they will be fine. What kind of mother does that make me?*

Awe. *Wow, this is actually beautiful. I am experiencing the fury of Mother Nature in all her glorious power. Look how heavy the rhododendron flowers are, sagging under their coating of snow. I am so high up here; I am practically in the storm clouds. Now that I have calmed down, I love this!*

Gratitude. *Thank goodness we are in Nepal, where there is a village every few kilometres up here. If we were in the West, where the vast wildernesses are devoid of human civilization, we would be toast.*

Grief. *How sad. I have lived my whole life believing that mountains are empty of human habitation by their very nature. But that is not true. If there hadn't been the genocide of Native Americans, American mountains would look more like Nepal.*

Concentration. *One step at a time, just don't slip, don't wander off the trail. Don't worry that my sneakers are soaked and squish like a sponge with every step. Doesn't matter. Keep walking.*

Silence. *My mind empty of thought. Clear and still like pure mountain air.*

Freedom and euphoria. *This is so real. I am here. I did it! I got back to myself... I AM ALIVE!*

Joy overtook me. The American life we left behind was a hamster wheel, and I was the hub. Multitasking before the sun was up, I cooked breakfast, made lunches, and hustled children off to school. I worked until three, and then drove kids to violin lessons and play rehearsals. Arriving home to "Mom! What's for dinner?" I rushed to get something passable on the table. I was on call for work constantly. Behind on yard work, laundry, house maintenance, dentist appointments, social commitments, and automobile upkeep, I fell into bed each night worrying about tomorrow, vowing to catch up and make a healthy dinner in the crock pot, too. Adam would complain, why was I always so tired?

Here, there was one task: keep going. My shackles of schedules and to-do lists were broken. The clarity of my precise, single goal—to stay on the trail—was a beautiful thing, like a meditation. One foot in front of the other, wiping the snow from my eyes, I felt free. My fear dissipated, the ache in my legs melted away, and my limp became a jog. I galloped along the trail now, feeling more alive than I had in years—wide awake, clear headed, and not just going through the motions. I decided to yell—using my voice to pierce the silence of the muffling snow.

"I am not driving the carpool today!" I sang out over the edge of the cliff.

"I am not at my computer paying bills" I called to the trees.

"I am not trolling the grocery aisles for the millionth time, wondering what's for dinner!" I shouted my utter relief into the void below.

"I am not reachable by phone!" I sobbed, "I am out of range!"

I ran faster. The trail descended into a valley and into a forest of towering pines. I pounded down the mountain, saw a house tucked into the trees, and made a beeline for the door. *I am a fully realized Heroine! I am powerful, like the storm! I can take these sopping wet sneakers off!*

"I made it!" I shouted as I burst through the door.

The room was full of people: my family, several other trekkers including the German family, and the Nepalis whose house this was. The mood in the room was calm, and everyone turned to stare at me. I was dripping with snow, face covered in tears, and had just come through the door yelling.

A fire blazed in a woodstove; wet clothes hung to dry, and bowls of soup steamed on the tables. Sophia grinned at me, a bowl of Maggi noodles before her. Bella glared her warning: *Mom, don't be embarrassing.* Adam warmed his hands over the stove.

"Namaste" I said to the Nepali woman nearest me, clearing my throat and wiping the tears from my face. She looked concerned.

"I am not upset," I mumbled softly. "These are actually tears of joy."

She looked at me, silently.

"Namaste," she finally replied.

I peeled off my wet clothes, ordered a chai, and noticed that Bella was playing cards with the long-lost German kids. Sophia had made friends with a British girl who had twinkling green eyes and a mischievous grin just like hers. Adam and I introduced ourselves to the two sets of parents, and we settled in to wait out the storm.

Adam pulled his ukulele out of our pack; we sang "Free Fallin'," "Hotel California," and Bob Marley's "Don't Worry about a Thing." This brought the extended multigenerational Nepali family out of the kitchen and bedrooms. They sang Nepali songs to us in return. The German kids had attended a Waldorf School, and knew the same songs our kids did, so they sang some of those together in a German-English jumble. Isur found a rickety boom box, popped in a cassette tape, and pulled me up to dance a traditional Nepali dance. When the storm had blown itself out in the late afternoon, we decided to continue the trek together, as a group. Bella and Sophia were delighted to hike with other kids. The Nepali family sold us warm fleece mittens and hats; we put on our now-dry shoes and headed out into the slushy forest, our band of chattering children leading the way.

*

Dena Moes's chapter "Annapurna Epiphany" is an excerpt from her full-length memoir, *The Buddha Sat Right Here: A Family Odyssey Through India and Nepal,* from She Writes Press April 2019.

Chapter 6

Long Haul Flight after a Visit to the Dali Museum

Jane Frank

The plane is chasing the sun
across a white desert,
a torn page floating in space.
Outside it is -43 degrees
but no mention inside.
I am marble,
my drawers opening
and slamming shut:
one brimming with reckless ideas
another leaking memories,
there's one of nurture,
and the dark one I can't close.
Through the round window,
past the waft of mass produced beef stew,
angels, shells, and fish
float in the light of a day
still to be born.

Chapter 7

Mexican Restaurants in Deutschland

Vanessa Couto Johnson

Honey I want to hold
your hand at the expensive
La Bandida where the Germans
spread sour cream across the tops
and sides of enchiladas.

Those little drink umbrellas,
I wonder if they realize how
much liquid's beneath them.

After Sex on the Beach I'm out
on the Berlin street leaning as though
the sand's on my ass
while in a kangaroo position,

and I laugh and laugh
at your expression and the Berliner
that goes by on his bike
laughs my laugh purposefully.

Chapter 8

As I Travel to Key West

Katharyn Howd Machan

I'm wearing clothes that are
too big, too loose:
turquoise stretch jeans
sliding down my hips,
a huge-shouldered jacket
painted with fish.
Even my watch with its
bold glass beads, face
a flamenco dancer.
Even my golden ring
so wide
it catches light through
the airplane window,
almost reflects how I'm
far past fifty,
a mother leaving her
children at home,
a woman comfortable
flying south in winter,
a little big,
a little loose.

IDENTITY

"No Ship Is Going to Sink with My Family on It": Motherhood and Travel in Jackie French's Children's Novel *How the Finnegans Saved the Ship*

Charlotte Beyer

Introduction: Travelling Mothers

The Australian author Jackie French's 2001 children's novel, *How the Finnegans Saved the Ship,* tells the story of how in 1913, just a few years before the Irish Easter Rising of 1916, Mrs. Finnegan and her seven children sail from Dublin, Ireland, to Australia to reunite with their husband and father and seek their fortune in the new world. The dramatic and life-changing circumstances as well as the uncertainty and upheaval brought by family migration are captured in the portrayal of the Finnegan family in the novel's opening: "There were eight Finnegans on the quay that morning in 1913, with their portmanteaus and their brown paper packages in their hands"(9)[1]. Jackie French is a widely-known children's author, and was the 2014-2015 Australian Children's Laureate. Although fictional, French's children's novel *How the Finnegans Saved the Ship* resonates with the real stories of many mothers who, with their children and belongings in tow, have embarked on strenuous and often perilous journeys to escape poverty and hardship and to make a fresh start in a new part of the world.[2] Nevertheless, more broadly speaking, cultural and literary representations focusing on mothers travelling are few and far between. The critics Marybeth Bond and Pamela Michael, the editors of the volume *A Mother's World: Journeys of the Heart* (1998), investigate this surprising gap in representation and explain why mothers seem to be absent from travel writing. In researching travel writing and the absence of maternal representation, Bond and Michael urge their readers to "search the book shelves of libraries or bookstores and you will find volumes and volumes of travel literature. But you will discover very few that depict women traveling with children or experiencing themselves in 'mothering' ways, nurturing others, or engaging in other women's mothering experiences" (xv-xvi). These important questions, regarding what has traditionally been perceived as the irreconcilability of motherhood and travel, are at the heart of the discussions and portrayals encapsulated by the image of the "travellin' mama." Yet critical and scholarly examinations have rarely concerned themselves with the topic of motherhood and travel in children's literature. My essay aims to redress this issue by examining how motherhood and travel are depicted in the context of migration in French's *How the Finnegans Saved the Ship*.

This chapter, as part of our book examining representations and experiences of travelling mothers, seeks to remedy the relative lack of scholarly attention paid to the figure of the travelling mother and to the complexities of representing maternal travel. These discussions are part of the effort to add further dimension to considerations of motherhood, mobility, and travel in literature, the arts, and the world. Drawing on critical and theoretical perspectives in relation to motherhood, travel, migration, and genre, my analysis of French's novel argues that children's literature plays an important role in not only portraying but also shaping and transforming readers' understanding of both maternal identities and travel. *How the Finnegans Saved the Ship*, specifically, explores postcolonial and maternal dimensions of intercontinental travel and the connections forged by mothers between Ireland and Australia. My examination of motherhood and travel in French's novel focuses on the construction of Mrs. Finnegan's maternal character and her role and function within the novel by foregrounding her specific qualities and strengths as well as the significance of these traits for the successful travel undertaken by her and her children. This reading is contextualised through the exploration of historical and cultural educational aspects of *How the Finnegans Saved the Ship* and of discourses of Irishness and Australian identity. The present focus includes an emphasis on the processes of travel, and their historical, cultural, and social contexts, specifically for a postcolonial country such as Australia, the population of which has witnessed continual growth and change facilitated by migrants from diverse global backgrounds (see Richards). The aim of this analysis is to underline the significance of French's novel in contributing to the representation in children's literature of strong, maternal female characters with the capacity to travel. Both topics—strong and inspirational maternal characters, and travel and migration—are subjects of crucial relevance to today's social and cultural debates. That they can be found depicted and investigated in a children's book further points to the important role that children's literature plays in contributing to and shaping these vital current debates surrounding travel and migration. Literature about travel involves confronting the new, encountering danger, trauma, disappointments, and challenges, as well as accepting and showing openness towards the other. In French's book, the mother figure Mrs. Finnegan is vital to these representations.

A Voyage of Self-Discovery

Traditionally, travel and motherhood have been conceived as irreconcilable, as maternal identity has been seen to represent traditional feminine values and as associated with home and permanence. Bond and Michael state that, conventionally, female travellers have been depicted as childless, reinforcing the idea that motherhood is irreconcilable with travel. They argue that women in conventional travel literature are often seen to abandon familial responsibilities, including children, as they embark on travel, rendering them "childless, solo adventurers—rootless" (Bond and Michael xvi). French's *How the Finnegans Saved the Ship* demonstrates how contemporary authors challenge these limiting stereotypes of motherhood that seek to restrict women's physical and symbolic mobility. Mrs. Finnegan's character highlights the contradictions of Irish motherhood, resulting from religious and social restrictions on female sexuality and the vilification of motherhood outside marriage. Raising her cousin's child born outside wedlock as her own, Mrs. Finnegan's resists these patriarchal cultural and religious norms, as she is determined to put her family first rather than to cast out this child in need of her care. As she emerges from the shadow cast by the symbolic figure of Mother Ireland, an embodiment of feminine submission (Clarke 1)[3], Mrs. Finnegan and her voyage to Australia represent the strength and courage of mothers everywhere embarking on travel seeking a brighter future for their children.

In telling the story of maternal and familial travel, and linking this narrative to the history of two nations, Ireland and Australia, French's novel demonstrates a strong educational dimension, evident in the text's structure and presentation. Laid out with chapters, the titles of which clearly demarcate the structure of the journey undertaken by the Finnegan family, *How the Finnegans Saved the Ship* also contains a number of realist black-and-white sketches that serve the important purpose of rendering the narrative more personal and compelling through the use of an appealing visual dimension. Through depicting the routines around the ship and in their family's cabin, and describing the food the Finnegans bring with them on the journey as well as the food served on board the ship, French creates a realistic travel writing discourse centred on maternal and intimate familial concerns. This narrative focus differs radically from the conventional male explorer narrative of the Victorian era, which portrayed travel as a masculine quest for transcendence and conquest (Bainbridge 452). Furthermore, the inclusion in the novel of an extensive appendix discussing the Irish famine and the cultural politics of food (Rowe) serves to historicize travel and the specific physical and political pressures that drove mobility between nations and continents. French, thus, explains how migration and travel overseas came to determine the lives of countless Irish families: "By the time the Finnegans emigrated almost half the Irish people had either died or left for the United States, Canada, South Africa and Australia" (French 114). Furthermore, French's recounting of traditional Irish food recipes further creates a link between Ireland, the country of origin and its customs and habits, and the new world, Australia. These links establish a sense of continuity and help to engender a sense of connection based on memory, which is arguably central to both postcolonial children's literature and to travel writing.

Such educational aspects demonstrate how *How the Finnegans Saved the Ship*, as reviewer Kelly Marie Rowe states, "seamlessly blends historical fact with fiction" and illustrates how travel fiction may be employed as an imaginative educational and creative tool. The novel also includes a drawing of a map that in easy-to-understand terms represents the probable route for the daunting voyage undertaken by the Finnegans. Starting in Dublin, the ship sailed past the Canary Islands, around Cape Town and Durban in South Africa, and the crossed the Indian Ocean to reach its final destinations—the Australian cities Perth, Melbourne, and Sydney. This visual representation of the Finnegans' journey further underlines the important educational aspect of the book—teaching contemporary child and adult readers the history of Irish-Australian travel and migration—provides an important opportunity for discussion of child readers' own families and their past and present personal experiences of events such as migration. Andy Bielenberg notes that "between the 1840s and 1914 about a third of a million Irish moved to Australia" seeking "economic opportunity" and "social mobility" (221). And Helena Wulff stresses that "emigration and exile, travel and mobility have been a vital part of Irish culture for a long time" (33). Thus, children's literature is not set apart from critical or revisionary engagement with history; on the contrary, it incorporates and problematizes these evaluative dimensions, providing a particular kind of prism through which to see travel and migration.

How the Finnegans Saved the Ship engages with the history of maternal travel by transporting readers back in time to 1913, when going to Australia from Ireland invariably meant a long and often perilous sea voyage. This historical view of travel serves to create a contrast with the present-day: "For most of the twentieth century, Australian identity as portrayed in children's books was grounded in the expansion of the British Empire through exploration, settlement and the transformation of local landscapes by the activities of pioneers and successive waves of immigrants" (Nimon 12). These postcolonial dimensions are central to the depiction of motherhood and travel in *How the Finnegans Saved the Ship*, as is the real-life historical sinking of the Titanic in 1912, just a few years prior to when French's story is set.[4] The tragic legacy of the Titanic weighs on the Finnegans' minds as they prepare for the voyage, which provides a negative and frightening master narrative for travel. Already before they have boarded the ship, the children ask whether the ship they are sailing on, the Anna Maria, will sink like the Titanic did (French 10). The striking contrast in physical appearance between the two ships, the Titanic and the Anna Maria, furthermore serves to highlight the impact of class and social status on the different modes of travel available to mothers and their children. The novel explains that "the Anna Maria was fat-bellied and shabby and made of wood, not like the Titanic's shining metal. She was a one-class steam ship, carrying a handful of immigrants and cargo to South Africa and then to Australia" (French 10). However, the tragic narrative of inevitable destruction symbolized by the Titanic is reimagined in French's novel into a narrative of challenge and eventual success engendered by a spirit of survival and communal resistance.

The representation of the experience of voyaging at sea from Ireland towards the new world, as a transitional phase that offers the potential for the renegotiation of identities, is a central aspect of the depiction of maternal travel in *How the Finnegans Saved the Ship*. In French's novel, the sea voyage marks an important symbolic stage of transition and highlights the perilous position of the individual subject at sea when confronted with the elements and the absence of land. *How the Finnegans Saved the Ship* gives realistic descriptions of the unpleasant physical effects of travel that had to be endured on early twentieth-century ships, such as extreme seasickness and suffering on board in cramped and poorly equipped conditions. These graphic represent-ations of discomfort and suffering are enhanced by the book's black-and-white illustrations, which show the conditions of travel for working-class passengers at the time, adding a sense of authenticity and social critique to the narrative. The novel's illustration showing the Finnegans' cramped rustic cabin with only the barest of basic comforts—the washing hanging to dry suspended in the room (French 47)—gives a realistic depiction of the realities of the Spartan conditions on board experienced by the lower-class travellers. The novel, furthermore, traces how the climate changes as they voyage on and the impact of these weather changes on Mrs. Finnegan and her children. During the voyage, Mrs. Finnegan and her oldest daughter Mary remove their stockings because of the warmer weather—an allusion to the potential freedoms, physical and mental, that travel can bring. This example forms a parallel to the reorganization and reimagining of individual subjective and collective national identities that travel engenders. However, *How the Finnegans Saved the Ship* also explores how the sea's volatility and mobility can threaten the stability of the self, echoing the point made by the critic Robert Foulke: "The environment of long sea passages promotes reflection. The thoughtful seafarer is enclosed irrevocably in the finite world of the ship with time on his hands. He must spend much of that time standing watch— literally *watching* and waiting for something, *or nothing*, to happen" (4). Echoing this insight regarding the meditative dimension of sea voyaging and the feeling of watchfulness it generates, Mrs. Finnegan is frequently described as looking out for icebergs and whales that may threaten the ship, which reflects a maternal need to protect her children reinforced by the memory of the Titanic tragedy.

Furthermore, the Finnegans' long sea voyage is characterized by constant change, a point also made by Foulke's description of a ship as "an unstable element that keeps [the traveller] in constant motion" (4). The novel's lyrical passages, depicting the ever-changing nature of the sea, contribute to making its descriptions of the voyage realistic: "All there was to see were sky and waves. When the sky was grey the sea was too, and when it was clear the sea was green and the sky was high and blue, with racing dark shadows on the waves as puffy grey clouds fled across the sky, dropping rain as they passed" (French 45). The changeability of the sea is echoed in the traveller acquiring a more perceptive state of mind and a heightened sensitivity in order to adjust to the constantly changing nature of their existence while voyaging— the changes in the weather, in the smell and warmth of the air, and the different nuances of light and sea water. Foulke comments on this dimension: "The seafarer's sense of time ... is both linear and cyclical, linear in the sense that voyages have beginnings and endings, departures and landfalls; time is also cyclical, just as the rhythm of the waves is cyclical" (4). However, the novel's title, which emphasizes the word "saved," also points towards the danger and risk that travel entails. *How the Finnegans Saved the Ship* builds in danger and tension, followed by a climactic moment of the struggle for survival, and then finally the safe arrival to Australia. This narrative structure enables the story to take in the myriad dimensions of travel—the boredom and sameness day in and day out as well as the moments of danger, hard work, struggle for survival, and tension that were all part of sea travel in the early twentieth century. Importantly, Mrs. Finnegan has a central function in keeping the family together and maintaining her children's safety and welfare throughout the high points and low moments of the sea voyage.

A vital dimension in Australian postcolonial children's literature is the reimagining of aspects of the country's history previously neglected, which is an important educational aspect of the novel in its depiction of the history of migration from Ireland to Australia. *How the Finnegans Saved the Ship* portrays the dislocation of migrant experience through Mary's growing realization of the great change travel affords. On leaving Ireland, Mary ponders how "Home was a long long way away now and every moment made it further away still. It was all different in Australia" (French 27). She understands that "even if the ship turned back there was no going home ... And slowly Ireland, even the idea of Ireland, faded like the stars" (French 95-96). Though hopeful, the Finnegan family quickly hear negative things about Australia. The next morning over breakfast, fellow travellers, the O'Gorman family, tell the Finnegans awful stories about Australia: "a terrible country it was, she said, a terrible place" (French 37). This portrayal not only contrasts with but directly contradicts Mr. Finnegan's stories about Australia that he has told his family—a welcoming society where they will be able to afford a large house with all modern conveniences and also access educational opportunities for their children. But the O'Gormans' view of Australia is very gloomy; they claim it is "sunshine and never a drop of rain from one month to the next, and bitter hot it is too, so the grass shrivels on the ground and your heart shrivels in you too" (French 38). Insisting that Australia is all things bad, the O'Gorman family embodies a negative and fearful attitude towards travel, which hints at the darker side of migration and the sense of despair and entrapment when things do not work out well. In contrast, the Finnegan family is determined to make the best of what awaits them, together. These contrasting attitudes reflect the complex circumstances that lead to travel and migration and the difficulties migrants encounter in adjusting to and settling in changed circumstances.

Later in the narrative, Mary bravely works through the night during a terrible storm that threatens to sink the ship. As she and her younger brother struggle alongside other passengers to save the ship from sinking, Mary begins to gain a clearer idea of Australia and what living there might mean. It is this image of the future and of hope that they're travelling towards that keeps her going and thus helps to save them all and save the ship from drowning, as she remembers her father's phrase, "it was always sunlight in Australia" (French 96). The postcolonial and feminist theme of freedom for the powerless and oppressed is extended when Mary frees an albatross that has been cruelly caught and tormented by a sailor for amusement (French 69). As she helps the poor trapped bird to escape its cruel capture, Mary whispers her mother's motto to herself: "A Finnegan always does her duty" (French 71). Just as the captured bird is set free, so too the Finnegan females are now able to seize the opportunity to leave an oppressive past behind and make a fresh start in Australia. The title of the novel, *How the Finnegans Saved the Ship,* underlines the theme of heroic travel, but, importantly, it is extended to women and children rather than the conventional depiction of intrepid male explorers and colonisers. Mrs. Finnegan and her family represent the quest for a new beginning across the ocean, away from the religious and political conflicts of Ireland during the period leading up to the Easter Rising of 1916. Through its educational aspect, the novel explains to children what travel was: "Humans are natural travellers. The history of every country is the history of who settled and who invaded or migrated and what happened then" (French 105). By asking why families would "venture into the unknown" (French 105), *How the Finnegans Saved the Ship* explores the inspirations for travel and examines attitudes towards the other and cultural difference.

Mrs. Finnegan and Representing Maternal Values

Mrs. Finnegan is vital in symbolic terms to *How the Finnegans Saved the Ship,* as she challenges the perception that in the early part of the twentieth century, travel was something that mothers only read about rather than something they undertook.[5] Through the representation of Mrs. Finnegan as a mother travelling with her family, her agency and voice take on particular significance, and her character is already firmly established in the opening chapter. At this point, Mr. Finnegan has already migrated to Australia and is awaiting his family's arrival. He is absent from the majority of the narrative; instead, we see the mother, Mrs. Finnegan, representing the family as the head and authority. Mrs. Finnegan, thus, provides a highly positive and extended representation of female and maternal authority rather than a helpless woman in need of male rescue. This is important, since in children's literature, according to Lisa Rowe Fraustino and Karen Coats, "often [the mother] is relegated to background noise as the focus understandably shifts to the development of the child character, but her influence remains significant and worthy of close consideration" ("Introduction: Mothers Wanted"). The reader gets a sense of the traditional gender roles of Mrs. Finnegan's contemporary society, which she has to negotiate as a woman and mother. These gender roles are explored in the representation between Mrs. Finnegan and Mary. Several significant mother-daughter bonding moments in the novel serve to cement their relationship and underline the importance of female relationships in women's writing, travel being the occasion that facilitates this bonding.[6] At night, Mrs. Finnegan and Mary lie awake in their cabin, talking about the future and trying to imagine what life will be like in Australia (French 58-59). These conversations provide opportunity to discuss the realities of motherhood and married life. Mrs. Finnegan tells Mary about the night she was born and talks about the lack of practical support she, as a rural farm wife, experienced as Mr. Finnegan was away in England working for the harvest. Mrs. Finnegan explains how women at that time were, "nothing but milch cows ... to the men sometimes," whereas the men would be the ones doing the travelling, "there for their meals and their children, and then away with them" (French 59). It becomes clear that Mrs. Finnegan hopes her daughter's opportunities may be improved in Australia. When Mary asks her mother why they have to go to Australia, Mrs. Finnegan gives her two replies. First, she stresses her sense of obligation (French 32); her second reply, however, emphasizes the importance of a fresh start overseas to enhance her daughter's life chances: "it was for your sake, Mary, that was why" and "there's a future for you in this Australia place" (French 32). Mrs. Finnegan's determination to achieve a better life for her children, not least for Mary, is a response to the oppressive conditions she endured in Ireland but is also an expression of a hope for change. During their conversation, Mrs. Finnegan also explains to Mary that it is necessary to embrace the unknown in order for these hopes to materialize, which are ideas at the heart of migration: "That's why you leave your country, why you go to a strange land ... You go for your children, even if it tears the heart out of you'" (French 32). Thus, the text shows how Mrs. Finnegan's maternal values of hope and determination sustain her children during the long and arduous voyage.

Through the portrayal of Mrs. Finnegan and her children, and their positive and determined outlook, French's novel writes back to the sense of fatalism reflected in the idea of the sinking of the Titanic, the intertext of the novel. Mary's reflection on "how could something as small as this sail such a long way" (French 14) echoes the book's critique of travel conditions for the poorer classes and the inadequacy of the transportation, but it also reveals an awe at the sense of the distance travelled to reach the new world in Australia. However, traditional sexism at times threatens to silence Mrs. Finnegan and her concerns about the ship's safety. When Mrs. Finnegan raises the issue of the leak in the boat which she has observed with the purser, he laughs and patronizes her: "Now Mrs. Finnegan, you're not to worry yourself about any of that. You just go down to your cabin and have a lie down and leave the ship to us" (French 16). This overbearing response dismisses Mrs. Finnegan's misgivings and observations; the request that she should take a lie down reveals the prevailing assumptions about women and their physical and mental capacity. Later, Mary attempts to speak to a sailor to ask him to report the alarming leakage that her family observed to the ship's captain. However, he merely dismisses her concerns and informs her that the leakage they saw was due to overboard drains emptying. Embarrassed at her treatment and the sailor's behaviour, Mary conceals the truth from Mrs. Finnegan, instead telling her mother that the sailor promised to inform the captain of the leakage. Thinking her pleas have been heard, Mrs. Finnegan tells her children: "If it wasn't for us, who knows what would have happened to it! We Finnegans have saved the ship, Mary, and don't you be forgetting it'" (French 22). This poignant phrase grows in significance as the novel goes on, when the Finnegans do indeed contribute significantly to saving the ship. The determination, resilience, and resourcefulness demonstrated by Mrs. Finnegan are central to the positive depiction of maternal authority provided in the book's travel narrative. Those qualities echo the assessment of motherhood made by Fraustino and Coats:

In her materiality as well as in the child's imaginary landscape, [a mother] plays many roles and bears many burdens: a place from which to launch and a home to return to; a secure envelope that protects or one that chides and stifles; a voice that guides and chastises; a surface on which to project the quest for self-understanding. ("Introduction: Mothers Wanted")

The vocabulary used by Fraustino and Coats in the segment above connects ideas of mobility with motherhood, which suggests a close link between travel and the mother's symbolic and physical role. Importantly, those Finnegan qualities include maternal compassion and a sense of duty to one's family. The reader is informed in the opening pages of the novel that Mrs. Finnegan has taken in her cousin's child born outside wedlock and is raising the girl as her own because of her sense of familial and sisterly solidarity. Here, Mrs. Finnegan's decision echoes the point made by feminist philosopher and maternal thinker Sara Ruddick, who has argued that mothering is a social function and a conscious decision that women make, rather than a biological essence. She has it that "maternal practice begins in a response to the reality of a biological child in a particular social world. To be a 'mother' is to take upon oneself the responsibility of child care" (Ruddick 17). According to Ruddick, "all mothers are 'adoptive'" (Ruddick 51); furthermore, Bond and Michael add in their introduction to *A Mother's World: Journeys of the Heart* that "When a woman becomes a mother she assumes ... a bundle of responsibility, duty, and delight" (xvi). As seen in French's novel, this may include the role and function of adoptive mother and/or "othermother." Mrs. Finnegan's nurturing of her cousin's child is all the more poignant in light of the fact that both the unmarried mother and her child would have faced a difficult life of marginalisation and condemnation in early twentieth-century Ireland. These terms and qualities resonate with Mrs. Finnegan's sense of responsibility, her capacity to mother, as well as her ability to manage the travelling process while retaining a sense of family unity.

The novel's descriptions of Mrs. Finnegan identify her as a woman and mother of physical and mental strength; she is protective of her family and is aware of her obligation as the main carer. Facing the sea voyage, Mrs. Finnegan "straightened her shoulders ... befitting a woman who was to take her family across wide and dangerous waters to a new land" (French 12). Through its portrayal of Mrs. Finnegan "shepherding her children like a fluffy Buff Orpington hen with all its chickens" (French 12), the book uses descriptions of her body language to reinforce a traditional image of maternal caring—the mother hen protectively guarding her brood—which is consistent with the historical time period the novel is set. Mrs. Finnegan's character represents traditional values associated with maternal practice, such as caring for the needy and weak, nurturing children emotionally and physically, and teaching them values and rules to live by. Mrs. Finnegan embodies a degree of cautiousness towards travel and a certain conservativism in her views of gender roles.[7] On the other hand, however, Mrs. Finnegan is also shown to possess the initiative and flexibility of mind and spirit to accept the need for the family's travel and to withstand the dangers and rough conditions aboard the ship. Mrs. Finnegan, alert and protective of her family, keeps a watch from the deck, asserting that she would never "let [her] family sail into danger without doing [her] bit"(French 41). When a frightening storm blows up, threatening to sink the boat, Mrs. Finnegan says, "God save us, if a storm's coming we're best together" (French 78). Gathered in their cabin, she makes the children sing: "it's a well-known fact that no one has ever been drowned while they've been singing" (French 81), which, thereby, distracts them from their fear and helps them to feel safe through the shared act of singing. When the ship crashes into an iceberg, Mrs. Finnegan gets her children up to the dining room where the passengers have been asked to congregate. Staying strong in the face of terror, she reflects on the importance of duty and resisting the urge to panic (French 85). The positive and communal values that Mrs. Finnegan embodies influence and set an example for her children and the other passengers on the voyage, especially in situations of crisis or danger. These active dimensions of Mrs. Finnegan's character are significant. For women who are mothers, such agency and active qualities are often diminished in travel writing, as Bond and Michael explain: "being a mother can render a woman invisible in society, can limit her career choices and advancement, and even diminish her own sense of herself. Never is this more apparent than in the realm of travel literature" (xv).[8] In the context of this erasure of maternal identity in travel writing—an absence which is also echoed in children's literature—Mrs. Finnegan resists erasure and invisibility. On the contrary, she emerges as an outspoken, protective, and courageous maternal character with a strong sense of duty and responsibility, as she pronounces: "no ship is going to sink with my family on it'" (French 11). The novel's postscript, "Notes on the Text," explains how the family arrived safely in Australia and how Mrs. Finnegan lived happily till the age of ninety-four, but she refused to ever go near the sea or the beach again, stating that "she'd had enough waves, she said, to last her all her life" (French 103). French's afterword explains that although *How The Finnegans Saved the Ship* isn't a true story, it was "inspired by a true story, that of my step-grandchildren's Nanna Mary, who told me how her family journeyed from Ireland to Australia in 1913 and helped save the ship when it hit an iceberg" (French 104). Such portrayals as this, of the Irish survivor family who (as the novel explains) do their duty, have become part not only of Irish constructions of national identity but also of Australian sensibility.

Conclusion: Encountering the New World

As Eleftheria Arapoglou et al. state, "not only people but also different cultural texts, projects, and ideas travel from one location to another, often transforming themselves in the process and resulting in new identities and narratives" (1). Jackie French's *How the Finnegans Saved the Ship* exemplifies many of the questions raised in children's literature representing travel and motherhood; it shows that the genre plays an important role in portraying and shaping but also transforming definitions of maternal identities and travel. As Bond and Michael argue, travelling and motherhood both have the capacity to offer continuous challenge and change (xvii). French's compelling novel uses the narrative perspective and educational outlook of children's literature to paint a realist and detailed picture of travel in the early twentieth century and the hazards and challenges that went along with it. The novel, furthermore, explores the dynamics of Irish-Australian migration, the history of Irish deprivation and oppression that lies behind it, and the long-term impact of this on Australian literature, culture, and history. In the "Notes on the Text," French comments on those driving forces behind Irish travel and migration, saying of the Finnegans and other migrants to the New World that "Like all families who seek new worlds they must have been courageous and determined to find a better land across the sea" (French 105-6).

The lack of specific attention to characterizations of travelling mothers in children's literature criticism generally suggests that this subject is due critical attention and also that French's novel deserves further scholarly discussion. Examining representations of motherhood in children's literature in their book *Mothers in Children's and Young Adult Literature: From the Eighteenth Century to Postfeminism* (2016), Lisa Rowe Fraustino and Karen Coats argue that not enough critical attention has been given to representations of mothers in children's and young adult literature ("Introduction: Mothers Wanted"). My chapter has sought to remedy this by extending these enquiries and examining how French's novel reimagines historical and maternal experience. In their commentary on motherhood and travel, Marybeth Bond and Pamela Michael investigate whether "it [is] necessary for a woman to shed all her uniquely female and maternal attributes in order to venture beyond her doorstep" (xvi). French's text suggests that, indeed, such "uniquely female and maternal" qualities are vital to the outcome of the voyage or journey undertaken. Mrs. Finnegan in many ways is depicted as a traditional warm, caring maternal figure and is symbolically linked to the continuity with the country of origin, representing values such as family, permanence, love, and acceptance. The sense of adventure she possesses is compromised by her fear of the ocean and by her reluctance to test her fears once arrived in Australia (French 94). This depiction, far from trivializing or dismissing her, shows Mrs. Finnegan as a nuanced character who has experienced the traumatic aspects of travel. As Foulke states, "Voyages are a natural vehicle for the human imagination exploring the unknown, whether it be discovering new continents, finding out the truth about oneself, or reaching those more perfect worlds we call utopias."(5) Within this life-changing vision of travel leading to the new world in Australia and a new life of opportunities for her children, Mrs. Finnegan is the maternal centre and emotional anchor of Jackie French's novel.

Endnotes

1   The title quotation of my chapter is taken from page 11 in French's *How the Finnegans Saved the Ship*.

2   An early version of this chapter was given as a conference paper titled "'How Could Something as Small as This Sail Such a Long

Way?": Recent Irish and Australian Children's Books Portraying Irish Migration in the Long Nineteenth Century,'" at the conference "Travelling Irishness in the Long Nineteenth Century," 28-29 August 2014, University of Limerick, Ireland.

3 See also my discussion of Mother Ireland in Beyer "Their Mother Was Waiting for Her."

4 I have previously discussed the representation of the sinking of the Titanic in Irish children's literature, in relation to trauma and history; see Beyer "Haunting the Text."

5 See also Day for a discussion of travel writing as an entertainment genre for mothers and children in the early modern period.

6 Travel and mother-daughter bonding is also discussed in the Introduction to this book.

7 For example, Mrs. Finnegan articulates the belief that book knowledge is harmful to girls and women on p.43 in the novel.

8 Also cited in the Introduction to this book.

Works Cited

Arapoglou, Eleftheria, et al. "Introduction." *Mobile Narratives: Travel, Migration, and Transculturation*, edited by Eleftheria Arapoglou et al. Routledge, 2014, pp.1-14.

Bainbridge, Simon. "Mountains." *The Routledge Companion to Travel Writing*, edited by Carl Thompson, Routledge, 2016, pp.444-453.

Beyer, Charlotte. "Haunting the Text: Nicola Pierce's *Spirit of the Titanic* and Irish Historical Children's Fiction." *Women's Studies: An Inter-disciplinary Journal*, vol. 44 no. 7, 2015, pp. 956-976.

Beyer, Charlotte. "'How Could Something as Small as This Sail Such a Long Way": Recent Irish and Australian Children's Books Portraying Irish Migration in the Long Nineteenth Century,'" at the conference "Travelling Irishness in the Long Nineteenth Century," 28-29 August 2014, University of Limerick, Ireland. Unpublished.

Beyer, Charlotte. "'Their Mother Was Waiting for Her': Mother-Daughter Relations and Irish Identity in Deirdre Madden's *One by One in the Darkness*." *Mothers and Daughters*, edited by Dannabang Kuwabong, et al. Demeter Press, 2017, pp.234-250.

Bielenberg, Andy. "Irish Emigration to the British Empire, 1700-1914." *The Irish Diaspora,* edited by Andy Bielenberg. Routledge, 2013, pp.215-234.

Bond, Marybeth, and Pamela Michael. "Introduction." *A Mother's World: Journeys of the Heart,* edited by Marybeth Bond and Pamela Michael. Travelers' Tales, 1998, pp. xv-xviii.

Clarke, Linda. "Mother Ireland ... The Myth." Paper given at Literature & Psychoanalysis in Dialogue, 9 November 2013. ICLO-NLS— Irish Circle of the Lacanian Orientation. http://www.iclo-nls.org/wp content/uploads/Pdf/Mother%20Ireland%20%E2%80%A6 The%20Myth.pdf . Accessed 27 January 2018.

Day, Matthew. "Western Travel Writing, 1450-1750." *The Routledge Companion to Travel Writing*, edited by Carl Thompson. Routledge, 2016, pp.161-172.

Fraustino, Lisa Rowe, and Karen Coats. "Introduction: Mothers Wanted." *Mothers in Children's and Young Adult Literature: From the Eighteenth Century to Postfeminism,* edited by Lisa Rowe Fraustino and Karen Coats. University Press of Mississippi, 2016. Ebook.

Foulke, Robert. "The Literature of Voyaging." *Literature and Lore of the Sea,* edited by Patricia Ann Carlson. Rodopi, 1986, pp.1-13.

Foster, John, Ern Finnis, and Maureen Nimon. *Bush, City, Cyberspace: the Development of Australian Children's Literature into the Twenty-First Century.* Centre for Information Studies, 2005.

French, Jackie. *How the Finnegans Saved the Ship.* Angus & Robertson, 2001.

Richards, Eric. *Britannia's Children: Emigration from England, Scotland, Wales and Ireland since 1600.* Hambledon Press, 2004.

Rowe, Kelly-Marie. "How the Finnegans Saved the Ship by Jackie French." September 2012. http://ellassignment1.blogspot.co.uk/. Accessed 26 March 2017.

Ruddick, Sara. *Maternal Thinking: Towards a Politics of Peace.* Women's Press, 1990.

Wulff, Helena. *Dancing at the Crossroads: Memory and Mobility in Ireland.* Berghahn Books, 2008.

Chapter 10

"Everyone Wants to Escape from Their Own Lives Sometimes, Don't They?": Motherhood, the Train to Edinburgh, and the Work of Kathleen Jamie

Melanie Duckworth

In *Sightlines*, the Scottish poet and nature writer Kathleen Jamie describes a time "when the children were small and the world had shrunk to the here and now … small people and toy cities built of blocks. Toy boats sailing the living-room floor" (*Sightlines* 131). She writes:

> I'd been kneeling on the carpet, putting Lego away and wondering which was the closest place one could go that was remote? Where an adventure could unfold—just enough to keep one's wits sharp, enough to let one taste an untamed grandeur, yet be back in a few days because, you know, of the children? I mean everyone wants to escape their own lives sometimes, don't they? (*Sightlines* 131).

Jamie decides to travel to St Kilda, an abandoned Scottish island difficult to reach by boat. She is away for a week, and on her return, she observes: "I'd been on the desert islands, my husband had been at home with the infants. He was the one that looked ravaged, like Robinson Crusoe" (*Sightlines* 135).

This vignette encapsulates some of the contradictions of motherhood: the shrinking of the world to toy boats and imagined journeys, the desire to escape this, the gruelling and relentless nature of caring for small children. The way Jamie overlays the miniature and the expansive here as well as the irony of comparing her husband rather than herself to Robinson Crusoe are characteristic of her work. Her essay collections *Findings* (2005) and *Sightlines* (2012) have been described as "conversation[s] with the natural world" and document journeys to remote Scottish islands and even Scandinavia. She leaves her children behind. For Jamie, however, the remote and the domestic are intertwined. Observing a cliff teeming with noisy gannets feeding their young, she remarks:

"It seems like a long time ago."

"What does?"

I gestured to the bird-crowded cliff face. I meant the time of breaking waters and nappy buckets and trails of milky vomit down one's shoulder. "Over!" I laughed. "That bit's over. For me, anyway." (*Sightlines* 76)

Motherhood colours her experience of the natural world, as at once something to be periodically escaped from and as a source of empathy and connection. Her writing chronicles the ambivalence of motherhood—the desire for it and the desire to escape it.

At the end of my maternity leave with my second child, I also had a desire to "escape my own life for a while." Travel was not new to me. I had left Australia several years before, studied in England, and ended up in Norway, where my children had been born. And there I was. Unable to leave my children behind as my partner was working abroad, I took them with me, to London, York, and Edinburgh. Felix was four; Antonia was ten months. We travelled by train. This is what I wrote.

York, June 2015

Twelve years ago, nearly to the day, I arrived in London with a huge backpack, a little backpack, and a brick of a laptop. I was brimming with excitement, anticipation, freedom, and nerves. Walking along the street, carrying it all, I felt like a giant turtle. I stayed in a grotty hostel in Earl's court. I went to the British library and marvelled at the medieval manuscripts and handwritten poems. I visited Southwark cathedral because a writer I knew told me she loved it. I went to Greenwich with a girl I met in the hostel. I went to the British Museum and looked at the loot from Sutton Hoo. I wandered around peering at maps and looking anxiously for tube stations. I was preparing to travel around for a while before starting a master's degree in medieval literature in York. I couldn't believe my luck.

Last week, I arrived in London with Felix and Antonia as my companions. Michael, my husband, was working in the U.S. for two weeks, and I didn't fancy staying at home alone for that time. I had wanted to come back to the UK for years and thought I'd better do it before my maternity leave was over. We stayed in a clean and shiny hostel near Hyde Park, opposite the Natural History Museum. Once again, I was excited and a little apprehensive. It felt so different. London was exciting the first time but also lonely and somewhat aimless. With all that time on your hands, how do you best spend it? And it didn't really matter if I got lost. Now I had two small beings to look after, and there was no time for loneliness or aimlessness. I felt myself ferrying them around in a little bubble of care. We went to playgrounds and the Natural History Museum and the Science Museum. We took a boat ride with my brother to Greenwich. It was nice to go to parks with a purpose—the promised playground at the end of the walk a mecca for all. I felt, in a way that I had not twelve years ago, like I belonged.

And early this week, I arrived in York. As we wandered around the town centre on our first day, my heart kept clenching in recognition. These were the streets I had walked and ridden my bike, the streets in which I had dreamed and longed and loved. I kept saying to Felix, "this is amazing; I feel so strange." "Why Mummy?," he asked, and I only said I lived here once, long ago, with Daddy. Arriving in York twelve years ago was a dream come true. After years of poorly paid care-work, I finally had time to read and think and study again, and forge friendships, and breathe the fairytale air of the north. That sounds romanticized, and I guess it was. In York, I did my master's degree and began my PhD, in York I fell in love. Felix and Antonia would not exist had Michael and I not met here.

So it feels strange and lovely to be back in this city that is at once pretty and mysterious, cosy and ancient, cradling and awe inspiring. It felt odd, to begin with, to have the little ones at my side and not be able to slip into uninterrupted reveries or read for hours in coffee shops. And I missed Michael. But I soon got used to showing the children around, collapsing exhausted in parks when I needed to. It was lovely to see Felix entranced by the stained glass window interactive displays in the Minster. "They cook glass like dinner," he told me. "Did they cook the glass in our house too?" There is a model train shop near our apartment, which I must have walked past hundreds of times but never noticed until now. We have to stop every time to watch the train go through the tunnel.

I have visited old friends and old places. I have walked old paths. It feels good to be here. I'm staying in an excellent little apartment just outside the city walls that just happens to be at a midpoint between the two houses I used to live in. It's just behind a huge painted sign visible from the city walls, which says "Nightly Bile Beans keep you healthy, bright-eyed and slim." It feels right to be tucked away just here in a place I rode past and walked past and spotted from the walls—here, now, with two little people. Here, in a place awash with history, I can almost touch my former lives, my former selves. I can wave but feel no need to go back. I can wave, also, at the self who may visit here in ten years, in twenty, but I am here now, this moment, and it is good.

***

We walked from our apartment to the station to catch the train to Edinburgh. My big backpack was strapped to my back; the little backpack was slung over the handles of the stroller, where Antonia sat, as Felix walked beside me. When he got tired, he sat in the stroller, and I strapped Antonia to my front in the baby carrier. We trundled slowly over the cobblestones like an oversized turtle. The train journey itself was less peaceful than I had anticipated, but there was a blissful moment when both children fell asleep on top of me until the conductor arrived and asked me to move my bags.

In Edinburgh, we discovered a fabulous museum. We went back two or three times. It was huge—two separate buildings connected by a tunnel. You could climb up on the roof. There were rooms set up with children's activities—enough to entertain them both. There were dinosaurs, a space room; there were trains, cars, and engines. There was, I discovered on our final visit, a whole level devoted to the Middle Ages, and below it, the Neolithic era. As Jamie puts it:

> Because of the earthfast notion that time is deep, that memories are buried, the Neolithic and Bronze Age artefacts occupy the windowless basement level of the National Museum. To visit the prehistoric, one must descend turnpike stairs, or travel down in a lift—either way, down—until the pressure of the building, of thousands of years of subsequent history, is piled on top. (*Sightlines* 43)

I wanted to have a look. "Let's go in here," I said to Felix. "No," he said. We had just spent an hour looking at steam engines. He wanted more. "Come on," I said. "Why don't you just sit in the stroller, and I'll put Antonia in the carrier, and you just relax for a little while. Just ten minutes. Please." For the first time, I felt myself growing frustrated. After two weeks of playgrounds and trains and kids activities, couldn't we just look briefly at something I was interested in? "No." He absolutely refused. There was nothing I could do. We went back to the steam engines for half an hour, then left.

If we had kept going, I might have seen a little bowl that Jamie describes in *Sightlines*, although I probably wouldn't have paid it much heed, displayed as it is, alongside a collection of other small bowls: "A load of old pots, the epitome of museum dullness, unless you like that sort of thing" (*Sightlines* 44). In an essay that I didn't read till later, "The Woman in the Field," Jamie describes going to visit the little four-thousand-year-old bowl in the museum. She tells how she was there when it was discovered on an archaeological dig in the summer of 1979 when she was seventeen and had just finished school. Incidentally, I myself was born only two weeks later, a few hundred miles south. It was found in a tomb beside the skeleton of a woman. She said it was a "very odd day": "Even as the crane swung the capstone aside and laid it on the spoil heap, the hills announced their disapproval and, as we moved forward to see what the cist contained, more thunder came, and huge drops of rain began to fall, so immediately a tarpaulin was dragged over the grave, concealing it again from sight" (*Sightlines* 64-65). She frames the unearthing of the pot as a kind of transgression and aligns it with her own transgression of choosing itinerant travel and poetry over secretarial college (*Sightlines* 66). I didn't see the little bowl. We went out through the museum shop, and I bought Felix a miniature space shuttle. Back outside, I manoeuvred the stroller and tried to ensure Felix didn't career off the footpath into a bus as he rattled along on the rusty scooter he'd borrowed from his cousins. I still felt annoyed. So when I saw the enormous Blackwell's bookshop, I said, right, we're going in here. Antonia fell asleep in the baby carrier, and there was a whole shelf of train toys to occupy the boy. I found the poetry section. I recognized Kathleen Jamie's name because I'd had to teach one of her poems once, as an adjunct in Oslo. So I bought two of her books. And that was the beginning.

***

Back in Norway and back at work, I read her essays and poems compulsively. In "The Tree House," Jamie describes climbing into a little tree house in her garden. The tree house itself, a small house built for children to play in, is described as cumbersome and unnatural, a burden that the tree must bear:

> a gall
> we've asked it to carry
> of its own dead, and every spring
> to drape in leaves and blossom, like a pall. (*Waterlight* 29)

A gall, according to the Oxford English Dictionary, can refer to a "painful swelling, pustule, or blister," "a sore or wound produced by rubbing or chafing," and "an excrescence produced on trees, especially the oak, by the action of insects." A "pall" is a cloth used to drape an altar, a corpse, or a coffin. In rhyming "pall" and "gall" to describe the tree's relationship with the treehouse, Jamie creates a curiously ambivalent image of pain, swelling, death, and encumberment, alongside that of life and rebirth. This ambivalence echoes the ambivalence Jamie ascribes to motherhood itself. Hiding inside the treehouse, "a dwelling, of sorts," Jamie briefly escapes her family:

I lay to sleep,
beside me neither man
nor child, but a lichened branch
wound through the wooden chamber,
pulling it close. (*Waterlight* 28)

In the treehouse, ironically built for her children, Jamie can experience what it is like to be apart from them, engaging instead with the nonhuman world. Here, away from the restrictive intimacy of man and child, Jamie can instead savour the closeness of a tree, a relationship that does not impinge upon solitude. The embrace of the tree branch reminds her of a friend who shares her wistful thoughts of a childfree life:

... a complicity

like our own, when arm in arm
on the city street, we bemoan
our families, our difficult
chthonic anchorage
in the apple-sweetened earth,

without whom we might have lived
the long ebb of our mid-decades
alone in sheds and attic rooms,
awake in the moonlit souterrains
of our own minds; without whom

we might have lived
a hundred other lives. (*Waterlight* 28-29)

Here, Jamie describes the families of herself and her friend as "our difficult / chthonic anchorage / in the apple-sweetened earth"—roots that tie them to the ground itself, prohibiting movement. Without them, "we might have lived / a hundred other lives." "Chthonic" refers to the earth itself, specifically, earth beneath the surface of the earth. It is a Greek word, associated with gods of the underworld or the harvest. Interestingly, in the imagined life without children, Jamie also returns to subterranean imagery: "souterrains" are Iron-Age underground chambers. The "souterrains / of our own minds," however, are weightless, transportable, and solitary.

As in the excavation of the Bronze Age bowl I discussed earlier, Jamie's imagination often extends earthwards, to caves, burial sites, and Neolithic chambers. In "Meadowsweet," she contemplates the Gaelic tradition of burying women poets face down. She imagines the seeds caught in the poet's hair growing upwards:

> towards light, so showing her
> when the time came,
> how to dig herself out—
>
> to surface and greet them,
> mouth young, and full again
> of dirt, and spit, and poetry. (*Waterlight* 79)

So while, like death, motherhood requires an anchoring, a stilling of movement, a precluding of possibilities, this is not all it offers. The deep earth holds within it the possibility of renewal, and stillness entails a different kind of journey. In "February," Jamie writes of willingly surrendering to "the heap of nappies," "the hanging out," and "the first / sweet-wild weeks of your life" (*Waterlight* 52). And in "Thaw," she writes of returning home from the hospital after the birth of her first child:

> ...and though it meant a journey
> through darkening snow,
> arms laden with you in a blanket,
> I had to walk to the top of the garden,
> to touch, in complicit
> homage of equals, the spiral
> trunks of our plum trees, the moss,
> the robin's roost in the holly. (Waterlight 51)

Although motherhood restricts journeys, it also enables and requires them—be they as simple as a walk to the bottom of the garden in the snow. Motherhood also casts light upon Jamie's identity as a member of the natural world, not a being distinct from it. The title of Jamie's collection of poems most closely related to motherhood, *Jizzen*, is an Old Scots word "meaning 'childbed'" (Simpson 77). In "St Brides," Jamie compares herself to "the hare in jizzen" and remarks: "a last sharp twist for the shoulders / delivers my daughter, the placenta / following, like a fist of purple kelp" (*Waterlight* 75).

***

My children certainly continue to restrict my movement, however. In my first autumn back at work, a series of seminars on ecocriticism and deep time at the University of Edinburgh tempt me greatly. I dearly want to go and get back there, but I am still breastfeeding Antonia at night, and it is too difficult. But we all go to Australia for Christmas. In January, I fly back with my children to Norway. The week we leave, there is a heat wave, above forty every day. The kind of heat where the gum leaves fizz and crackle, the ground radiates, and the rocks ought to split. The light hangs in sheets; it seems the barest ripple should spark the whole lot into flame. How is it possible for the thick skin of the earth to be so fiercely warm, so dry? We hide in air-conditioned cars and houses, and peer at the heat through the glass. When we step outside, the heat is a physical thing, like thick water, it slows you down. The thought of the trees and rocks and koalas and birds out in it, all day long, is hard to grasp. After twenty-four hours in the bellies of planes, we arrive home to Norway in the middle of a cold snap. "Look at the snow!" I say to Felix, pointing out the plane's window as we come in to land. "That's not snow," he says cheerfully, "that's the sand on the beach." It is minus twenty degrees. The world glitters. The trees are crystalline. Gazing at it all, again, through glass, it is the thought of the earth itself that haunts me, the frigid ground, the rocks clenched with cold.

I discover some of my colleagues are arranging a conference on the theme of "Going North." Hah, I think to myself, I know a bit about that. I decide to write about Kathleen Jamie, whose work I cannot get enough of. She travels repeatedly to the north, to remote Scottish islands, to Bergen, and far up the coast of Greenland to glimpse the northern lights. My journey from Australia, the hot earth and the cold earth, wavers in the back of my mind. And that other journey up to

Edinburgh. It all feels oddly connected. I couldn't go back to Edinburgh, but a conference at my own college is manageable. While I am working on the paper, I hear about another conference, in Kristiansand, Norway, in May. It is the triennial conference of the Nordic Association for English Studies. That's not so far away, I think, maybe we could all go, my husband and the kids. And then I discover who the guest poet is. Oh.

We do go, and it is wonderful, but combining family and travel and work is not straightforward. We buy a Lego boat and ice creams on the ferry and watch the round granite islands through the windows. Taking the kids to dinner at the local pizza place is noisy and challenging. My husband and I argue on the journey home. I miss the final afternoon of the conference, as it's a meeting I'm not sure I need to go to but later wish I did. I come and find my family instead, and we go to the swimming pool, but my daughter is distraught as she has missed her nap, so after an attempt to swim, I wrangle my screaming toddler very slowly back out through the change rooms, and she falls asleep on my lap on a bench outside. Other parts work well. There is a famous animal park here, and my husband and the kids spend a successful day there while I am at the conference. I am a bit nervous speaking about a poet with the poet herself in the room. But she smiles. It's ok. It's a thrill. Later she tells me it felt odd to be referred to as "Jamie." And as I fuss about getting an audio recording of one of her poems ready to play, she wonders if she should just stand up and read it for me. At the end of the day she gives a reading, forty-five minutes that remain among the magical minutes of my life.

York, October 2016

In the summer, I wean Antonia in preparation for my very first journey without her. I am taking a group of students to the Norwegian Study Centre in York. She screams in the airport when I say goodbye. But it is, I discover, easier than expected to slip back into this other skin, this former self, who falls asleep and wakes up alone, who can have a shower and wander off to breakfast at the canteen without a second thought. It is autumn, and in York, it is the smell of the place that hits me most, the wet leaves, wet stone smell that is somehow so very different to Norway. I hire a bike; I roam the streets, and I catch up with some old friends. But in the bookshop it is the children's shelves that hold my attention. Felix is getting old enough for longer stories now—our shelves already bulge with picture books—so I search for titles I remember: *Pippi Longstocking, The Magic Faraway Tree, Flat Stanley*. In the clothing stores, I buy presents for Antonia, gloves with little cat faces, flowery leggings.

Towards the end of the week, I sit in the corner of a warm café on a low bench crammed with cushions, scanning the menu for something that doesn't make me queasy. I take out my computer and look listlessly at the article I am supposed to be writing. It's called "Travelling North Together: The North, Whales, and Intercultural Communication in Kathleen Jamie's Essays and Poems" (Duckworth 2017). It's nearly overdue. The thought of tying up all its loose ends is overwhelming. I close my computer and open up Jamie's *Selected Poems* instead. I read:

Our baby's heart, on the sixteen-week scan
was a fluttering bird, held in cupped hands.

I thought of St Kevin, hands opened in prayer,
and a bird of the hedgerow, nestling there,

and how he'd borne it, till the young had flown
—and I prayed: this new heart must outlive my own.
(*Waterlight* 56)

Out of nowhere, I start to cry. Hot tears over the crusts of my sour-dough toast. I am pregnant, eight weeks. Enough to be invested in it. Enough to be nauseous, and exhausted, and faintly nostalgic for the few brief weeks after weaning Antonia when I had my body to myself. But too early to say anything. Too early to be sure. Jamie writes, in "Ultrasound":

Oh whistle and I'll come to ye,
my lad, my wee shilpit ghost
summonsed from tomorrow. (*Waterlight* 49)

I think of all my ultrasounds. The flickery, ghostly, improbable movements. Or stillness. I have two children, but this current pregnancy is my seventh. In my fifth pregnancy, ten weeks along, I sat stiffly, frightened, in a tired hospital corridor on a plastic chair. I longed desperately for a second child. There had been some blood. I tried counting to ten, over and over, to make the time pass. I couldn't focus on the Norwegian parenting magazine on the table beside me. I clenched and unclenched my hands. I breathed in and out. I counted some more.

The scan, when it came, showed an indistinct shape like a stone. I knew immediately. I knew for sure. The doctor didn't seem to realize this. "There is no heartbeat," he kept telling me. "Look, I can show you. There is no heartbeat." He showed me image after image after image. Eventually I interrupted him. "I've got the picture," I said. I somehow had to drive back home. At that point, I did not know if there would ever be another. After the initial numbing grief, a coldness settled about me, a shadow. After three consecutive losses, I qualified for tests, which revealed nothing. But my next pregnancy, half a year later, resulted in my daughter. Jamie writes:

If Pandora
could have scanned
her dark box,

and kept it locked—
this ghoul's skull, punched eyes
is tiny Hope's,

hauled silver-quick
in a net of sound,
then, for pity's sake, lowered. (*Waterlight* 49)

I sit in the café in York and cry and cry. And hesitantly, inevitably, I remember my first pregnancy. During the twelve-week scan, which lasted a good two hours, they discovered a problem. The problem was tiny but serious. The baby would require surgery following birth and had only a small chance of survival. After more tests and research and much deliberation, we decided to terminate.

It is strange to think back on that now. I had just finished my PhD and moved to Norway from England, but I was in Australia for Christmas. I remember, between the diagnosis and the decision, presenting a conference paper on Randolph Stow's novel *The Girl Green as Elderflower* and the story of the Green Children, as recorded by the twelfth-century chroniclers Ralph of Coggeshall and William of Newburgh (Duckworth 2011). The children are discovered next to "certain very ancient pits" and appear to come from another world (Stow 182).

> A certain boy was discovered with his sister by the inhabitants of that place, lying by the edge of a pit which exists there, who had the same form in all members as the rest of mankind, but in the colour of their skins differed from all mortals of our habitable world. For the whole surface of their skins was tinged with a green colour. Nobody could understand their speech. (180)

The villagers adopt them. The boy quickly wastes away and dies, but the girl grows up to become "lascivious and wanton," "the girl green as elderflower" (Ralph of Coggeshall 181). It is an odd thing to find oneself speaking of these children, when the life of the child within you is just as precarious. These children have come from far away. They cannot find their way back home. We fail them.

I remember feverishly writing poems. I wrote: "You are much more real, than, say stars, / for who can speak for things so far away." I wrote of all the names I longed to give my child: "have them all," I said. "I'll weave them into a coat of many colours / Fit for a favoured child... / And if, where you are going, you do not need it, well, / leave it behind." Impossible to think of death as anything but a journey, a going on without me. I remember the plane journey back to Norway, the desolation of leaving my mother at the airport, my body scraped clean, weirdly alone, my breasts producing colostrum for a baby who was not there.

Norway, March 2017

I am writing now from my kitchen table at home in Norway. It feels like the first day of spring—the snow has melted overnight. The fields are coppery gold; there is sunlight all over the fjord. The trees clench tight to the rocks. I am tired. Michael has been away all week, working in America. I may resemble Robinson Crusoe when he returns. In half an hour, I need to pick the kids up from kindergarten. Just last week, I finally forced myself to email the organizers to withdraw from the conference in Manchester in June that I badly wanted to attend. But the little one within me, just a flickering promise last autumn in York, is now thirty weeks and expected to arrive at the end of May. I had hoped that the baby and my Mum could have come to the conference with me, but there is no way to get the baby a passport in time.

In his novel *The Girl Green as Elderflower*, in addition to the story of the green children, Stow draws on the medieval image of the "green man," part human and part tree. Jamie, of course, is familiar with this image, and when she describes a larch shed built by her husband in her garden, she mentions that "above its door he hung a plaque with a green man with fronds of plum tree issuing from the mouth" (*Findings* 104). In Stow's novel, the "girl green as elderflower" is the most compelling character—the surviving green child, forever exiled from her home. And in *Jizzen*, Jamie writes not about the green man, but "The Green Woman":

> Until we're restored to ourselves
> by weaning, the skin jade
> only where it's hidden
> under the jewellery, the areolae still tinged,
> —there's a word for women like us.
>
> It's suggestive of the lush
> Ditch, or even an ordeal,
> —as though we'd risen,
> tied to a ducking-stool,
> gasping, weed-smeared, proven. (*Waterlight* 76)

I think of the green children. I think of the little clay bowl I didn't see in Edinburgh. I think of my own "chthonic anchorage / in the apple-sweetened earth" (*Waterlight* 28). I am not to be restored to myself quite yet.

Works Cited

Duckworth, Melanie. "Travelling North Together: The North, Whales and Intercultural Communication in Kathleen Jamie's Essays and Poems." *Travel and Intercultural Communication: Going North*. Edited by Eva Margareta Lambertsson Björk & Jutta Cornelia Eschenbach. Cambridge Scholars, 2017, pp. 51-68.

Duckworth, Melanie. "Grievous Music: Randolph Stow's Middle Ages." *Australian Literary Studies* 26(3), 2011, pp. 102-114.

"Gall." Oxford English Dictionary, 2019, https://en.oxforddictionaries.com/definition/gall. Accessed 25 Jan. 2019.

Jamie, Kathleen. *Findings*. Sort of Books, 2005.

Jamie, Kathleen. *Sightlines*. Sort of Books, 2012.

Jamie, Kathleen. *Waterlight: Selected Poems*. Grey Wolf, 2007.

Simpson, Juliet. "'Sweet-Wild Weeks': Birth, Being and Belonging in *Jizzen*." *Kathleen Jamie: Essays and Poems on Her Work*, edited by Rachel Falconer. Edinburgh University Press, 2015, pp. 71-82.

Stow, Randolph. *The Girl Green as Elderflower*. 1980. Text Publishing Australia, 2015.

DISCOVERY

Chapter 11

Voices from the Oublie: Ghostings of Dutch and Portuguese Colonization

May Joseph

Coda:

Writing has a sea faring element about it. I write frequently with a hazy image in my mind, rather like the Playa de Plata that drew Ferdinand Magellan relentlessly southwards towards the tip of South America to undertake the brutal journey across the tip and around what would come to be known as the Strait of Magellan. What began as a historical excursion into the archaeological past of the Malabar region of South India, morphed into a project in montage history, an Instagram of multiple moments mapping a particular region's fractured social imaginary through the self-ethnography of one woman traveller.

These fragments have the uncertainty of the early expeditionist, sounding her way along the shores of a coastline. The Strait of Magellan is possibly the most arduous of the sea journeys I have read about. It offers a visual prompt for the challenges of writing the Indian Ocean.

i.

Cabo de Tormentoso, later Cape of Good Hope, is a mythic, elemental place of my Tanzanian childhood, where I had been told modernity's shock reverberates, collides, converges, and transforms into something new. It is a place of colonial violence but also of great calm and intensity. Everything changed at this place where two oceans meet.

Even the sea at this place churns a frothing divide, separating two oceans of different sea hues, colliding temperatures, one cold, the other warm. The merging oceans generate inverting currents. Those treacherous currents capture the turns of history and memory. They toss up the cultural obsessions born of the moment of colonial violence—that moment when everything altered for people living at the tip of Africa and at the tip of India along the Malabar Coast, where Vasco da Gama first landed. *Cabo de Tormentoso*, the Cape of Storms, was a place of dreams for the Portuguese and later the Dutch. It became a landscape of hauntings for Africa and Asia.

ia.

The delirious feeling of standing at a nerve point of the world's greatest involuntarily nomadic journey, the slave trade routes, is concretized high up on a hill in the Bo Kaap district of Cape Town. Amids grass, shrubs and dry brush, lies an ancient cemetery. The grassy knoll, poised on a hill overlooking the Cape Town waterfront, exudes an otherworldly ambience. It is deserted, and remote, despite its centrality within the city. Here above the city, spirits lie in respite, tended by the faithful. The spirit of the Tana Baru is at once of the past and the present. The Tana Baru are a group of holy men or saints of Cape Town's seventeenth-century Muslim community. Their resting place up on the hill is both poignant and disruptive—reminding one of journeys through which human cargoes were transported, from Batavia to Cape Town, via the Maldives and Cochin, and onwards to Pernambuco.

These journeys are now remote and forgotten. But the serenity of the Tana Baru draws the past into a retracing of the present. When? How? Words rise. But for the living around the cemetery, the Cape Malay community, the quiet resting place is a thing of the past, along with the forbidding of Islam and the recitation of the Quran. The tombs of the Tana Baru remind of the slave ships carrying their Malay cargo from Batavia all the way to Cape Town. These early Muslims were forbidden to carry their Qurans with them. They were denied the holy book. The first Qurans in Cape Town were recited from memory. Some of the first imams were imprisoned on Robben Island and died on the island, leaving behind the first Kramats of Cape Town, located on Robben Island. The Tana Baru evoke the many spaces of the nomadic dead of Cape Town. The Kramats, memorials of holy men from the Cape Malay community, mark this history of migration—forgetting a diasporic sacred tradition forged out of exile and death. Their burial sites remain a testament to earlier migrations to Cape Town.

ii.

Around the Cape of Good Hope lies the crossroads of the world. Bartolomeu Dias and Ferdinand Magellan, Vasco Da Gama and Ibn Battuta, Africans, Arabs and Indians. But it is Fernando Pessoa who draws this sea faring world into a singular vision. Pessoa's journey from Cape Town through East Africa, and linking Daressalaam to Zanzibar and Lisbon, shrinks the great distances of time and space into the stance of the poet, standing at his bureau, writing of what he saw and lost. The oceans swell in Pessoa's writings, spilling beyond the Tagus River into the many oceans that lie between Lisbon and Cape Town. Pessoa's imagery traverses the western coast of Africa southwards and travels up the eastern seaboard through Zanzibar and Mombasa.

In the poem "The Stone Pillar," he chronicles the striking navigational pillar of Bartolomeu Dias that marks the southern African landscape at the western tip of the Cape of Good Hope, a journey of derailments that led to the accidental discovery of rounding the Cape. Pessoa invokes the Portuguese sea, "Mar Portuguese," as a sea of reinventions, where lives and maps collided. "O salty sea, so much of whose salt/Is Portugal's tears! / ... Whoever would go beyond the Cape / Must go beyond sorrow." A brutal but imaginative empire of the seas emerges through Pessoa's poetry, shaping new epistemologies of becoming. Again, Pessoa: "I, Diogo Cao, a navigator ,/ Left this pillar by the swarthy strand/ And sailed onward. / ... This pillar is a sign to the wind and skies/ ... The limitless sea is Portuguese."

iii.

Pessoa's writings chronicle the history of modern shock from a particular trajectory. One cannot embrace the aesthetics of the historic avant-garde without coming to terms with the history of shock that shaped it. Traversing the history of shock leads me to Lisbon, where the historic connections between the Portuguese colonization of Africa and India lie nestled along the Avenue das India and the Casas da India.

A walk through the city of Lisbon is a journey into autoethnography. Lisbon puts images and feelings back into the archives of colonial administrators, the notes of expeditioners and navigators. In the streets of Lisbon, there are many ruins of former lives from the colonies. India, Africa, and the Malabar hover along its elegant streets. The grandeur of Lisbon's avenues and buildings contrast with the decrepitude of the decaying city. An ochre patina fills the city's hues alongside the red tiled city. A warehouse reminds me of the tea factories of Cochin's Mattanchery Island. The scale of the Castello of Lisbon reminds me of Fort Aguado in Panjim, Goa, of Fort Thangassery in Quilon where my mother comes from.

Lisbon is a dreamscape of the past. Walking at twilight along the ramparts of the old Castello high up where the fort still remains is a journey in cultural shock. Moments of recognition. A curve in the stone wall brings me to a scene that reminds me of Bagamoyo, the old slave port of East Africa. The view of Lisbon from the sea is the unforgettable juncture of the Tagus River and Atlantic Ocean, where a city on the hill rises strategically, with a sweeping view of the sea. I am startled by the visual repetition of the image: Fort Jesus at Mombasa, at the junction of Tudor Creek and the India Ocean. Fort Cranganore (Kodungaloor) along the Periyar, at the opening to the Indian Ocean. Fort Aguado at the juncture of the Mandovi River and the Arabian Sea. At Galle, Ceylon, the spectacular junction of ocean and promontory.

iv.

It is 1973, and my family is spending the day in Bagamoyo, a sleepy coastal Tanzanian village at the time. It is a historic place that shaped heart rending narratives in our history books at school in Dar es Salaam about the extreme brutality of Portuguese slavery. We kids in primary school could not visualize the horror that tormented the languorous Swahili coast we called home. Now at Bagamoyo, a terrifying unease I can still feel years later, grips me as I wander through the mythic, desolate town with my father. Bagamoyo literally means "lay your heart to rest"—a cryptic warning to the unfortunate people whose lives were forever destroyed by slavery. It is also a welcoming note to take respite to the thousands of porters who wandered through this "end of the journey" town by the sea, after carrying brutal amounts of cargo on their shoulders for weeks.

Bagamoyo, a peripheral coastal village in the early 1970s, boasted a spectacular unspoiled beach front. Its ambience is deceptively placid. Bagamoyo's violent past, however, is etched on its somnambulistic landscape. Ruins of Portuguese slave fort design, Omani details, Afro-Arab residential architecture and Indian arabesque facades connect the medieval Swahili town to Lisbon, Muscat, and Calicut. It is the lesser known Arab docking ground in the elaborate slave trade leaving East Africa for the North and Western Hemispheres. An old mosque in town and the old slave holding piers with pockmarks in the concrete offer reminders of a different era of human trade. Late eighteenth-century shipments of human cargo to Zanzibar for the New World colonies and the Caribbean. Comings and goings between Oman, Malabar, and East Africa involving spice, slaves, and silks. Burton and Speke, Stanley and Grant, all setting out in search of the source of the Nile, from Bagamoyo. The gateway to the Indian Ocean. Now, the decaying site is strangely vacant of commemoration or acknow-ledgement. Its stark silence a reminder of the ghosts of history.

The heat of the afternoon sun leaves one thirsty by the sandy shore. There is no shelter around the slave pen. Even the trees fear the place, wrought by its dark past.

v.

In *Message* (1998), Fernando Pessoa writes of *Mar Portugues*—that vast oceanic imaginary that evokes Portuguese mastery of the sea by the sixteenth century. This vast oceanic imaginary, at once heroic and nationalistic for Portuguese, is simultaneously a dark sea for Africa and Asia. At Bagamoyo, this Portuguese sea is a zone of irreparable loss, horrific crossings. At Lisbon, the Portuguese sea is a faded glory. At Belem, the Portuguese sea is liquid dreams. It is where Da Gama leaves for the Indies, where Bartolomeu Dias leaves in search of a sea route to India. Washed away by centuries, *Mar Portugues* is for our time the great unknown, that moment of unknowing but seeking, of curiosity left unanswered by distance and the limits of the visual. Thinking about that moment in the mid-1400s where the scale of imagination was vast, unimagined, megalomaniacal, and hallucinatory, this is what *Mar Portugues* invokes. Now, standing at Cape Point in 2015, *Mar Portugues* liquifies into the ghosts of the sea. The ocean of shock is a fluid archive whose watery pasts bear secrets best left at the bottom of the sea. Yet the past tugs at the present.

vi.

Crumbling fort walls of Portuguese solidity frame the waterfront of Fort Cochin near my parents' home. Once a major colonial fort port for the Portuguese, then later the Dutch, the city of Cochin now maintains Fort Cochin as a repository of the historic past. The waters around Cochin are placid with a dark, murky hue. Grey green and opaque, light bounces off the ripples whipped up by the diesel boast ferrying people to work and back across the archipelago. A distinct odor of toxic fumes lingers around the dock as the ferry swings by the quay to pick up commuters heading home. Standing at the pot holed little quay waiting to catch the boat, the aura is one of time in its own frame. Nothing arrived here swiftly. Nothing leaves in hast. The mould assails everyone.

vii.

Under the shadow of the largest fort the Portuguese built in the Malabar, Fort Thangassery, there is a grand old *tharravadu* (family home), now derelict, ghostlike, built on what was originally the site of a Hindu temple. It sits on a hill by the Ashtamudi Lake, surrounded by rolling gentle hills of coconut plantations. In 1965, this desolate ruin used to be a lively place; it had a large outdoor kitchen bearing six stone fire hearths that burnt coal to prepare food for the large home of nine children and the numerous grandchildren all living in the dispersed family property around the main mansion of my mother's father. Evenings in this provincial hamlet centred around the family *tharravadu* with informal gatherings, high teas, and large dinners served every day for the random assortment of extended family showing up. It was a place deeply connected to the lake—a sea people with a rich history of a traumatic past that was buried in the silt along the coastline that marked the edge of their property along the Kollam waterfront. Over the years, the layers of fragmentation, the violent discontinuities invisible to my child's eye slowly registered over the years—like a classic Chekhov play, with dying ways of feudal life replete with serfs and a communist ethos reshaping a colonial landscape. Now, the serfs are land-owning communists, the once bustling dwelling a derelict remnant of the past.

The slow decay of my mother's family home *Valia Veedu* or "big house" fascinated me as the years wore on, for its atavistic "swamp people" obsessions, as I was wont to think of them and their very entrenched preoccupation with coastal life, the sea, mould, and the maritime past. At the source of my deepening fascination with the Malabar Coast was a tale divulged to me late one monsoon afternoon, sitting under the swaying coconut trees, the fishy stench of the Ashtamudi Lake wafting up the mouldy bank. I was in Quilon on one of my rare visits. My loquacious Grand Uncle, a Jesuit priest well trained at the Vatican, felt it opportune before he died to reveal a never discussed family secret. He recounted quietly that there was a family myth that one of my great-great-great grandmothers was a "kept woman," brought on the ships from Indonesia. "Being Catholics, however," he said, "we don't discuss such things. It was a family secret."

viii.

All families have rumours and hearsays. Coastal families along the Malabar Coast have more than their fair share of stories to tell. The family home on top of the hill on Ashtamudi Lake was intriguing for more reasons than the distant past.

I grew up in Quilon's fort city of Thangassery as a child, visiting my mother's home town from Dar es salaam, Tanzania. My Thangy cousins and I would wander among the sixteenth century Portuguese and Dutch cemeteries and were fascinated by the living ecological remnant of a complex multilayered historical past that shaped the

Malabar Coast. The rumoured revelation years later, about the possible Batavian connection—a conjecture I made based on shipping documents of the Dutch East India Company archives at The Hague—opens up a hidden history buried inside the fort walls of medieval Quilon. It dawns on me that the mythical Batavian great-great-great grandmother would have probably come through this fort port as a slave in the seventeenth century, as it was the largest harbour in the region and the main port for Portuguese and Dutch cargoes.

I try to imagine this grim scene:

A Dutch ship from Macao via Malacca filled with rough seamen unloads an unspeakably distraught group of women from Batavia, most likely Muslim. The scene is hard to visualize. The Quilon beach at Thangassery is spectacular—its wide open sandy shore a mesmerizing background to the unfolding scene of violence. The fort is still unsettling, with its cavernous moat and Portuguese Moorish "*cerca mura*" or Moorish encirclement in reasonable shape despite the centuries. Its forbidding walls continue to keep the tempestuous sea out, and the wails of the abject women within its fortifications.

Haunted by this elusive, tactile image every time I walk the old ramparts of the fort city, I begin research to corroborate the mythic reference to the supposed "Indonesian" ancestor. I begin work on the Dutch East India Company's entrepots.

The Dutch East India Company exiled numerous ship loads of populations from Southeast Asia, from as far flung as Tidore, Aceh, Ambon, Ternate, Java, Malacca, Patani, and Moluccas, to the South African shores, via Quilon and Galle. Political insurgents, anticolonial rebels, and radical agitators among the Muslim populations from Batavia, what is now modern Indonesia, were a large demographic.

A footnote buried in the archives of the Dutch East India Company mentions two shiploads of Batavian women brought as comfort women on board Dutch ships from Batavia, disembarking in Quilon. No further mention of this unfortunate consignment is made in subsequent accounts. The minor footnote amid the detailed documentation of military personnel, spices, slaves and commodities is chilling. The archival fragment from the 1700s makes the present infinitely layered. My jovial Great Uncle the priest was not fabricating. There was evidence that the Dutch transported slaves from the East Indies to Cape Town via Galle and the Malabar. His whispered revelation in the monsoon twilight about the Indonesian grandmother who was a "kept woman" was entirely probable. The anecdote spurs me to study the exposed ramparts of Quilon and its terrifying *oublie*—the space of shock in the Indian Ocean.

ix.

Fort Thangassery still stands tall and foreboding. Its solid buttressed military walls of red stone built by the Portuguese in the style of the Castello of Lisbon, remain the tallest structures of the low lying port. Reinforced and fortified by the Dutch during the seventeenth century, with a deep moat separating the fort from the mainland, the grim spectacle dominates Quilon's spectacular coastline. The star-shaped fort's regulatory planning with its circular pathway up the hill, repeats the shape and movement of Lisbon's Sao Jorge castle. Fort Thangassery's central artery designed for heavy cannons is constructed of heavy stones with picturesque homes in bright colors fringing. Its battlements echo the urban pattern along Lisbon's medieval Castello. Walking up the Castello Sao Jorge, one is reminded of Thangassery. Strolling around the quaint streets of Thangassery, one recalls the uneven cobble stoned streets of Lisbon's Sao Jorge. My cousins still live inside the now languorous contemporary fort city of Thangassery; its ramparts are now filled with hanging laundry and potted plants of its current denizens.

The Quilon region was known for it "black gold," as the coveted spice of black pepper was called in medieval times. The lure of this deceptively petite pod of flavor was such that entire empires colluded and competed with each other, seeking access to the exquisite pungency of black pepper. Drawn by the aroma of the species, traders from Aleppo and Zanzibar and Canton sailed the treacherous seas to Quilon. Many stopped at Quilon and never turned back. Others travelled further ashore, embracing new gods. Quilon was the first safe harbour one encountered if one was sailing the long stretch from Aceh across the tip of India where the waters were volatile, furious. Quilon offered a safe, spacious harbour that ecologically mirrored another similar cove around the other major land mass in the southern hemisphere—the Cape of Good Hope.

In scale, strategic accessibility, and shelter from the axis of sea currents and oceanic disturbances, these two coves mirrored each other. This synchronicity of the two coves was not missed by the colonizing powers, both the Dutch and the Portuguese, and later the British. Hence, the connectivity between Quilon and the southern coast of Africa exceeded the merely tactical replications of colonial administrative practices. They reproduced habits of colonial recalibration, consolidation, and strategic outreach, which both coves enabled sea faring military powers, such as the Dutch and the Portuguese, to achieve.

X.

It is a beautiful spring day. The Dutch countryside is picture perfect as the train rolls out of Amsterdam towards The Hague. Perfectly tended, the flat rolling landscape of canals and water and farms lull me into a dream space. I feel as though I am inside a Dutch painting.

I have embarked on the trip with the elusive goal of finding ship records that track the ships that travelled from the Zuider Zee to Cape Town and from there across the Cape of Good Hope to the Malabar Coast and onwards to Batavia carrying slaves and pepper from India. On their return journey, stocked with nutmeg, cloves and the wealth of the Indies, the ships would stop at Quilon and then onwards across the Indian Ocean through the Agulhas and Kaap Staad back to the Zuider Zee and Rotterdam.

At the VOC Archives at The Hague, I am transfixed by the meticulous cataloguing of the VOC's shipping archives. All commodities including slaves, comfort women, and other goods were carefully logged onto the ship's sea log. I begin my painstaking search of the VOC's eight thousand journeys, looking for clues, trying to understand their routes, their preoccupations, their cargoes. Sitting at the computer, I ask the patient archivist how I would track down the possible cargo of women from Batavia to Quilon in the seventeenth century. He replies I should scour the ship's logs.

I envy the Dutch their precise archives, their cartographic sweep of the world by the fifteenth century, their grasp of value and mercantilism that so shaped my past as the underside of their future. As if to echo my thoughts, a group of four paintings hang in the colonial room at the Rijksmuseum. They are a series of city views from the sea, painted by Joan Vingboons. The first is of Kaap Staad (Cape Town), the second of Cochin, the third of Pernambuco, and the fourth of Batavia.

A view of Batavia from the ocean painted in the seventeenth century with incredible detail show a string of islands of strategic interest to the Dutch. Yet another detailed map of the notoriously evil Elmina Castle in hues of green and browns captures a scenically impressive scene of rolling hills and a large fortress along a splendid coast. If one didn't know what the map represented, only the most heinous of human constructions, it would pass for a lovely tourist destination. Another vivacious map of Cape Verde, the view is from the ocean looking inland. Another, very detailed map of the elaborate fort town of Calicut, immediately communicates the strategic importance of the site to the cartographer. These are only some of the nearly six hundred maps that Joan Vingboons painted meticulously with great precision regarding the scale of streets to fort and of the colonial ports environs to the uncharted territories lying outside the Dutch borders. Vingboons' maps are remarkably detailed, visually suggestive renderings of entire urban lifeworlds along the global trading routes of the Dutch Golden period. Each of the illustrations is executed with the intuitive eye of the cartographer inventing a fictive worldview made real through the production of the maps.

Centuries later, Vingboons' early illustrations provide the first visual depictions of Manahatta under the Dutch, and of Quilon, Calicut, Cochin, and Cananor during the Dutch period, as well as other international ports of call from the medieval era, including Aceh, Macao, Kaap Staad, Recife, Sao Tome, Panaji, Galle, the Maldives, and Colombo, to name a few from the southern hemisphere. For the contemporary urbanist, reading these colonial renderings against their emergent landscapes is a practice in decolonizing the city, and revisualizing its future. Vingboons' maps are intriguing for their imagistic depictions of lost histories.

xi.

It is another rainy day on Singel Street. I decide to ride my bicycle down the thirteenth-century part of Amsterdam, and en route, I run into a picturesque map shop. A story book map maker's dream world, the compact store reveals a bespectacled man buried behind a pile of maps.

A step away from the busy pedestrian activity of the tiny street, Mr. D's shop is a flashback into the historic past of the Brabant region and the Netherlands. I wander amid the antiquarian maps, and, uncertainly, I ask if he has any maps of the Dutch colonial era, particularly of the Dutch East India Company's holdings in Asia. Mr. D looks up with sudden interest and asks what exactly I am looking for. I ask for Joan Vingboons's maps. I tell him I am following a family rumour of a great-great-great-grandmother who was brought by the Dutch from Batavia to Quilon.

The story captures Mr. D's interest, and he steps away from his desk at the back of the packed store of maps from every corner of Europe. He approaches me and says he might have a few. He says that he too has a tale to share: his ancestor from the 1700s was a VOC captain who travelled from Texel on the Zuider Zee through Cape Town and Cochin to Hooghly, where he eventually climbed the ranks of administrative office to head the VOC at Hooghly. Mr. D. speaks of how the old money of modern Amsterdam was really the new money of the 1700s, made from the colonial trading ports in Asia and Africa. They were new money of the time. Today, the handful of Dutch families of old wealth remain the descendants of the Dutch Burghers whose vast wealth was acquired across different parts of the southern colonies in Asia, Africa, and Brazil.

Mr. D. looks me in the face and says: "May, I am sorry we Dutch did this to your ancestor. How terrible the story. I feel perhaps maybe we are even related." Then, disappearing momentarily into the recesses of his store, Mr. D. returns with a map of thirteenth-century Amsterdam and gives it to me as a gift of a shared history, of a mea culpa across time and a potlatch of reconciliation. I am disarmed by the gesture. Mr. D's ancestor of the same name buried three wives in India. He lived in Hooghly for thirty years, finally returning to the Zuider Zee to live the rest of his life back in the cold Northern Sea. A painting commissioned by the VOC commemorating the elder Mr. D's sea journey back to Texel through the Bay of Bengal still hangs in Mr. D's home.

Work Cited

Pessoa, Fernando. *Fernando Pessoa & Co. Selected Poems.* Edited and translated from the Portuguese by Richard Zenith. Grove Press, 1998. Digital Edition.

Chapter 12

Twilight

C.M. Clark

Her obsession became full-bodied
and round—a melon straight
from the tilted garden tracing

the lowland's curve. The silt-heavy
rivers helped carry her throat's sore lump
along, careening rock to rock, riverbed

to tired tributary. Even slogging these foothills,
distant Loulan no more than nightmare
than memory, she nursed each sour swallow.

A stunted child fed on gruel, barely
grain, barely milk, barely
water and redolent with clanging insects.

Chapter 13

Pomegranates in Tehran

Laura Foley

They sell them whole or weeping halves in the street. Room service brings caviar by the pound. Civilian-dressed police patrol the halls, yank a scarf around my head. Khomeini's dead, our balcony's riddled with bullet holes, government-sanctioned walls blazon *Down with Israel, Kill U.S.A.,* as shopkeepers urge us to sip the fresh-squeezed, red juice, stroke our *Satanic* blond-haired sons.

Family Trip

After hours in a jeep feeble as our marriage, jostled on a rain-rutted road, we're directed to hold our baby up high, wade with our two young sons through flotsam and filth up to our waists, towards an old wooden boat anchored in the bay, our passage south. We travel eight hours in this rickety craft without food, life-rafts, or jackets, to Ujong Kulon, home of the last great white rhinoceros none of us will see.

WORK

"Was It Not Lucky That the Boy Was with His Mother?": A Travellin' Mama in Bangladesh

Anne Hamilton

There is silence—*save for the shouts of hawkers, horns of motor-rickshaws, and the late afternoon call to prayer—as the wedding party leans in to hear the most important question of the day: "What do you think of our country?"*

Simon, guest of honour, doesn't need time to think about it. "Bangladesh is rattling," he pronounces with all the gravitas a five-year-old can muster. Then, duty done, he turns his intention to important things— playing hide and seek with his friends, Shahdot and Rihan, big boys at twelve.

"He is right. He is right," the mystified villagers agree, then turn to me, "Sister, what is rattling?"

There was a time, many years ago, when I was a mystery in rural Bangladesh: a fair-haired (therefore Western), lone female traveller, neither young nor old. Where was my husband? My children? I couldn't possibly have left my children behind, could I? No, I'd explain, it was even worse than that; actually, I didn't have any children. The more times I said it, the more times I was tempted to create a parallel universe comprising five whopping sons, two beautiful daughters, their adoring father and grandparents ... all currently at the beach in Cox's Bazaar while I Did Some Good Works here.

The curiosity I didn't mind at all, and I was happy enough to be an oddity. What was harder was the genuine pity, the whispers of sympathy reverberating around the villages, the offers of prayer. Soon, *Inshallah*, I would have the family I must want however much I pretended otherwise. Meantime, mothers and aunts thrust their swaddled babies and naked toddlers into my arms for a consoling cuddle. It's hard to say who was more terrified—the screeching infants being inexpertly clutched by a ghostly-pale foreigner or the ghostly-pale foreigner inexpertly clutching the screeching infants.

Fast forward a decade and I rode into town triumphant. Not only did I have a fine, fat specimen of a ten-month-old baby in tow, but it was also a boy baby—how clever was that? There were delighted, approving nods all round; now, I was part of the club. The smiles fell only slightly on my subsequent visit. The baby had grown into a three-year-old, and I had yet to produce a little brother or sister; oh well, there was still time.

When he became five (and a half) and our little family showed no sign of expanding, I was greeted with resignation and a shadow of that former pity—aided and abetted by said five-year-old. He hoped, he told the community, we could take home with us a handful of boys—the girls were too "kissy"—to give him the big brothers he really, really wanted. It would never happen, I told both parties firmly, babies or big brothers. To this day, they don't believe me.

The Bangladeshi approval of me, travelling singleton turned travelling mama, is less understood back home. In 2001, friends recognized my (relatively) young, free and single statement of volunteering overseas. Their preoccupation was the likelihood of primitive toilets without recourse to toilet paper in a country where I would— no maybe about it—suffer terrible, explosive diarrhea. Being contrary, I didn't. Moreover, I fell in love with the place, wrote a book about it, and helped establish a home and school for children with disabilities. That I then kept on returning was widely (if tacitly) believed to be fulfilling the mothering instinct of a thirty-something, childless woman.

When, in 2010, I had a child of my own, the same people assumed that would be the end of my relationship with Bangladesh. After all, I wasn't going to take a baby there, was I? The food, the heat, the weather, the travel. My flippant reply of "they do have children there too, you know" was largely shrugged off as another example of me being, if not exactly an irresponsible mother, certainly an eccentric one.

Travel to Bangladesh, we did (with no ill-effects), and we continue to do so. These days, I am not a novelty; that mantle has fallen on my son. It is his job to say the country rattles (i.e., is noisy, full of commotion, and boats and rickshaws shake and jangle) and mine to translate.

We're on a slow, slow train somewhere between Dhaka and Sylhet, allegedly a five-hour journey. The carriage is designated first class, a small box off the main corridor, with two plastic-covered bench seats and a glass-less window. Simon is leaning out, watching the pop-up villages adjacent to the railway line: tarpaulin and cardboard tents, children his age stirring rice cauldrons on wood fires, cows alarmingly within patting distance. From the youngest to the oldest, the boys and girls pause in their tasks to nudge each other, grin and wave to him.

"Are they playing houses, mummy?" Simon asks. Then, longingly— it's hot and dusty on the train, and he's not allowed on the roof with the horde of young men cadging a free lift—"I wish I could go and play with them."

It is never easy explaining destitution, and it's particularly challenging when it looks like so much fun. These children can't go home to their toys, to dinner, and to a cosy bed, I tell him, because this is their home. Carefully, we deconstruct what such oddness means, until, for him, we come to the crux of the matter: "But it's alright if their grown-up is with them because they won't be scared," Simon says, with utmost confidence.

It's gratifying that such a sense of security is instilled within him. It's also terrifying, since I am his one and only day-to-day grown-up and the responsibility of that is immense— perhaps more so here with the lack of coherent infrastructure. That aside, for me, his philosophy captures the success of being a travelling mama-child duo.

I've learned that if I am going to change dramatically his parameters of country and culture—of his life, in fact—then there must be some reference points that are constants. On a short visit to poverty-stricken, rural Bangladesh, the points that most structure his five-year-old life—what, when and how he eats, where and how he plays, when he goes to sleep and gets up—aren't that straightforward to maintain. Here, he has to eat rice, rice, and more rice, and he eats it with his hand (okay, not so hard that one), and he eats it late at night when usually he'd have been long in bed, which is fun for a day or two until the crankiness sets in. Then, he gets up and washes in a bucket of cold water and negotiates a toilet he views as a hole in the ground. Of course, he can play, but his playmates have their chores as well as lessons and the indoor toys constitute half a cupboard of battered building bricks.

The benefits are obvious. Simon has no hang-ups about weird toilets or having spicy vegetables instead of cereal for breakfast. Skin colour is down to the sun, and disability is the body working in a different form; sign language is as valid a language as verbal communication. Those beliefs are probably not unusual in a small child, but the privilege of seeing it all first-hand surely widens his frame of reference about normality and, hopefully, will foster his acceptance of difference. Sound angelic? Hmm. Here, his preferred diet is plain rice and pomegranates; at home, he has no qualms about doing a poo in the park, and yes, he left his toys and games behind in Bangladesh because his new friends had none but only after negotiating a trip to the toy shop back home. Swings and roundabouts.

Adjusting to our trips is like doing a jigsaw puzzle, getting all the pieces to fit—as any parent or carer knows, a holiday is never a holiday; it's a matter of doing what you do at home in strange surroundings. For Simon and me, the security that underpins our travels here (and there and everywhere) is that the constant point of reference is the presence of his grown-up.

The travelling mama is the same person, doing the same things, but doing them differently—and saying that's okay.

First, the girls dress me in a purple and orange sari and then they try to oil my hair, making me resplendent for the picnic party. Then they watch me stirring a cauldron of rice and rolling out roti in the stifling heat of an outdoor kitchen, clapping at my mediocre attempts. My long dupatta is trailing on the ground again, and someone rearranges it again.

Simon, impatient to board the truck-sized tractor for the ride to the riverside, shakes his head:

"You look funny being looked after when you are a grown-up, mummy. You are my mummy, but they are being like your mummy because you can't do things even though you are old."

My first visit to Bangladesh was a leap of faith. As a volunteer with an international but very low-key nongovernment organization in an unfashionable and little known (in the West) country, I knew what to expect. At least, I did in theory—so mirroring my experience of becoming a parent for the first time after years of working in the field of child development and protection; the practice was light years from the textbook.

Arriving in Bangladesh was like reverting to being three years old but with the mortification and deskilling of adult awareness. I could not speak or read the language; I could not properly dress myself in the baggy salwar kameez; I could not easily sit cross-legged on the floor and eat my dinner with my right hand. Slowly, with infinite patience and much good-nature, those around me took responsibility for teaching me the basics of what I needed to know.

Fifteen years on, I'm still being actively looked after—mothered—by those original friends and colleagues and now by women young enough to be my daughters and probably (gulp) by Bangladesh standards my granddaughters. The feeling of security, of luxury, is immense. At home, I have an unwritten, self-imposed rule that I should always manage alone; it's rare I'd ask for help, but in Bangladesh, it's like going to a mythical childhood home. For a little while, I can concentrate on the handful of things I can do well; there is always someone else, far more qualified and keen, to cook, to fix the fan, to call a rickshaw, and arrange the money.

Yes, it can be frustrating when people don't listen to me, or they misunderstand my words, or ignore me because they think they know better (and they usually do), but I can deal with that—it's worth it—by retreating into my own little world for a bit. The unexpected bonus of having this time to stand and stare brings me so much closer to the life experience of a five-year-old; I'm just doing what Simon does to survive in an often confusing world. And he sees that while mummys know best about lots of things, they certainly don't know everything—and that's okay. It's also okay to ask for help. As his very supportive school says, we are all learning together.

"When is a mummy not a mummy? When she is in Bangladesh."

I've always had a sneaking yen to live a communal life. I'm fairly sure that born just a few years sooner, I would have been off to Woodstock with flowers in my hair. These days, when I visit our home school, I get to experience that sense of community—the highs and the lows. Like any intergenerational, extended family set up, it throws a new light on the practice of parenting and puts the emphasis on the old adage, "it takes a village to raise a child."

These children and young people are away from their family homes. Indeed, they might not have a family home. The older children parent the younger ones, and they are adept at doing so—a child only a few years older than Simon is proficient with caring, cooking, cleaning, gardening, and laundry—and the adults take communal responsibility for their overall care and protection.

I am never a mother to the children and young people here. We've already established that my abilities fall far short of those exhibited by their excellent house mothers. I am, instead, a quirky big sister; I am afforded respect for age and for an "away" life they can barely comprehend. (Western TV and general Internet has not yet infiltrated this corner of Bhola Island.)

But even as I write that, I realize it's my perception; the distinction would be largely immaterial in Bangladesh where the line between being a birth mother, a sister, an aunt, or a cousin is far more blurred than any I make in the West. Here, extended family living is the norm, and it is the women collectively who do the mothering; there is a deeply inbuilt, frequently hidden, female power in domestic life (This is despite the patriarchal society where, legally, the father is paramount and a child whose father is dead—even if he or she has a whole network of female relatives—is still considered an orphan.).

If living in a community affords me the security and company of shared roles, it equally expects that I take on board all that that means. I have to let go. I can't hover over Simon, worrying, in that infernal way I do at home. If he's to enjoy the family atmosphere, I have to let him live in it, and I have to accept the communal mothering.

On extreme occasions, my opinion will be sought (*"Is it okay for him to swim in the pond ... climb the coconut tree ... help kill the goat?"*), and whatever my answer is, the question serves to make me question myself in the mothering role: when I make decisions, what's about him and what's about me?

Simon says I worry too much. In his words, "You are a worry pot." But in Bangladesh, he goes on, I worry less. Because he is less reliant on me one to one, he isn't party to any fallout from my internal agonizing. (What if he swallows half of the filthy pond water, falls out of the twenty-foot-high tree, or is squirted with the cute little goat's blood and is traumatized forever?) It's a fascinating discrepancy in our mutual perception.

> *Back at the wedding, the bride looks like a delicate china doll, weighed down under her gold jewellery and silk drapes. Her head is demurely bowed, and she resembles a brightly-coloured butterfly beside the solid presence of her new husband. They are being fed pieces of cake, hand to mouth, a symbol of the joining of two families.*
>
> *"Why do they look scared, mummy?" Simon asks, standing on his chair to get a better view. "Why is the granny crying?"*
>
> *I open my mouth, but the very splendidly dressed auntie next to him, grabs him, and much to his horror, she plants a smacking, red lip-sticked kiss on his check. "The grandmama's little girl grew up," she says, "and that is happy and sad. You will understand when you are a daddy and then it will be your mama's turn to cry."*
>
> *"Oh," says Simon. "I thought maybe they didn't like the taste of the cake."*

Why wouldn't these newlyweds look nervous? This is an arranged marriage—with which both are happy—and despite having known each other for several years, they have never been properly alone. The bride is only fifteen, the youngest daughter who has never been away from her mother. Now she's expected to join a strange household equally as wife, third daughter-in-law, and young mother-in-waiting. There is excitement, kudos in the match, and a whole lot of wedding jitters.

Through sustained visits to Bangladesh, I've made many friends and have more or less surrounded myself with my own Bangladeshi family. It still comes as a shock that those I first met as children younger than Simon are now grown up enough in law and custom to marry and have their own children. Asha, the bride today, I knew as a seven-year-old. She's profoundly deaf (back then, she and her group of friends taught me the rudiments of sign language), but she has overcome what was once seen as a major, stigmatizing disability to achieve her proudest moments so far—a primary school diploma and a husband. She tells me how she hopes soon to become a mother; maybe on our next visit, Simon will have a new playmate. I smile at that because part of me still sees Asha as his playmate. Yes, it's her youth, but, partly, I suspect it's simply that a mother or mother figure (or even a much older foreign "sister") always finds it a challenge to see her child come of age.

Motherhood at fifteen? Motherhood at thirty? Whatever is the cultural acceptance, it's life changing.

As Asha's wedding party progresses, it's clear Simon and I have the privilege of being part of the family. But I am offered a very fond seat on the side lines—more coach than player now, my fifteen minutes of fame over—and the spotlight is on my son. My identity is as his mother: the one who brought him here. I'm happy with that. It allows me the anonymity to get on with my job here. These days, this is to ensure that the children temporarily or permanently resident in our home and school are cared for and protected in the best possible way. Our aim is that they, and their own families, grow in confidence and see possibilities. Fundamentally, it's about mothering—by whoever (female or male) and wherever that is and in whatever way it happens.

It has worked for Asha. I hope it is working for Simon.

Meantime, Simon and his friends Shahdot and Rihan are taking tradition to heart and stuffing each other with wedding cake. Then, they'll go off and play some more, and I'll stay here with the other proud and indulgent mamas. It would be the same back in the UK because if the most important question here is "how does Simon like our country?" There, it's simply rearranged as "how does Simon like Bangladesh?"

Just before they run off, the three little boys turn to me with a tissue full of cake crumbs. "We saved you some," Simon says. "Just because you are my mummy."

Every Bangladeshi knows the writing of Rabindrinath Tagore, the national poet. There's not one person here present who wouldn't agree with his line from "The Hero": "Was it not lucky that the boy was with his mother?"

The travelling mama is home to roost.

Chapter 15

Negotiating Fieldwork and Mothering

Angela Castañeda

"Wouldn't it be great if there was a rent-a-child business for anthropology?" This was a joke I heard often while in graduate school. At the time, I was perplexed as to why bringing a child to the field when conducting research was seen as involving so many perks. But now, nearly two decades and two children later, I have a whole new appreciation for what it means to travel to the field with children.

In this chapter, I use my experiences over the past decade travelling throughout Latin America to highlight the ways in which mothering affects my identity as an anthropologist. I found, as other scholars have before me (Butler and Turner; Cassell; Flinn et al.; Cupples and Kindon) that mothering is a useful tool for anthropological research; it provides the ability to be seen as a real person, someone that others can immediately identify with and place within their own cultural landscape—a mother. Mothering also marks moments of cultural judging, as different mothering techniques and strategies are put under the microscope of a mothering gaze. In my case, the complexities of travelling with children shaped my own research agenda, as at one point I made the difficult decision to refocus my field site to the United States due to feeling it was just too complicated, too expensive, and too exhausting both mentally and physically to travel with my children. But overall, since as an anthropologist my job is to balance multiple perspectives and gather many voices, the role of mothering in this process has only strengthened my ability to become an active witness in the lived experiences of culture.

Intersections of Ethnographic Methods and Motherhood

Nearly each fall semester, I teach a course titled "Ethnographic Methods" in which I help students unpack the role vulnerability plays in anthropological research. Drawing upon Ruth Behar's work *Vulnerable Observer,* I teach the value of reflexivity in my research and I emphasize the role my identity plays as one of my most important research tools. Over the past two decades, my identity as an ethnographer has changed along with both my marital status and association as a mother. These changes are especially important given the cultural context of my research in Latin America, which is a place where motherly images of saintly virgins are always within reach. As a Latin Americanist, I devote time to living and conducting participant observation in various countries—including Brazil, Colombia, Cuba, and Mexico—and the scope of my research within these spaces revolves around questions of power, performance, religion, ritual, health, and healing.

In this chapter, I use autoethnography to examine the intersections between fieldwork and mothering as I reflect on the ways travelling with my children affects my work. The formal use of the term "autoethnography" began in the 1990s, when Deborah Reed-Danahay provided one of the first detailed histories of its use as both ethnographic research conducted within one's own community and the use of autobiography in ethnographic writing. In my own work, autoethnography has always played an important role—whether it was translating Afro-Brazilian religious rituals through my strict Catholic upbringing or rediscovering my family roots in Central Mexico while negotiating my identity as a Mexican-American. Most recently, my rite of passage as a mother had me once again turning the anthropological gaze inwards as I worked to balance fieldwork and mothering.

As an anthropologist and mother, I juggle the pressure to be both good at my profession, which translates to being active in the field, and also good at being a mother, which implies being present for my children. In this sense, a mothering presence includes "being physically and emotionally present, being accessible, available and responsive in times of need" (Farrelly et al. 8). To fulfill both of these expectations, I either have to travel with my children to the field—which can also be critiqued if the fieldsite is one that others perceive as dangerous or inappropriate for children—or make my home my fieldsite.

For anthropologists, fieldwork involves an intimate process of bearing witness not only to, most often, a new culture, but also to an unveiling of their own identity, as layers of who they are as fieldworkers are often exposed during fieldwork. The history of fieldwork in anthropology typically presents the anthropologist as a "solitary fieldworker," and the presence of others is often left to a few words of appreciation in the acknowledgment section of books (Cupples and Kindon; Gottlieb). Yet the lived experience of conducting fieldwork is anything but solitary. I recognize that there are moments when a fieldworker feels isolated and alone, but the experience is filled with personal exchanges and relationship building. In this way, I find the process of fieldwork and mothering very similar. As a newcomer to fieldwork or motherhood, the institutional weight to get things right can feel overwhelming, yet the processes involved with each endeavour brings forth opportunities for transformative change. These spaces can be viewed as "sources of power" as Adrienne Rich identified mothering to be in her work *Of Woman Born*:

> The term "motherhood" refers to the patriarchal institution of motherhood that is male-defined and controlled and is deeply oppressive to women, while the word "mothering" refers to women's experiences of mothering that are female-defined and centered and potentially empowering to women … In other words, while motherhood, as an institution, is a male-defined site of oppression, women's own experiences of mothering can nonetheless be a source of power. (qtd. in O'Reilly 2)

In this chapter, I unpack the power dynamics involved with mothering and fieldwork by focusing on my autoethnographic experiences as an author-mother.

Mothering as Ethnographic Entrée

In the summer of 2000, I began the first of what would be many fieldwork experiences in Veracruz, Mexico. I was a young graduate student and newly married to a Mexican citizen. The decade I spent working in Mexico on my dissertation and postdoctoral research was mostly spent childless, yet questions surrounding my identity frequently involved my nonmother status. In Mexico, not only did I have the general cultural pressure to conform to the ideal role of woman as mother, but I also had familial expectations from my husband's family. Early on in my career, my gender and national identity combined with my marital status made others view me as nonconforming and *extraña*, or strange. As much as I tried to gain insider status, my nonmother self only emphasized the American part of my Mexican-American identity, and not in a good way. This all changed in 2008 after the birth of my first child.

As other anthropologists have noted, taking children to the field can enhance rapport building (Schrijvers; McGrath; Sinclair; Cupples and Kindon). My first fieldwork experience as a mother was, indeed, marked with a newfound sense of belonging and acceptance. My infant son was the immediate source of smiles from strangers and an opening for conversations with new research participants. When riding the bus or waiting for a taxi with my son in tow, I was met with approving nods, instead of questioning looks. For example, when my son fussed at the Veracruz state archives, causing sweat to drench the back of my shirt as I worried we would be asked to leave, a librarian came to my aid offering her air-conditioned office as a safe space for us to cool off and recharge.

In one particular case, my early attempts to network with an important anthropologist at a national research institution were met with fierce guardedness—when the anthropologist learned of my U.S. citizenship, she literally grabbed her books from me and nearly pushed me out of her office. In a later encounter at a local conference, my son nestled in my arms, this same anthropologist was not only friendly but generous—she shared her presentation and notes, and introduced me to her research team. What had changed? I concluded that like many others in my fieldsite, she was reading me differently. I was not just a *gringa* researcher anymore, I was a mother. As Trisia Farrelly et al. state, "By providing a common standpoint of 'parent,' children are useful in the building of trusting and meaningful relationship and dismantling differential power relations" (2). As a mother, a familiar and comfortable category to locals, I became the "repositioned other" (Rosaldo; Gilmore; Cupples and Kindon) with a new and stronger rapport-building identity.

Mothering under the Cultural Microscope

Shortly after my son turned one, I travelled to Brazil with my family for fieldwork on the secularization and commercialization of Afro-Brazilian religious traditions. As I planned our travels, I worried tirelessly about the nearly ten-hour flight down to Rio de Janeiro. Those worries were unfounded, as my son slept the entire flight, thanks entirely to breastfeeding. The downside was that I dared not move during the flight for fear of him waking, which left my right breast numb upon landing. The good news was if I thought rapport building was better with my son in Mexico, it felt far better in Brazil. Walking down the street in Rio de Janeiro, I was surprised when people half a block away would begin to call my son's attention to greet him and interact, but what I found most interesting was the reaction from men. Adult men of all ages seemed so pleased to interact with my child, which ultimately opened doors to conversations related to my research.

One of my main goals during this fieldwork trip was to obtain an interview with a local artist and religious leader. This was my third trip to Brazil in search of this elusive interview, and I was determined to make it happen. After multiple phone calls, visits to abandoned shops, and tips from neighbours, I managed to contact my participant, Adalena. She reluctantly agreed to an interview at her home but not before stating several complaints about her negative experiences of being interviewed in the past. My journey to Adalena's home took me across town and included a bus, metro, and trolley ride, not to mention the long walk up a steep, cobblestoned street. Knowing the distance needed to travel to her house and because I didn't feel comfortable leaving my toddler all day, my husband accompanied me with my son. Since I was so determined to complete this interview, I didn't dare ask Adalena if I could bring anyone else to her home, so I felt the pull between mother and researcher, as I left my family and slipped into the courtyard behind the large metal door of the building.

I finally found Adalena's home, her door open wide, soothing samba music lofting outside and colourful flags dancing in the breeze of her doorway, which signaled the June celebration of the *festas juninhas*. I glanced at the clock when our interview began, as I knew I had only an hour or maybe a little more before I would need to return to my family. Things started slowly, with basic questions about her artwork; the interview felt forced. I didn't feel Adalena opening up to me. How could she when I was nervous myself, worried about what my husband and son were doing locked outside on the street of an unfamiliar neighbourhood. The pressure of making this interview work pushed me forwards, and as we neared the hour mark, I heard a familiar sound. It was a baby crying, not yet loud, and not just any baby but my baby. It must have read all over my face. Adalena stopped talking, and it took me a moment to realize she was sitting silently. Naturally, she asked if something was wrong, and before I could explain, the weight of the interview coupled with feelings of guilt at not being able to comfort my baby became too much, and I broke down in tears.

Fast forward. I'm nursing my son on Adalena's couch while she shows my husband her small terrace with views of the famous Christ the Redeemer statue. As my son toddled nearby with a *biscoito*, or cookie, in his chubby hand, Adalena chided me for leaving him outside. "Why didn't you just bring him in?" she questioned, since this was obviously the culturally appropriate thing to do. And even more curious to her was my decision to leave my baby with my husband. Adalena seemed shocked that I didn't employ someone for childcare. This question of childcare supported my observations at parks and around town where women, mostly Afro-Brazilian, dressed completely in white uniforms were seen pushing babies in strollers or on swing sets. I was well aware of *faxineiras*, or domestic workers, as class markers; however, I was more inclined to employ my observation skills rather than participant observation skills when it came to engaging with this particular part of mothering culture in Brazil.

After I reunited with my baby, Adalena and I were able to continue the interview, but this time the interaction was more open and engaged; her responses to my questions were more detailed. When my son reached for a doll on her bookcase, Adalena began to describe vivid memories of her own mother working long hours as a seamstress.

With little extra money for toys, her mother would use scraps of fabric to make dolls as gifts. These dolls fostered Adalena's own creativity and imagination. Lovingly crafted by her mother's hands without glue or stitches, each knot represented the love and dreams she had for her daughter. And before I could tell my son to stop, Adalena gently placed the doll in his hand as a *presente*, or gift. Five years later, after the birth of my second child, a daughter, I received a lovely children's book written by Adalena, a reminder of our special friendship.

Mothering as Absent Presence

As my research projects have changed over the years, so too has my mothering style and my ability to travel with my children. After the experience travelling to Brazil with my son, I came to the difficult realization that fieldwork abroad was now too complicated, too expensive, and too exhausting as a mother. And because I did not believe in travelling without my family or employing outside help, I decided to start an entirely new project in my home state. Leaving Latin America behind for a domestic project was a hard decision but a necessary one for me to continue as an active researcher and ultimately obtain tenure at my institution. With my identity still firmly grounded as a Latin Americanist and my children quickly growing, my absence from the field was thankfully temporary.

Most recently, I was invited to travel to Cuba—a place I had always dreamed of visiting—on a preliminary visit for a new course at my university focused on public health. This was an opportunity I could not miss, yet it also meant it would be my first time travelling without my children. At the time, my children were seven and two years old, and the first of multiple visits to Cuba would only be for five days. I packed lightly for this first short visit, but at the last minute, I decided to rush out and purchase a cheap manual breast pump. My daughter still nursed but only at night, so I didn't think it would be a problem. My flight took me to Miami for an overnight stay, my first night sleeping alone in over two years, and then I boarded an early morning short flight to Havana. After passing immigration and customs, exchanging money, dropping bags at the bed and breakfast, and touring the neighbourhood, I finally sat down for lunch. Sitting there I felt a strange yet familiar feeling, a tingling that started slowly but quickly grew to a burning ache. I realized what was wrong: my breasts were engorged. I had no idea that my body was still producing enough milk to make this happen. After a quick lunch, I told my hosts I needed to rest and rushed back to my room in desperate need of that breast pump. I sat on the edge of my bed, cursing myself for buying such a cheap pump, as tears of frustration and pain rolled down my cheeks. In addition to my painful condition, I was also unable to communicate with my family for days due to a telephone issue. All of this left me feeling angry at myself for being unprepared, for underestimating my body, and for missing my child. I felt that I had made a big mistake. I should have never made the decision to travel without my family but that would have meant giving up what felt like, at the time, a once-in-a-lifetime opportunity.

Eventually I managed to adjust physically and emotionally, enough so that I could do my job and make the necessary arrangements for the next trip down with my students. However, the power of my child's "absent presence" was never more real to me. In "Being There: Mothering and Absence/Presence in the Field," Farrelly et al. write about the power of absent presence: "their [children's] absence is made present by various material objects (for example, our bodies, breast pumps, phones, computers, buses) and non-material traces (for example, our emotions and how mothering is conceptualized by ourselves and others), and these have given their absence agency" (21). I have since travelled four times to Cuba, each time for a bit longer and always without my children. After that first trip, my daughter began to say, "Mamí, Cuba no," whenever she saw me take my suitcase from the closet or heard someone mention the word Cuba. I felt horrible about having created this adverse reaction in my child to a place that I was growing to love more with each visit. I have plans to one day travel with my children to Cuba, and I promised myself I will change my daughter's sentence to "Mamí, Cuba sí!"

Early on as a new mother, I made the conscious decision to always find ways to travel with my children. It was a decision that felt good to me. Today the field is ever changing, as anthropologists can almost always be in the field by using increasingly advanced forms of global communication. The field is becoming less of a "bounded discrete entity separate from everyday life" and more of "a leaky space in which our relationships with participants shape and are shaped by our relationships with the co-researchers, friends, partners and family members who accompany us in the field" (Cupples and Kindon 212). My role as a mother affects every stage of the research process—from defining the research agenda and making arrangements for fieldwork, to conducting participant observation, to building rapport with participants, and to finalizing the results (Brown and Masi De Casanova). Negotiating travel with my children when conducting research highlights the relational nature of fieldwork as well as the intersecting identities of a mother-researcher.

Works Cited

Behar, Ruth. *The Vulnerable Observer: Anthropology That Breaks Your Heart*. Beacon, 1997.

Brown, Tamara Mose, and Erynn Masi De Casanova. "Mothers in the Field: How Motherhood Shapes Fieldwork and Researcher-Subject Relations." *WSQ: Women's Studies Quarterly,* vol. 37, no. 2, 2009, pp. 42-57.

Butler, Barbara, and Diane Michalski Turner, editors. *Children and Anthropological Research*. Plen, 1987.

Cassell, Joan. *Children in the Field*. Temple University Press, 1987.

Cupples, Julie, and Sara Kindon. "Far from Being 'Home Alone': The Dynamics of Accompanied Fieldwork." *Singapore Journal of Tropical Geography,* vol. 24, no.2, 2003, pp. 211-228.

Farrelly, Trisia, et al. "'BEING THERE': Mothering and Absence/Presence in the Field." *Sites: A Journal of Social Anthropology and Cultural Studies*, vol. 11, no. 2, 2014, pp. 25-56.

Flinn, Juliana, et al. editors. *Fieldwork and Families: Constructing New Models for Ethnographic Research*. University of Hawaii Press, 1998.

Gilmore, Sheila Seiler. "Both Ways through the Looking Glass: The Accompanied Ethnographer as Repositioned Other." *Fieldwork and Families: Constructing New Models for Ethnographic Research*, edited by Juliana Flinn et al. University Of Hawaii Press, 1998, pp. 35-44.

Gottlieb, Alma. "Beyond the Lonely Anthropologist: Collaboration in Research and Writing." *American Anthropologist,* vol. 97 no. 1, 1995, pp. 21-26.

McGrath, Barbara Burns. "Through the Eyes of a Child: A Gaze More Pure." *Fieldwork and Families: Constructing New Models for Ethnographic Research.* Edited by Juliana Flinn, et al. University of Hawaii Press, 1998, pp. 60-70.

O'Reilly, Andrea, editor. *From Motherhood to Mothering: The Legacy of Adrienne Rich's Of Woman Born.* SUNY Press, 2012.

Reed-Danahay, Deborah. *Auto/ethnography.* Berg, 1997.

Rosaldo, Renato. "Grief and a Headhunter's Rage." *Text, Play, and Story, 1983 Proceedings of the American Ethnological Society,* edited by Edward Bruner, 1984, pp. 178-195.

Schrijvers, Joke. *Motherhood Experienced and Conceptualised.* Routledge, 1993.

Sinclair, Karen. "Dancing to the Music of Time: Fieldwork with a Husband, a Daughter, and a Cello." *Fieldwork and Families: Constructing New Models for Ethnographic Research,* edited by Juliana Flinn et al., University of Hawaii Press, 1998, pp. 110-129.

Chapter 16

Ink Black Sky Bright White Page

Holly Anderson

Mondello and San Vito Lo Capo, Sicily 21 June –10 July

2 July 10:00 a.m.—Because I enter these pages more and more infrequently, the sequences begin to read like a psychedelic series of jump cuts. Today, I'm not crying to myself on a Times Square-bound 7 train but sitting on a beach of marble bright stones in a half-moon cove on a nature preserve near San Vito, Sicily. Sitting under a bent brimmed hat, watching my Lucyfruit shovel stones as small as corn kernels into a bucket with my other beloved, Jonathan, reclining beside her. This morning at half past seven when we took last night's supper trash and wet diapers to the dump site, Jonny and I stopped and swam naked in a tiny little fingernail of cove. Adam and Eve redux. If Lucy wasn't covered in twenty-five plus brilliantly red and angry mosquito welts (the fucking *zingara* as vicious as anything in the north woods) and nursing the last of a summer snotty kid cold, I'd be half certain we'd all died and finally made it into some version of heaven after a very dark-tunnelled winter.

We arrived a week ago so stunned with exhaustion from the blamblamblam of New York life, and then Jonathan went straight off the plane and right into rehearsals for a 100 Guitars performance on 28 June, and I walked back and forth to Mondello beach with Lucy in a kind of coma for some days and slept dimly, dumbly in a decent hotel, bathing at 5:00 a.m., hoping not to wake the baby girl and trying to remember whose life we are living at this moment. It does seem like a reward or a respite after the horrifically sudden death in our family.

Now, Isa is here from Paris with her young daughter fending mostly for herself because Rhys becomes the invisible man in family life leading up to a concert. And the concert was a huge, huge success: a two-thousand-seat amphitheatre sold-out and five hundred more people wanted tickets! Our Sicilian *fratello* Fabio pulled off a major coup with his new production company, and now we're spending the week in a nature preserve paradise with him and Anna and fifteen-month-old Agnese celebrating. The six of us tight in a white-washed version of an up-north cabin. Same cruddy beds and gas ring for cooking. Same *Off* smeared on before bed for the above-mentioned mosquitoes and the taste as always makes its way into your delish outdoor dining same as Minnesota. But the differences are these: the front walkway consists of a tight arbour of olive trees on one side and small cedars on the other. Directly out the door is a garden of peach and plum trees, banks of prickly pears, geraniums past their prime but still spicy, shrubby rosemary, and thick-stemmed basil. The ink-black sky is still eloquent with stars, the sound of slapping clapping waves pushing you towards sleep, the early morning swim the same sort of perfection as childhood lake summers in a life you thought you'd forgotten how to live.

Lulu travels beautifully. No problems on the Atlantic flight or the shorter one from Milan to Palermo. No problems eating later in the evening than she's used to and not getting to bed before ten or very much later. The night of the concert, I insisted on taking her to Malaluna club afterwards with a crush of guitarists drinking free beer provided by the city and the mayor there with all his bodyguards for the video opportunities. After that, a fish dinner on the harbour with the core band and wives and partners. Not home 'til 3:00 a.m. and Jonathan near furious, but rebellious mommy and baby had a blast!

Now, it's critical to simply relax. Feed our souls and feed our bellies. Not think too often of the fresh hells at home that probably await us. I must try and work on the long narrative for voiceovers for Bebe Miller's *Tiny Sisters*.

3 July—The Sirocco came last night like a furious blast furnace and around 2:00 a.m., Lucy woke up screaming, inconsolable for close to an hour. Nothing worked until her gesturing towards the door, beyond incoherent, we took her outside to look at the trillions of stars scattered like buckshot. The night sky calmed her immediately, and then she slept.

Not me, these mistrals make a black rash on the brain.

4 July—The ocean's temperature dropped at least ten degrees yesterday because of the winds, and today the jellyfish drifted in like deadly pink corsages. I've attempted two inchoate and clanking sentences for *Tiny Sisters.* Maddened by the clean, clear opening I dreamt one morning in Mondello and then completely forgot, not a trace remained the moment I woke up. These hourly skirmishes that involve motherprotector vs. writerpoet whatever I was/am trying to regain become be creator, but mother isn't always producer in the same way someone without children might be can be.

The grassy green lizards with the Morse-code-patterned backs that turn toad brown and dun by midday.

The herring-sized fish that mimic the black shadows and green patterns dotted with dashes of turquoise to match the Mediterranean shallows.

The squat, pebbled-like-a-toad lizard living in our tiny bedroom.

The trails of green capers spilling over volcanic rock and the Tom-Thumb-sized purple flowers like micro orchids.

The huge purple thistles of artichokes scratching at our cotton sarongs drying on the crooked wash line.

The blood red or burgundy agates on these beaches shot through with marble chips white as tooth or bone.

The volcanic stone rising out of the littlest bit of bay resembles nothing so much as huge branches of dead coral.

The nautilus shells no bigger than a newborn's toe and utterly rare on these stone beaches. I think I've found five now.

6 July—Our dear heart went to bed at 6:30 p.m. on her birthday yesterday—no more the sacrosanct two-hour Sicilian nap with mommy and daddy; oh, how I wish we could import this habit home but maybe she's already shifting back into east coast time and tempo—and so she slept thirteen hours straight. Nothing like it since infancy. Therefore, no pasta all'Amatriciana cooked by Fabio, no fruit crostata driven fresh over endless curls and curls of road from San Vito. It was melancholy for us, but we'll celebrate soon enough at home with her buddies. Lucy clearly needed to log the hours, our beautiful baby girl sprinkled with bites and bumps, a waterfall of snot leaking into her pouty mouth.

And will she ever remember that as a soon-to-be two-year-old she heard a 100 Guitar Orchestra playing *An Angel Moves Too Fast To See* outdoors on a cloudless night in late June at Teatro di Verdura in Palermo, Sicily, sitting absolutely motionless in my lap, transfixed for an hour watching her father play the drums?

Urbana, Illinois: The Erlanger House

5 September 9:40 a.m.—Sparrows periodically hurl themselves at the glass wall behind me, and one mourning dove murmurs in the enormous sycamore I can get lost in by tipping my head back just so if the creaky neck allows it. Bebe's been gone an hour to audition forty-odd dancers down to nineteen for a newer piece she's putting on them. We're both out here at University of Illinois to present a workshop on the collaborative process with nine dancers and nine writers. (Mostly grad students or faculty, many published—some poets and some fiction writers, one older woman who until very recently raised thirteen possums at home. Of course, I'm most interested in her, but the dance department director seems to think she may be the most trouble in terms of expectations and possible agendas. Huh?) Bebe and I getting stoked—finally—yesterday afternoon at O'Hare talking about our far flung and somewhat random process and then again last night at this fantastic house talking to faculty and department friends about what we made, what we did in *Tiny Sisters*, and how to convey all that in workshop.

Now about this house: a mid-sixties Japanese-influenced brick box with polished broad board floors and poured pebble walkways. A sleeping loft with two Goldilocks beds slung over a "great room" with twenty-foot ceilings. Teakwood tables and desk and hardware-less closets and built-in cabinets everywhere. A broken-neck trap for toddlers for certain, but my Lucyfruit is safe at home with her daddy, and I'm enjoying the first completely unstructured day I've had alone in two years. Bebe's not due back until four and no class tonight until 7:00 p.m. Heaven is here right now.

In Appreciation and Gratitude, Holly Anderson, 1955-2017

Caroline Beasley-Baker
16 February 2018

"Out on deep reconnaissance into the spirit crack, please send
info back" —Holly Anderson

Holly Anderson is one of my closest, long-time friends. Losing access to her voice, her "Holly-says," and her "Holly-ness" is hard to take-in—all of her bits and pieces of info—advice—adventures—her everyday-ness—those spinning/glorious-evermore words and stories and poems—that before Holly, I didn't know I needed.

It does leave me bereft, but the size of her—her kindness and generosity (her nurturing) as a friend. The simple things—her love of cast iron skillets, her red barn and blue and white perennial garden—(Bovina)—and feeding her Kanovskys (her sweated-onion pasta). Our French fries and beer. Her dear hearts, dearies, and darlings.

When I wake up at 2:00 a.m. unable to sleep, I won't be counting sheep—I'll be counting Holly's silver trout streaming up my modern walls, watching the firelight, and thinking about Holly here in the sky/smack dab in the centre of the Milky Way, where she said she will be.

(It's nice to think of Holly and John Cage and Prince all having tea.)

There is body and math and music in Holly's work—a populated kingdom of Holy-ness—magical and pagan, celebratory, swooning and lost to be found. There would never, ever have been enough time for Holly in the world, for her to be and say all that she is. But we live with all that she has given. Her fierce/funny/brilliant/adamant spirit lives—and for me, she will remain endlessly present and unfolding.

So Holly/Holly—signal back, I know you can.

For Mom

Lucy Anderson Kane

The night before I sat down to write this, I had a dream that my mom and I were talking on the phone. While my mom positively impacted the lives of so many and will be remembered by everyone as the prolific artist, tireless advocate, and selfless hero that she was, I have the unique privilege of being the only one who will remember what Holly Anderson was like as a mother. Of course, she was exceptional at it.

She and I spent a lot of time together, just the two of us, when I was growing up. Shared memories that might seem banal—Dunkin' Donuts dates as a toddler, binge watching TV series on DVD as a preteen, and countless long, lazy summer days in Bovina—I saw as moments of quiet significance. These moments dominated the first eighteen years of my life, when my mom and I spent more time together than we did apart. When I left for college, and moved between St. Paul, Cape Town, and Boston for the next five years, my mom and I replaced our face-to-face moments of quiet significance with long, rambling phone calls that spanned hours, topics, and time zones. This, despite the fact that neither of us especially liked talking on the phone. I'd been putting off writing this for weeks, simply because I did not know where to begin, but my dream about our phone call seemed like a sign that it was time to get started.

My mom influenced me in more ways than I can verbalize or even conceptualize. Most of my greatest simple pleasures—the bagel and lox breakfast special at Zabar's, burnt orange accent pieces, the perfect combination of potato chips and Sauvignon Blanc, and a staunch refusal to comb my hair or wear a bra unless *absolutely* necessary— were all taught to me by mother.

And she also taught me some of my greatest loves—a love for a rich vocabulary, a love for the number five, a love for cooking from scratch and feeding friends and family, and a love for her home state of Minnesota, a place where I spent four formative years and fostered some of my most significant relationships, only because my mom scheduled a tour of the Macalester campus for me in November of 2009. There was a moment of time when I felt such a deep sense of belonging in the Land of 10,000 Lakes that I had the outline of the state tattooed behind my right ear. Of course, this was only after extensive discussions about it on the phone with my mother because I have truly never made a major decision without her sometimes unsolicited but always valuable advice.

No collection of adjectives can accurately describe my mother, but here is my best attempt: warm, sage, bossy, hospitable, creative, loving, passionate, empathetic, intellectual. The list could go on infinitely. But perhaps the best word is unique. I have never met someone like my mother. I think we can all agree on that, which is why so many people loved her even after only meeting her once. Her energy lit up each and every room she entered; her bright blue eyes never missed a moment, and her indispensable advice impacted so many, whether it be for only a second or for decades. I see glimmers of my mother in myself, but she has given me so much to aspire to be. I aspire to be as brave, as confident, as resilient, and one day as tender of a mother as she was throughout her life.

My mom and I spent a week in Chania, on the island of Crete, the summer after I graduated college. Each day more or less took the same format. We would wake up and eat fresh fruit on the balcony of our hotel room, the same hotel she had stayed in years before on an early trip to her beloved Greece, before making our way to a local beach where we would lie in the sun, read, drink cheap Greek beer, and swim in the Aegean Sea. Eventually, we would make our way back to town, rinse off the salt water, and watch the sunset while we drank three-Euro glasses of white wine on the harbour. Then we would stuff ourselves on fresh seafood, dolmas, tzatziki, and feta, and marvelling each and every night at the hospitality of the people of Crete. The predictability of these days allowed my mom and me to have some of our most significant conversations. During that week in Chania, I turned twenty-two, and we realized that we had also been in the Mediterranean when I had turned two—that time in Sicily. We spoke about returning, twenty years later, for my forty-second birthday— me, her, and the grandchildren I promised to give her. While this trip will not go as initially planned, it is still something I have every intention of doing—to honour my mother in a place she loved so deeply. Despite being from the shores of Lake Superior, my mom felt a deep connection to the crystal blue waters of the Mediterranean. I would like to close by sharing a poem my mom wrote while in Sicily, on 4 July 1995:

"The grassy green lizards with the Morse Code-patterned backs that turn toad brown and dun by midday.

The herring-sized fish that mimic the black shadows and green patterns dotted with dashes of turquoise to match the Mediterranean shallows.

The squat, pebbled-like-a-toad lizard living in our tiny bedroom.

The trails of green capers spilling over volcanic rock and the Tom-Thumb-sized purple flowers like micro orchids.

The huge purple thistles of artichokes scratching at our cotton sarongs drying on the crooked wash line.

The blood red or burgundy agates on these beaches shot through with marble chips white as tooth or bone.

The volcanic stone rising out of the littlest bit of bay resembles nothing so much as huge branches of dead coral.

The nautilus shells no bigger than a newborn's toe and utterly rare on these stone beaches. I think I've found five now."

CULTURE

Chapter 17

Attached Bodies: Movement, Babywearing, and the Travelling Mother

Maria Lombard

Global representations of women who mother can be analyzed through the connection between textiles and movement. I will thread my own story of motherhood and travel together as I discuss babywearing—a simultaneously imposed and chosen symbol of motherhood that encompasses a piece of fabric mothers around the world use to attach their children to their bodies. In this chapter, I discuss babywearing both in the West and in the parts of the world where babywearing is perhaps more authentic, and I offer my own experiences with and observations of babywearing. The multiple roles I have as a mother, as with most women, can come with many labels. At work, I am a teacher and a colleague, whereas at home, I am a mama, daughter, wife, and neighbour. Another, more complicated, label that I wear might be expat, or is it migrant worker, or maybe economic traveller? As with the labels that I wear, babywearing is complex, and is socially and economically dependent on where the mother is coming from and going.

Once defined by how many countries I had visited, my life of travel is now delineated between trips before becoming a mother and our travels as a family since. Before motherhood, I didn't mind going into countries just out of turmoil or those that were clearly headed that way. Just after the Arab Spring, I went to Egypt for the first time, visiting Tahrir Square in Cairo and taking a *dahabiya* cruise from Luxor to

Aswan on the fabled Nile. I have been on treacherous mountain sides in Pakistan, with barely a road beneath me, leaving the Swat Valley just a few months before the Taliban made the area impassable for the tourists, hikers, skiers, and climbers who used to frequent the area surrounding K2, the second highest mountain in the world. Paris and London were checked off my list early in my journey, but it was always the call to less travelled places that I wanted to answer most. I thought that less visited places would provide me with more genuine experiences.

My journey took me down a path from travelling the world with my husband to going back home, via Seoul and Doha, to Alabama to give birth to triplets. After having Isaac, Daniel, and Sophia, travel clearly had to change for me. The kids changed my modes of transport—from tuk tuks in Sri Lanka and a camel caravan in the Sahara to full-size vans and Audi station wagons with three child seats. They also changed my accommodations from a noisy apartment next to a night club in the old town of Dubrovnic to country houses with pools and chefs in France and Italy. What motherhood changed most for me, though, was the meaning of travel. While I still wanted the excitement of exotic travel, I wanted my family to connect with the places we visited.

An image that began to change my perceptions of my own life and travel even before I was expecting triplets was the faces of mothers I saw abroad in distant lands, who were far removed from any ideas of motherhood I had. Motherhood means different things around the world. A Western notion of motherhood can mean dropping off the kids at nursery early in the morning, or taking them to the mall in a folding stroller tucked in the back of a minivan, or feeding them packaged food full of unpronounceable ingredients. In Sri Lanka, I stayed in a tea plantation that coordinated the schedule of workers who picked and processed tea with the school timing of their kids. The women of the plantation carefully plucked clusters of bright green leaves and put them in large baskets on their backs. The men processed the leaves, drying them, sorting them, and preparing them for auction. The children had their job to attend a school built to educate the children of the plantation. After they all finished their work, the families could be seen together in the evenings, eating aromatic fish curry through the open doors of their small homes, then walking together all in plastic flip flops among the green hills.

The most compelling, almost instinctive image of motherhood I came across in my travels was babywearing. Babywearing is an ancient custom of motherhood practiced in Indigenous cultures in Africa, Asia, and the Americas, in which the mother carries infants in a cloth on the front or back of her own body (Blois 30). As a conceptual fourth trimester of pregnancy, babywearing is an external womb and allows the child to be visible, audible, interactive, but still attached. As textiles of movement, the woven wraps facilitate travel for women who mother. When worn on a mother's back, the child faces forwards with her. When the child is wrapped on the mother's chest, the child faces the mother, ready for feeding, nurturing, and touching.

In Bhutan, mothers wrap their babies in a large scarf called a *rachu* and carry the child on their back wherever they go, on normal errands to gather vegetables from the garden or to do household chores (Altmann 60). I distinctly remember two women in rural Bhutan walking through a golden rice field, recently harvested, with their babies tied to their backs facing forward. The red *rachu* held the babies close, as though the fabric was extending the gestation period. The almost organic image of family extended to the home of a local teacher I visited in Bhutan. The children were the centre of the daily life of the family but not themselves the centre, which is so often the case when I plan my day entirely around the children. In Bhutan, the children go along for the ride, but the ride is not orchestrated just for them.

The same image of Indigenous babywearing was repeated for me in Zanzibar when I boarded a ferry to Dar Es Salaam. A Tanzanian mother travelling alone had her toddler son strapped to her back in a colourful scarf, leaving her hands free to carry heavy bags. Women in Tanzania use the *kanga,* or traditional scarf, to carry and cover their child (Zawawi 27). These large scarves often have inscriptions on them in Swahili or in another language, which are religious, social, political, or cultural in nature (Zawawi 31). I watched this mother on the ferry adjust her son, who nearly fell out of the *kanga* at one point because he was wiggling so much, maybe excited about the trip he was taking with his mother. She carefully adjusted him, bent forwards, and bounced him back up towards her shoulders. She finally retied her *kanga* to keep the young boy more tightly secured. I wondered where they were going. Were they visiting family or relocating for her work.

After having my triplets, the image of the child on his mother's back seemed daunting. Gone was my daydream of easy travel with my baby wrapped tightly to me and a plane ticket in my hand. I wondered how I would ever carry three babies. Fears of multiple strollers, car seats spread across Mercedes vans, and booking an entire row of an A320 filled my head. Determined and resourceful, I found suitable wraps that would hold my babies. While searching Amazon, the online shopping site, not the jungle, I stumbled upon a vast selection of baby-carrying devices, and I made my purchase. One at a time, I carried a child on my back, while one toddled or rode in an umbrella stroller, and my husband carried the third baby in his own wrap. I managed to carry them in a wrap until they were about two years old. Mobile, attached, and connected, the wrap seemed to connect me both to the places I had been and the places we were going together as a family.

In both Bhutan and Tanzania, a mother carrying a child on her back was not recreational. It was a necessity—for work, for chores, or for transport. The women were not hopping on the metro in New York to go to mommy and me yoga, but neither could I for that matter. Life was incredibly different for the mothers I saw in Tanzania and Bhutan than what I am used to seeing in America or Europe. The complexities of babywearing in the modern world mean different things in the Global South than they do for Western women. In the Global South, or developing countries in Asia, Africa and South America, babywearing is functional for carrying water, working in fields, and walking long distances. The Global South is a term that displaces more negative phrases like "third-world countries" or "developing nations" and is defined by unemployment, poverty, food insecurity, and other economic and social issues that are particularly challenging for women (Prashad 130). Considered as almost synonymous with postcolonialism (Harindranath 109), the Global South frames the spaces of babywearing in developing nations as colonizing of women. It seems that in addition to the everyday burdens women face in the Global South, the babies being worn on their mothers' backs are colonizing them. Alternatively, Western women, like me, buy expensive, often organic textiles woven for consumption and chosen for the freedom they provide in city life, housework, or leisure travel. The economic and social constructs of life in the Global South mean that mothers must take their children along, but for me, babywearing reflects my conception of travel as a space for movement and exploration. Babywearing liberates me as a traveller and a mother to move in and out of spaces, while reminding me that travel, like babywearing, can be colonizing.

As I started to plan my first trips abroad with my children, I began to reassess how I typically think of travel with children. The wrap frees the mother in ways that strollers cannot. In her travelogue of a family trip to Italy, Katie Cantrell laments the airport arrival in Rome and asks her husband, "Do you want to unpack the stroller here or let the kids run loose until we get in the cab" (24). Cantrell says she was "never ... so excited about a piece of luggage as when [her] stroller came bumping along on the conveyer belt (25). Admittedly, for Cantrell, with a one-year-old and a three-year-old, babywearing was a solution for the smallest, as she put baby Charlotte in the carrier on her back when they left the plane (Cantrell 26). Babywearing is a simpler way to carry a child on a journey. As a mother travelling with a woven wrap, my babies are safe, comfortable, and close. I can move through spaces that a stroller cannot. I can ride in transport that doesn't accommodate car seats. I can have an evening meal at an outdoor café in Athens, motorcycles buzzing by, with my child sleeping obliviously. Or like Cantrell, I can select between the available means of transport at a given time to suit my needs and capabilities as a traveller. After all, the title of Cantrell's book is *Have Stroller Will Travel,* and the cover of the book is a photo of her children in a double stroller in front of the obelisk in Piazza del Popolo.

The paradox, of course, is that the freedom and choices that babywearing provides also connect mothers endlessly to the time-enduring image of attachment parenting. Parenting philosophies over the last few decades have wavered between attachment parenting, helicopter parenting, and just-let-them-do-whatever parenting. As I saw mothers on my travels with babies on their backs, I began to see how key babywearing was to attachment parenting. A wrap, a scarf, these textiles connect mothers with their children in a way that only their bodies had done before. Children remain close to the mother during the travel experience; they are physically and emotionally close for care, nursing, sleeping, and comfort. Like Katie Cantrell, I travelled with both a double stroller and wraps when my husband and I took two of the triplets to London when they were six months old for a doctor's checkup. The wrap was our first choice when going out in the city because we were freer than with the bulky stroller that was difficult to manoeuvre on the crowded streets of London. Babywearing allowed us to connect with our children and to nurture them in the rain under our own umbrellas.

Although I do value the historical connection to babywearing as a traditional, attachment sort of parenting approach, I do not want to oversimplify the significance of assigning the role of babywearer to the mother alone. From a feminist perspective, the mother's body attached to her child's through the wrap can certainly be a sign of oppression or social construction of the female's place in society. Simone de Beauvoir famously said, "One is not born a woman, but rather becomes a woman. No biological, psychological or economic fate determines the figure that the human female presents in society; it is civilization as a whole that produces this creature" (301). De Beauvoir's description of society producing the female is in line with the representation of the mother as caretaker in the Global South. A shift in terms of Western, or maybe Global North, travel parenting is that it is not necessarily the woman doing the babywearing. My husband has carried our triplets, one at a time, in his own wrap—a wrap equally selected for its durability and a masculine gray tweed fabric than my own pink and purple striped wrap. During a recent trip to Barcelona, I saw nearly as many fathers as mothers wearing their babies. Male tourists had front carriers, baby backpacks, and other kinds of branded babywearing products, freeing the travelling mother through partnership in babywearing. The notion of babywearing transcends parental gender and identification in the Global North and can free parents to engage with the child and the spaces they travel together.

The image of the travelling mother is complex, particularly in a postmodern world. Although technologies of travel have reinvented the modes of transport, humans have also been reimagined as technological beings, mediated by iPhones and tethered by cables for endless devices of communication and leisure. Part of the reimagining of the technological human is also a retelling of origin stories. When Mary Shelley created the monster in *Frankenstein*, she was retelling one of the oldest creation stories: birth, a god, or a man giving life to a creature, and then setting it out into the world to fend for itself—

abandoned by his creator. Shelley gave birth prematurely only to lose the baby girl shortly before writing her enduring tale of birth, *Frankenstein* (Marshall 107-110). She would go on to finish her novel while pregnant again. Birth and travel were connected for Shelley, as she struggled to come to terms with loss, birth, and her own movement. Shelley's *Frankenstein* was a story of travel, but more importantly, Shelley's own stories reflect her strength as a writer, a woman, and a mother: "Bringing Mary Shelley out of *Frankenstein's* shadow revives the woman as a confident writer in her own right" (Sharp 71). Documenting her own life experiences through journals and letters, Shelley told her stories of travel as a legacy of women's travel writing which reflects ownership of the experiences women have as mothers and travellers.

In retelling the birth story, a traditionally biological tale of a woman carrying and giving birth to a child, Shelley can be seen as what Donna Haraway has called a "cyborg writer" who uses the "tools to mark the world that marked [her] as other" (Haraway 175). These "tools" that Haraway refers to "are often stories, retold stories, versions that reverse and displace the hierarchical dualisms of natural-ized identities. In retelling origin stories, cyborg authors subvert central myths of origin in Western culture" (175). I wonder if the wrap, a textile and technologically simple in its making, could be a tool of a cyborg, since it displaces myths in the Western world of what it means to travel with a child in a stroller. In retelling stories of mothers and fathers who carry their children on their backs, the concept of naturalized identity as a parent becomes less hierarchical and more collaborative and communal. Travelling as a parent might be seen as difficult at best, encumbered by the products of infancy and toddlerhood, strollers, high chairs, plastic pacifiers or dummies in the baby's mouth to keep him satisfied. All of these images are supplanted with a natural closeness in babywearing. The implication for travel and parenting is a new naturalness, a cyborg parent who displaces accepted Western myths of parenting to create a new identity as a connected and naturalized traveller.

Travel is often done in search of meaning and companionship. Stories of finding love in a faraway land, like Elizabeth Gilbert's *Eat, Pray, Love*, reflect a desire to make a connection. Particularly for women's travel writing, the conventional role of romance is a theme revisited over and over, whether it is the search for companionship in Gilbert's work or the struggle to make sense of romance, even a failed one. In *Wild: From Lost to Found on the Pacific Crest Trail,* author Cheryl Strayed hikes over one thousand miles to discover what was left behind of herself after the death of her mother and a failed marriage. A *New York Times* bestseller and an Oprah Book Club selection, Strayed's travelogue is an example of the kind of women's travel writing seen since the end of the nineteenth century: women going alone and searching. Women travel writers like Gertrude Bell, Isabelle Eberhardt, and Freya Stark were all European women who braved the late nineteenth and early twentieth century notions of male dominated travel to insert their voices and experiences into the annals of travel literature. Contemporary male travel writers like Paul Theroux and Thomas Swick may also suggest that travellers go alone. Going alone may give travellers more time to think, free from fretting over tiny travel companions, itineraries, and lost luggage full of baby formula. The explorer going alone into the jungle is the one who comes out with a story of being nearly eaten by a lion. Maybe he really was nearly eaten or maybe he just doesn't have anyone else to deny the story. Stories of motherhood are not tales of travelling alone. Travel and motherhood intersect in spaces of companionship, community, and connection. This companionship is certainly not always straightforward. Maybe that's why other travellers choose to go alone. Travelling with children often means finding the nearest playground rather than seeking out unexplored parts of Paris. I have to pack enough of the kids' favourite Weetabix cereal before we leave home and to find the blue toy car that rolled under the sofa. I know that when I walk out the door, the suitcase will be missing something that the kids want or need. The journey is still a search with children, but for women's travel writing, stories of motherhood and travel need to be told as an addition, a contradiction, and an alternative history to the woman who goes alone.

Travel and movement across spaces can be about escaping the mundane and finding one's self. For others, travel is about the journey into the unknown. For me, travel has been many things—from a way of life, flying off to a new country every chance I had, to a way of connecting with the people I travel with, the places I go, and with myself. As a teacher working abroad, I have loved making new connections and redefining what home means to me. Not because I don't value where I come from but because I want to understand the lives that people live outside of the suburban Midwest of America where I went to graduate school and away from the perceptions and misperceptions about the American South where I grew up. Travel for me is not about escape but about connection and attachment to something that is just beyond my everyday reach. For mothers, connection can be a strong reason to start babywearing—a material bond that supports the maternal bond.

While my own mother and I had dinner at a café in Athens, motor-cycles buzzed by as Sophia slept in my wrap. I have been to Athens a dozen times, and I have seen many economic changes over the years, from austerity leading to the closure of neighbourhood *tavernas*, to the rise of Greek ecofashion brands like Heel and MuMu. The vibe in Athens is consistently alternative, hip, and a bit gritty. Athens is not glittering like Paris, nor is it as Eastern as Istanbul, mired by empire and gentrification as suggested in the literary descriptions of Orhan Pamuk's memoir, *Istanbul*. Athens is the product of thousands of years of travel. Sailors, explorers, and philosophers left and came to a city on the vanguard of travel. As I sat in the café that night, with Sophia wrapped tightly to my body, I was keenly aware of the place we sat in history—a very modern family, in a very ancient world, still impacted by the places we have been, those that have gone before us, and yet to be moved by the places we were headed.

The Greek goddess Leto was without a doubt the goddess of the travelling mother. Known more commonly as the Titan goddess of motherhood and modestly, Leto gave birth to twins, Apollo and Artemis while travelling, and she continued to wander with the babies in her arms once they were born (Ovid). She did not want to travel but was on the run from Hera, the wife of Zeus who was the father of Leto's twins. Leto went to the island of Delos where she delivered her babies under only a tree, and then she had to continue on her journey to Lycia, where the temples to Leto and her children still stand, though in ruins today. Finally finding a place of rest in Lycia, Leto, nevertheless, struggled with the carrying of her babies on such a difficult journey. A depiction of Leto by French painter Merry Joseph Blondel shows Apollo and Artemis wrapped in Leto's golden robe, held close to her body. Other paintings, like that of Italian Baroque artist

Francesco Albani, show similar images of Leto with her children draped in her own robes. Clearly an image that struck painters of myth was the way in which to depict a woman travelling with two babies. The myth of the travelling mother, as seen through Leto's story and paintings, represents the complexities of a mother facing the challenges of travelling the world with her children. The myth of Leto is a rich source of imagery of a travelling mother, with two babies under her arms, a harsh and vast world around them, searching for a place to stay and trying to meet the basic needs of herself and her children while in a faraway land that does not necessarily welcome them.

Though not a myth, my own travel experiences with multiple babies may be more like the retelling of origin stories that Haraway talks about. My triplets have been to Greece, the UK, and Italy; they have spent a summer in a lavender field in Provence and have eaten *churros* in Barcelona. I have walked through the crowded streets of Vienna with Isaac, the smallest of the triplets, on my back, facing forwards in my wrap just like the mothers in Bhutan and Tanzania. Sophia was with me in Athens, and Daniel loved being on his dad's back, which is a testament to contemporary parenting, free of the gender restrictions that I think might seriously impact mothers in developing nations who continue to carry their babies not out of attachment but out of necessity. The origin story for my babies has been less tied to a naturalized identity about how children should travel in a Westernized world.

As I look back over the trips we have made as a family, my travel philosophy has remained one of connection. Although the wrap and the attachment that comes with it may symbolize for me the phrase that was reiterated throughout E.M. Forster's *Howard's End* "only connect," I know that travel itself is more complex than only connecting. The journey, the people I meet, their own contexts, and baggage accompany them in much the same way that ours as travellers follow us. The wraps I bought are a link to ancient motherhood and movement. It is a historical textile made almost entirely postmodern.

Works Cited

Altmann, Karin. *Fabric of Life: Textile Arts in Bhutan: Culture, Tradition and Transformation*. De Gruyter, 2016.

Beauvoir, Simone De. *The Second Sex*. Edited by H. M. Parshley, Vintage A Division of Random House, 1974.

Blois, Maria. *Babywearing: The Benefits and Beauty of This Ancient Tradition*. Praeclarus Press, 2016.

Cantrell, Katie. *Have Stroller Will Travel,* CreateSpace, 2014.

Forster, E M. *Howards End*. Knopf, 1991.

Gilbert, Elizabeth. *Eat, Pray, Love: One Woman's Search for Everything Across Italy, India and Indonesia*. Riverhead, 2007.

Haraway, Donna. *Simians, Cyborgs and Women: The Reinvention of Nature*. Routledge, 1991.

Harindranath, Ramaswami. "The View from the Global South: An Introduction." *Postcolonial Studies,* vol. 17 no. 2, 2014, pp. 109-114.

Marshall, Florence Ashton Thomas. *The Life and Letters of Mary Wollstonecraft Shelley, vol 1*. Bentley, 1889. eBook Collection (Project Gutenberg) http://www.gutenberg.org/files/37955/37955-h/37955-h.htm. Accessed 26 Jan. 2019.

Ovid. *Metamorphosis, Bk VI:313-381 The Story of Latona and the Lycians*. Translated by Anthony S. Kline. The Ovid Collection. University of Virginia Library. http://ovid.lib.virginia.edu/trans/Metamorph6.htm#480077263. Accessed 26 Jan. 2019.

Pamuk, Orhan. *Istanbul: Memories and the City*. Translated by Maureen Freely. Vintage International, 2006.

Prashad, Vijay. *The Poorer Nations: A Possible History of the Global South*. Verso, 2013.

Sharp, Michele Turner. "If It Be a Monster Birth: Reading and Literary Property in Mary Shelley's *Frankenstein*." *South Atlantic Review,* vol. 66, no. 4, 2001, pp. 70-93.

Strayed, Cheryl. *Wild: From Lost to Found on the Pacific Crest Trail*. Vintage, 2013.

Zawawi, Sharifa. *Kanga: The Cloth that Speaks*. Azaniya Hills, 2005.

Chapter 18

A Taste of the Good Life: Expatriate Mothers on Food and Identity

Lynn Mastellotto

Introduction

For expatriates, travel fulfills the axiomatic imperative of broadening the mind with which it is conventionally associated since the experience of "dwelling-in-traveling" (Clifford 108) enables the development of an expanded sense of the world through the experience of building a new life in a new land. The seemingly oppositional notions of routes and roots converge in the expatriate experience, revealing that travel can contain both an impulse to move (flux) and an impulse to stay put (fixity). Although some expatriates are short-stay travellers who move mainly within compatriot enclaves, never seeking integration in their host country, this chapter addresses transnational writers who engage deeply with locals and local culture in their adopted homelands through long-term foreign residency. Peter Hulme refers to this practice as "deep immersion." He notes that as travel writers immerse themselves in foreign cultures for extended periods, they acquire "the sort of intimate knowledge which gives them access to people and places unknown to short-stay travellers, let alone tourists" (97).

Identity reformation emerges as a central theme in narratives of travel and resettlement; it is especially resonant in the case of female travellers who become mothers while living abroad and who detail this identity transformation in memoirs about their mothering experiences. For these travelling mamas, the experience of displacement is multi-layered and complex as they navigate a new mothering role within a broader journey that takes them far from home and from the certainties of their home cultures. The sense of dislocation they feel is immediate in relation to food and eating practices as they confront foreign foodways in an effort to feed themselves and their families upon resettling abroad.

Beyond the biological significance of eating as necessary for survival, sociologists point to the highly symbolic function of food as a formative activity in the definition of self-identity, as well as an imprinting of family, class and ethnic status. As Sarah Sceats notes, eating is the first thing we do as humans; it is "our primary source of pleasure and frustration, the arena of our earliest education and enculturation" (1). In Western culture, the identification of the mother as fulfilling a primary role in feeding children and socializing them into a food culture means that eating is a highly gendered domain of human activity. According to Sceats, women are ascribed a dual role as "feeders" through their biological capacity to manufacture food for infants and as "nurturers" through their socially assigned function in nourishing and caring for others, "with all that this implies of power and service" (2).

The relation between food and mothering is further problematized for expatriate mothers who enact this feeding and nurturing role within new cultural contexts according to unfamiliar rules and customs. Reminding us that "encoded in appetite, taste, ritual and ingestive etiquettes are unwritten rules and meanings, through which people communicate and are categorized within particular cultural contexts" (1), Sceats signals how food acts as both a material and metaphorical object of consumption. For the expat mother, foreign food offers a direct taste of cultural difference and functions as a portal into deeper understanding of the layered cultural contexts and subtexts of placed-based practices. Examining the practices centred on feeding and caring for children, Pamela Druckerman and Jeannie Marshall depict how their experiences as expat mothers form a unique kind of deep immersion in foreign place. This immersion is at once "disorienting and orienting," to borrow Justin Edwards and Rune Grauland's phrase describing the fundamental double-sidedness of travel (3), as it displaces old affiliations and yields a multilayered sense of self and other through the emergence of dialogical identities.

In *Bringing Up Bébé* (2014), Pamela Druckerman, an American journalist in Paris, learns about French food habits and Parisian table manners while raising three children according to parenting precepts in her adopted France. In *The Lost Art of Feeding Kids: What Italy Taught Me About Why Children Need Real Food* (2013), Jeannie Marshall, a Canadian writer in Rome, learns from local mothers, grandmothers, and market vendors the importance of fresh food in raising healthy and happy kids. Both transplanted North Americans develop an intercultural competence by learning to shop, cook, and enjoy food according to local traditions. As mothers who play a central role in feeding their families, the new food cultures they encounter through relocation present opportunities to rethink nutrition and the social identities related to food habits. Their memoirs present the centrality of food in the overall process of cultural accommodation, which unfolds according to three general phases of acculturation: first, a confront-ation with place that focuses on cultural difference and novelty; second, a negotiation with place that juxtaposes contrasting cultural paradigms; and third, an accommodation with place that involves deep and sustained engagement in local community over time.[1] Becoming cultural insiders takes on an urgency for Druckerman and Marshall, as they seek to decode the symbolic associations of food in their adopted homes in order for their children to participate fully in its food culture: their journey towards fitting in begins with learning to eat like locals.

French Manners

Pamela Druckerman moved to Paris with her British husband in 2002. She had a daughter then twin boys in quick succession and wrote about the experience of raising a young family in a transnational context in her bestselling book *Bringing up Bébé*. The subtitle to the American edition — *One American Mother Discovers the Wisdom of French Parent-ing* — suggests a whole-hearted embrace of French parenting practices. In fact, Druckerman has been criticized, especially in the American press, for her perceived uncritical acceptance of French manners.[2] However, a close reading of her text reveals that she juxtaposes competing cultural paradigms and uses her journalistic skill to probe their respective sources and contexts. Druckerman sums up French parenting as a combination of unyielding expectations and an insouciant approach, explaining how a *cadre*, or frame, sets firm limits for French children on such matters as food and sleep, but "within those limits, the kids have a lot of freedom" (70). This is a difficult mix to achieve, especially for a foreigner who cannot rely on any instinctive understanding of the balance of rights and restrictions underpinning such complex cultural practices.

At the outset of her deep immersion in the Parisian every day, Druckerman observes with incredulity and awe the French approach to food and mealtimes, which she claims act as an "invisible, civilizing force at their tables" (4). She notes that French children, unlike American children, are not presented with a special "kid's menu" or permitted "mono-diets" based on a narrow range of their food preferences, but they instead eat whatever their parents are eating, including fish and vegetables (5). While observing French families eating calmly and convivially in restaurants, she notes that French children seem to sit contentedly waiting for their food to arrive and then eat everything without a fuss. In contrast, she recounts her own experience of dining out while on holiday with her eighteen-month-old daughter as a special "circle of hell." Imploring the waiter to bring them everything—appetizers and main courses—at once, she and her husband rush through their meal, eating separately in order to take turns chasing their toddler who will not remain seated. Meanwhile, on the other side of the cultural divide, "there's no shrieking or whining. Everyone is having one course at a time. And there's no debris around their tables" (4). Druckerman observes that "quietly and *en masse*, French parents are achieving outcomes that create a whole different atmosphere for family life" (5), and she sets out to uncover the recipe for their success. This difference in French parenting and in child behaviour related to food habits is indicative of different social norms, which as an American mother abroad she is eager to understand and assimilate.

Isaebele De Solier and Jean Duruz note that "the material culture of food, and its associated practices and taste formations, have long played a key role in the creation and maintenance of social identities based on ethnicity, nation, gender and class" (4). It is especially revealing to see how food culture plays a central role in the identity reformation of expatriate mothers. The domestic consumption of food is a means of producing and regulating family life and relationships within the family. The differences in the way Druckerman's own family eats compared to the French families she observes are indicative of different relationships within the family and different expectations regarding the socializing influences of food. Druckerman's daughter is allowed to get down from the table and run around as soon as she has finished eating; consequently, the parents must rush through their meals to keep her company. By contrast, the French children she observes learn from a very young age to eat meals in courses, generally with a starter, a main course, and a dessert; this applies to whether they are eating with their families or at school (67). Besides helping them appreciate a variety of food served in healthy portions, this approach teaches patience, and it teaches that meals are not to be rushed through, since they are times for socializing with others. She notes that daily rituals around mealtimes in France act as "an ongoing apprenticeship in how to delay gratification" (67).

Citing UNICEF data, Druckerman explains that 90 percent of French fifteen-year-olds eat the main meal of the day with their parents several times per week, compared with only 67 percent in the USA and the UK (67), so they are learning to eat well and convivially at the table. Moreover, from time spent in the homes of French friends, she observes that children take part in the preparation of meals and, especially, in the weekend ritual of baking. They generally start by learning to make a simple cake like *gâteau au yaourt* by measuring all the ingredients, mixing, and pouring—in short, "they actually make the whole cake themselves" (65). Druckerman claims this baking ritual teaches self-control—with "its orderly measuring and sequencing of ingredients, baking is a perfect lesson in patience. So is the fact that French families don't devour the cake as soon as it comes out of the oven, as I would. They typically bake in the morning or early afternoon, then wait and eat the cake or muffins as a *goûter*" (66). She observes that it is mainly French mothers who impart these early lessons in restraint, shaping the way children eat and avoid over-eating.

Druckerman seems to applaud the role of French mothers in imparting limits to how food is consumed (how much, when, and with whom) and in regulating appetite by modelling socially learned body boundaries in relation to food and eating (or not eating). Her use above of the self-deprecating phrase "as I would" suggests that she has to unlearn one set of cultural assumptions in order to learn a new one. Her willing adherence to a new cultural norm also extends to snacking, as she notes that outside "the official and only snack time" of four o'clock at the end of the school day—a ritual that is "universally observed"—French children do not snack (66). Learning to eat and sleep according to a fixed schedule, learning to be self-reliant and to control emotions, and learning to wait are all important aspects of a child's life in France. French mothers invest time imparting a set of strict rules, *le cadre*, so that childrearing does not become an all-consuming activity leading to maternal stress and depression.

Druckerman embraces the new food practices even while admitting these represent for her a paradigm shift: "It's hard for me to imagine a world in which moms don't walk around with baggies of Goldfish and Cheerios in their purses to patch over the inevitable moments of angst" (66). French mothers do not treat food as a way to distract or pacify children and there is no culture of food on demand; instead, French children eat only during the official *goûter* and, consequently, they are hungry at mealtimes. Druckerman reflects that this regulated form of snacking teaches them the importance of waiting, since the after-school *goûter* may be baked at home the day before or bought in a shop that morning, but children have to wait until the appropriate time to consume it. This difference in parenting approach emerges from a different view of the nurturing role of the mother: more permissive on the one hand and more regulating on the other. Although Druckerman tends to indulge her children and give in immediately to their whims, she observes French mothers being less yielding and more inclined to impose restrictions in an effort to impart self-control and autonomy.

Learning to be on their own and to cope with frustration is regarded as a core life skill for French children: besides self-soothing in the night, French babies are taught to wait "long stretches from one feed to the next" (59), and when they are older, they wait until the four o'clock *goûter* for sweets and cakes (66). In fact, children get used to waiting until their mothers finish their coffees, their conversations, and other activities that should not be interrupted by their impulses and desires; instant gratification is not the French way, Druckerman notes (63).

French mothers are nurturers but are also individuals with separate lives, and children are taught to respect this. Learning to wait, Druckerman observes, "is a first, crucial lesson in self-reliance and how to enjoy one's own company" (55). To believe in it, you need to also believe that a baby is capable of learning and is able to cope with frustration, which is an attitude that comes down from Rousseau to Françoise Dolto, a paediatrician and psychoanalyst, regarded as the modern "Titan of French parenting" (89). Druckerman notes that in the 1970s, Dolto helped change the traditional, authoritarian notion that French children should be *"sage comme une image"*—should be seen but not heard—by encouraging parents to educate children to be well-behaved and self-controlled as well as able to express themselves (88). According to Dolto, speaking to them is important: "children are rational beings capable of understanding the world and respecting limits when these are carefully explained by a caring adult" (95). From this perspective, parenting is about boundary setting and social training for self-control, a core life skill.

Whereas parents in America at this time were being told by Dr. Spock to rely on their own instincts and to treat children with flexibility and permissiveness, Druckerman reflects that Dr. Dolto in France was advocating a more systematic approach based on the belief that parents should trust in their children's ability to behave rationally, and, consequently, they should impart a system of expected behaviours. This cultural parenting gap is highlighted during an episode Druckerman recounts in which her ten-month-old daughter pulls down all the books on a shelf. The pattern of misbehaviour is regularly repeated until one day, a visiting French friend kneels down and calmly but firmly explains to the child "we don't do that" and then shows her how to replace the books *"doucement,"* which she does (96-97). As a result of believing the child could understand language and could learn to control herself and do things with care, the little girl changed her actions. Druckerman had previously thought good behaviour was not so much a learned social skill as a matter of temperament and luck, but she changes her parenting precepts upon observing how French mothers model expected social manners and teach these to the children from a tender age. Druckerman observes a different notion of maternal nurturing at play, one not based on satisfying immediate needs but on imparting responsibility—the responsibility of eating at prescribed times, of coping with frustration, and of behaving in a polite manner. French mothers model restraint rather than indulging children's whims; this notion of nurturing implies forming a child's behaviour, not satisfying needs on demand.

These cultural differences in parenting are not merely incidental but instead are formative experiences for Druckerman who is invested in learning from her new environment how to be a good mother. In becoming a mother abroad, far from her own family, Druckerman cannot rely on a network of familiar child-oriented services or practices. Instead, she plunges into a new culture of childcare—new services, new assumptions, new practices—which is both disorienting and, at the same time, instructive. That Druckerman must unlearn American parenting precepts to learn new French ones illustrates the extent to which the mothering role is socially constructed. As Nancy Chodorow argues, gender roles are not natural or intrinsic manifestations but are social constructs rooted in place and time. By thinking one way of mothering seems natural (i.e., the American style) and another way foreign, Druckerman signals the social embeddedness of particular patterns and their imprinting on individuals. Although she admires many aspects of French parenting, Druckerman thinks these norms and values still feel foreign, and she cannot fully condition her American instincts. Learning to be a mother abroad involves her juxtaposing two different socially constructed roles and seeing how these can become her own with time.

All around Paris, at playgrounds and parks, Druckerman notices how readily her French peers detach from their kids, leaving them to play on their own. "I've never seen a French mother climb a jungle gym, go down a slide with her child, or sit on a seesaw—all regular sights back in the United States and among Americans in France" (131), she writes. One French mother describes how she mentally disconnects for half an hour while her young sons enjoy going round the old-fashioned merry-go-round by the Eiffel Tower: "I spend thirty minutes in pure relaxation"; in contrast, Druckerman spends the half-hour there "waiting to wave at Bean each time she comes around" (146). Drawing on Sharon Hays's analysis of "intensive mothering," this child-centered and time-consuming parenting approach is part of a contemporary American ideology that presents the good mother as all-giving and all-present. The good mother puts her child first, sacrificing her own interests and pleasures to attend to those of her child. The good mother expends an abundance of energy, time, and resources for the child, often acting as the single caretaker. This ideology of intensive mothering conflicts with that of the workplace, and it presents mothering as an all-consuming vocation. Hays notes that, consequently, many educated, middle-class white women in America opt out of paid employment to stay home and care for their children.

Druckerman self-consciously weighs these two models. She notes her instinctive tendency to over-parent and envies French mothers who sit at the edge of the playground chatting calmly with friends while their toddlers play independently. She remarks on her own tendency to hover, a pattern of behaviour that is culturally inscribed. Jean-Anne Sutherland argues that the cult of "new momism" in the U.S. expects women to "approach motherhood joyfully and completely)i.e., physically, intellectually, emotionally and psychologically), while sacrificing themselves to the demands of motherhood" (314). Comparing herself to her French peers, Druckerman acknowledges her own inability to unplug from her mothering role and enjoy a half-hour relaxing and socializing with other mums in the park; instead, she sacrifices her own needs to satisfy what she perceives as her daughter's need for her presence, since this is what a good mother does.[3] Dawn Marie Dow contends that hegemonic mothering ideologies like that of the "good mother" permeate American society and act as a regulating gaze in women's lives. Mothers consequently judge themselves according to this perceived social standard and feel guilty when they fail to measure up in their own estimation. Dow emphasizes that mothering practices, in fact, vary according to race, ethnicity, and social class structures, which undermines the notion that a single standard exists. However, approaches to mothering are conditioned by the regulating gaze of the social groups to which one belongs.

Druckerman displays growing ambivalence towards the way the American mothering role is constructed. Unlike some American mothers that she observes narrating a play-by-play account of their toddler's actions in the park, she does not engage in such monologues she finds foolish (140). Her ability to set the American and French approaches side by side and examine their different norms and values is an intercultural competence acquired over time as she grows into her mothering role abroad. Dislocation enables Druckerman to experience French mothering practices as constructs, not as automatic or instinctual patterns given her different cultural background; this recognition, in turn, enables her to see the constructed nature of the American mothering approach and question her own cultural certainties. She begins to see parenting through a dual lens: on the one hand, she is thrilled that Bean is "growing up bilingual," but on the other hand, she is "ambivalent about Bean growing up French" and worries that her daughter may be "internalizing the rules a bit too much" (161).

Druckerman, too, seems, at times, to internalize the French rules too readily, arguably in an effort to fit in in her adopted home. Yet she finds the process of acculturation frustrating, since no matter how well she adapts, she will never reach full integration; she notes, "Though Paris is one of the most cosmopolitan cities on earth, I feel like I'm off the grid. In French I don't understand name-dropping, school histories, and other little hints that, to a French person, signal someone's social rank and importance. And since I'm a foreigner, they don't know my status either" (23). This statement clearly expresses the dilemma of Druckerman and other expats like her who aspire to an insider status they can never fully achieve because of a cultural gap. As an expatriate mother, she is distant from the cultural certainties she grew up with concerning parenting practices as well as from the conventions of her new home; thus, she occupies a liminal position that does not fully belong to either but takes in both perspectives.

Although she lacks the cultural literacy of a native-born Parisian, Druckerman achieves an intercultural competence through her experience of long-term accommodation to French life. In particular, she acquires a knowledge of place, develops attitudes that value local practices, compares French manners regarding childrearing to U.S. ones, and engages in bilingual and cross-cultural interactions demonstrating an evolving intercultural awareness. By explicitly foregrounding her experiences as a displaced mother raising children on foreign terrain, her memoir destabilizes a monological, Anglo-expat reading of the French as cultural others; her story, instead, offers a complex reading recognizing socially constructed mothering roles across cultures. Druckerman's mothering memoir is one of her own identity reformation in France and is written from a dialogical perspective that sees cultural differences as bidirectional and multi-faceted. She becomes aware of motherhood as a socially and culturally constructed role by becoming a mother abroad.

Italian Taste

A freelance writer from Toronto, Jeannie Marshall left Canada for Rome in 2002 and had a son there three years later. Raising him within a traditional Italian food culture, she learns about the pleasures of fresh, seasonal food while exploring Roman street markets and gathering local ingredients and recipes from farmers, butchers, and grandmothers. She discovers that the cultivation of taste starts early in Italy—when babies are still in the womb—but she also learns that even a food tradition as established as Italy's is threatened by a processed-food and marketing industry that is changing children's diets by reforming their tastes. Marshall's book *The Lost Art of Feeding Kids* is a celebration of the *cucina povera*, the simple, wholesome food she finds in Rome and in Italian regional cuisine generally—a food culture based on readily available, seasonal ingredients linked to a peasant past of abundant fresh produce and meat scarcity—as well as a celebration of the sensual and convivial pleasures of food. Her account is steeped in nostalgia for the past (or soon to be past) of package-free food and unhurried meals, aspects of Italy's food culture that are changing with modernization. Her mothering memoir recounts how the personal becomes political for her in her role as a new mother abroad. In trying to find the best way to feed her own child, she uncovers how parents and communities play a vital role in creating a food culture that places children's health and nutrition above the interests of the modern food industry.

Marshall's apprenticeship to local, traditional food culture begins on a Roman holiday that stretches into a prolonged period of foreign residency when her husband is offered a job with the International Fund for Agricultural Development, a UN agency based in Rome. She notes that from the outset, the idyllic image of Italy "was attractive to two Canadians who grew up in modern cities without a clearly defined cultural food heritage" (3). Beyond this surface attraction, she comes to understand that "food in Italy is more than just something to eat. It is embedded in life here. It's a simple pleasure on the surface, but one that is in reality a complex web of history, place, religion, family, health, and community. It is a cohesive *food culture*, which is much greater than the individual cooks and eaters who live within it. And we wanted to be part of it" (3). A first step in her process of acculturation involves understanding that learning to live like an Italian begins with learning to eat like one, and the role of taste formation is primarily the responsibility of mothers. The gendered role of women-as-mothers-as-feeders-and-nurturers defines a maternal archetype in Italy, in which the giving of food and love are inseparable and are inseparably bound to women.

When Marshall's son is born, she is taught that breastfeeding her baby is best—not only for the well-documented health benefits of mother's milk but also for the role it plays "in shaping children's food preferences" and the way it "influences what they eat later and how that consequently affects their health" (26). Breastfeeding is a way to pass on food flavours at the earliest stage of life and to help babies cultivate a taste for healthy foods. This is so obvious to Italian mothers that everyone assumes Marshall already knows that taste formation begins while the baby is still in the womb and continues afterwards through breastfeeding. Whereas during her pregnancy Marshall thinks of what she eats mostly in terms of the developing baby's nutrition, she learns from her Roman midwife that a fetus begins to swallow around six months in utero and tastes the amniotic fluid and, through this, the flavours of the food the mother has been eating. Consequently, eating "the freshest foods possible and taking advantage of what each season had to offer" is the "first step in teaching the baby to like the foods of its culture" (24). Embracing this feeding and nurturing responsibility whole-heartedly, she is careful throughout her pregnancy to eat a range of fresh, seasonal foods that are local and regional.

Marshall does not seem to question the conflation of biology with a socially constructed parenting role. Sceats notes that in the Western tradition the mother is, as a rule, "the most important figure in an infant's world, able to give or withhold everything that sustains, nourishes, fulfils, completes" (11). In this role, a mother shapes or socializes a child's appetite and expectations of the world "by feeding on demand or adhering to a rigid schedule, by the cultivation of table manners, through the provision of fish fingers or porridge, raw fish or curry" (11). Along with nutrition, a mother "feeds her child love, resentment, encouragement, or fear" thus representing "a figure of limitless, irresistible authority … Yet the maternal role in Western society is ambiguous, if not ambivalent: mothers are overwhelmingly powerful but at the same time are socially and domestically disempowered by their nurturing, serving role" (11).

Overlooking the gender politics of the mothering role, Marshall, like Druckerman, is keen to learn how to be a good mother and perform this role well in accordance with local norms and expect-ations. Marshall's journey into Italian food habits leads her to observe that tradition and nutrition are two different ways of approaching food: the first focuses on the pleasures of tasting and sharing food convivially; the second focuses on the nutritional value of various foods. Although her Canadian instincts lean towards modern food science concepts of nutrition, her immersion in the Roman ritual of shopping for and cooking fresh food every day teaches her the value of traditional Italian food culture. Describing a simple lunch consisting of spaghetti with fresh San Marzano tomatoes chopped and lightly cooked in a skillet with hot olive oil, a pinch of salt, and fresh basil thrown in at the end, with the dish then topped with salted ricotta cheese, Marshall muses: "none of us thought about the flavonoid content of the tomatoes or about the protein, calcium, or vitamin A in our meal," but instead they about the pleasure of eating good, simple food with friends (51). In the Italian context, a good mother imparts the pleasures of eating good food in good company.

Marshall notes that Italian parents tend to think more about what tastes good and what their children will enjoy rather than what is "good for them"; this emphasis on taste and pleasure "rather than on an abstract notion of nutrition or fear of allergies is really about passing on culture." Marshall continues, "Italian parents think about nutrition in a broad sense and try to ensure that their children eat a wide range of foods, but they also assume that the foods of their culture are healthy" (40). Marshall admits that she has been thinking primarily about nutrition—"about getting vegetables into the baby like a dose of medicine"— whereas she sees Italian mothers training their babies' tastes and knows that this will "lead them to the foods that [are] good for them" (38). Initiating children into a food culture involves helping them discover the flavours of fresh food grown locally as well as the daily food rhythms at home and school. She sees Roman children learning to love pasta with lentils on Wednesday, gnocchi on Thursday, and fish on Friday. These predictable rhythms punctuate the week and give a sense of participation in a food culture that is larger than the individual, one that connects eaters in a community through a shared tradition.

Given the emphasis on early taste development, Marshall is heartbroken when her son Nico has problems latching on and cannot immediately be breastfed. She notes that it is "painfully ironic" that after all the healthy and fresh food she ate during her pregnancy and after enduring natural childbirth with no pain medication so that her son "would start his life without any foreign substances in his system" (29), she is unable to feed her baby with her own mother's milk. Instead, Marshall has to resort to buying a box of infant formula to feed her son during the first week of his life; she disparagingly calls it "paediatric fast food" and acknowledges that it is "the first industrially produced food for children that begins to interfere with the food culture" (29). She observes that milk from Nestlé or Similac tastes exactly the same every day, whereas a breastfed baby tastes different foods at each meal: "that baby is tasting garlic, rosemary, basil, sage, olive, lemon, tomato, eggplant, bitter greens, melon, squash, *prosciutto crudo*, cod, turbot, anchovies, octopus, and so on." These are varied flavours which "make him more inclined to eat the foods that are found in plenty in his environment"; moreover, since "traditional diets from long-established food cultures tend to be healthy, the child is likely to grow up healthy" (30). Collective wisdom recognizes that tastes are formed in the earliest stages of life and, consequently, there is considerable pressure on mothers given the indispensable role they play in the transmission of food culture. By internalizing this responsibility, Marshall experiences feelings of inadequacy when she cannot live up to social expectations regarding breastfeeding.

Erin Taylor and Nora Wallace provide a framework for under-standing infant-feeding-related maternal guilt and shame in the context of feminist theoretical and psychological accounts of the emotions of self-assessment. They argue that whereas breastfeeding advocacy has been critiqued for its perceived role in inducing maternal guilt, the emotion women often feel surrounding infant feeding may be better conceptualized as shame in its tendency to involve negative self-assessment—a failure to achieve an idealized notion of good motherhood. Whereas maternal guilt arises from a perceived inadequacy related to a private act of parenting, maternal shame is social, as it is linked to a mother's perceived failure to measure up to a societal paradigm of idealized motherhood. Taylor and Wallace further note that mothers often feel shame because "they hold themselves up to a certain standard of motherhood and judge themselves as falling short, as failing" (37).

One of the widespread tenets of good mothering is that breastfeeding is the best way to feed babies and to impart to them a food culture. Marshall agrees but falls short of being an ideal mother when she cannot easily breastfeed her baby; however, she overcomes this setback and redoubles her efforts to introduce her weaned son to healthy foods that are grown locally and seasonally. Like Druckerman in France, Marshall also notices the absence of packaged snacks and fortified processed foods for small children. Instead, she observes Italian toddlers developing "their fine motor control while eating cooked chickpeas and cannellini beans at their designated snack time" (45). The after-school *merenda* usually consists of fruit or yogurt rather than a packaged snack. She reflects that children in Italy are not seen as separate marketing demographics (babies, toddlers, and young children) with each requiring its own special foods, since children typically eat whatever the family is eating. For babies, the ingredients of the family meal are mixed together with some homemade broth and a drizzle of olive oil with some grated Parmesan cheese added in for flavour. They do not need fortified foods or food supplements, since their meals are based on fresh, seasonal ingredients that naturally contain all the vitamins and nutrients to meet their health needs.

As her son grows, however, Marshall begins to notice that this traditional food culture is under threat as more processed foods become available and are marketed to children. The daily rituals of shopping for and cooking fresh food at home as a way of educating her son's palate and cultivating pleasure in eating take on a missionary zeal as Marshall puts her journalistic training towards investigating the food industry and uncovers its unsavoury aspects. She observes the emergent monopoly Nestlé has in places especially designed for children's entertainment—water parks, amusement parks, and seaside resorts—where Western kid's menu items like hamburgers, French fries, hotdogs, soft drinks, and packaged ice creams replace traditional Italian foods. She notes that the food landscape is slow to change in Italy and that processed food products still co-exist alongside more traditional, wholesome, family meals, but she wonders for how much longer. She worries that the "Western diet" is being exported worldwide (along with its attendant health problems, like child obesity) and could become normalized even in a place like Italy. She sees the consequences of shifting children's tastes away from fresh foods in the direction of processed foods as "tragic" (83).

Marshall is also critical of the way so-called healthy packaged foods with added nutrients are marketed to Italian parents who put their trust in experts and their faith in product labels. She notes that by encouraging parents to get their children "to take supplements and eat fortified foods," the food industry is causing them to mistrust their own collective memory and cumulative knowledge passed on through generations—"our sense of smell, taste, and texture, to ignore the visual delight of multicoloured fruit and vegetables"—and instead is using science to promote its products and training "children to think this method is not only normal but superior" (63). Instead, she advocates for shunning all convenience food that comes in packages because the process of industrial packaging is itself unhealthy and ecologically unsustainable. By becoming an outspoken advocate for "slow food," Marshall assumes a responsibility not only for feeding her own son and educating his tastes but more broadly for preserving the national food heritage of her adopted Italy. In this sense, she appears as a kind of Ur-mother who embraces her role as feeder and nurturer very seriously and performs it in both the domestic and public spheres of life.

The way Marshall becomes politicized through food in Italy and the zeal with which she embraces her mothering-as-nurturing role are commendable. Yet she does not seem to question why mothers have the primary responsibility for the preparation of family meals and the transmission of food culture. The gender politics of mothering remain unexamined in her text, as they do in Druckerman's memoir, likely for the same reason: both transnationals embrace local food orthodoxies in an effort to fit in. They do not question local food practices, or transgress the socially prescribed mothering role that actively supports these, since they are seeking a cultural accommodation in their adopted homes. Druckerman's and Marshall's food forays act as a structuring device for their process of identity reformation as they accommodate to new selves and new lives abroad. It is clear that food and food habits—what one eats, how and why one eats, and how and why one prepares food in a certain way—are personal and cultural expressions that embody deep meaning in their journeys of self-transformation. As mothers learning how to care for their children in foreign contexts, food is a primary point of entry into new cultural norms and social acceptance.

Food, Mothering, and Identity

The culinary knowledge one acquires by travelling abroad and eating foreign foods is a form of social distinction through which one displays the mastery of new lifestyle habits.[4] Germann Molz suggests that "food figures prominently in the ongoing symbolic struggle to distinguish oneself as a 'traveller' rather than a 'tourist,' with the former searching out the most exotic (to them) new tastes, whereas the latter searches out bland and familiar (to them) foods abroad" (87). Building on John Urry's notion of the tourist gaze, Jennie Germann Molz suggests that culinary tourism often becomes a form of "gazing with the tongue," which involves a cursory engagement with foreign foods as symbols of diversity, ways of tasting foreignness without engaging deeply with it or being transformed by it (88). However, in pursuing a sustained engagement with the food cultures of France and Italy, Druckerman and Marshall distinguish themselves as something more than travellers or tourists in search of novel tastes; they are, in fact, transnationals who gradually acquire insider knowledge by apprenticing themselves over time to local food culture through their role as mothers.

Druckerman's and Marshall's gastronomic forays are both a form of sustained physical engagement with another culture's foodways and through the narrative reconstruction of these adventures, a way of displaying local culinary connoisseurship for global readers. The way food is generally mobilized according to Germann Molz in order to create belonging or estrangement—eating to feel at home (eating familiar foods to feel connected to home while away) or eating to feel displaced (trying strange or unfamiliar foods to feel exotic while at home)—is rendered more complexly in these expatriate accounts. Marshall, for example, consumes authentic Roman food (grows, cooks, and eats it) as a way of increasing her sense of belonging there while feeding and nurturing a family; she then reconstructs these food experiences to enable her Anglophone readers to enjoy a vicarious taste of Italian authenticity. Germann Molz maintains that "food materializes a cosmopolitan sensibility toward the world. Indeed, we might think of foods as cosmopolitan objects that travel" (90).

This travelling of material culture involves a process of trans-culturation in which Marshall and Druckerman act as interpreters for readers who lack their intercultural insight. That these observations derive from their own experiences as transnational mothers grounds their accounts in the everyday—rituals of shopping, cooking, snacking, and family meals— making these accessible to readers who may lack first-hand knowledge of what it means to raise children abroad. The conceptions and constructs of foreign authenticity that gather around Druckerman's and Marshall's tables raise some important questions regarding cultural difference. The defining experience of international relocation and the long-term process of identity reformation shape a strong ethical discourse running through their narratives, which pivot around the same ontological question: "How should I live?" This question takes on a more layered significance when posed by two expatriate mothers seeking a happy and healthy lifestyle for themselves and their families through a negotiation of local and global practices—a process which is, in the first instance, mediated by food and food culture as they resettle their lives in new locales.

In becoming mothers abroad, Druckerman and Marshall negotiate their role as feeders and nurturers in accordance with new cultural paradigms while not losing sight of older familiar conventions. The uncertainty involved in parenting decisions is, in their case, amplified, since they are performing the mothering role in foreign contexts while seeking integration within social groups where new norms apply. The pressure to conform to expected behaviours, actions, or beliefs is an inescapable part of contemporary motherhood, according to Jane Swigart, since mothers operate continually under the gaze of society and its construction of the good mother, with tremendous weight given to each decision and each outcome concerning the lives of their children; consequently, the guilt many mothers feel "is endless and tyrannical" (66).

Judith Warner describes the stress-laden demands of contemporary mothering, which can lead mothers to experience guilt and shame in different social contexts; these stress factors are perhaps even greater for transnational mothers trying to "do motherhood" in foreign contexts where they are subjected to unfamiliar conventions regarding expected behaviours and beliefs. Both Druckerman and Marshall want to perform as good mothers under the gaze of society and, thus, gain acceptance and belonging. This necessitates their first learning to challenge some home certainties in order to understand the precepts that define the mothering role in their respective cultural contexts. As travelling mamas, they must learn to decode cultural mandates in their adopted homes to perform their role as mothers abroad; the inter-cultural competence they develop is central to the identity reformation they undergo, a transformative process which their mothering memoirs explore and detail.

Conclusion

Defining cosmopolitanism as "an intellectual and aesthetic openness to divergent cultural experiences" in which a "willingness to engage with the Other" is demonstrated through a "search for contrasts rather than uniformity," Ulf Hannerz signals openness and engagement with diversity as core values in a cosmopolitan orientation (239). In addressing parenting practices in France and Italy, specifically in relation to food and food habits, Druckerman and Marshall display a cosmopolitan engagement with cultural difference. Bronislaw Szerszynski and John Urry similarly claim that cosmopolitan predis-positions involve "a willingness to take risks by virtue of encountering the Other" (470). In Druckerman's and Marshall's relocation experiences, foreign food culture is the gateway through which the authors engage with diverse cultural norms as transnational mothers. Arguably, Druckerman's interactions take fewer risks; she remains insulated within a class bubble in which multiplicity and complexity are more attenuated. Hers is a more modest form of cosmopolitanism, and her engagement with cultural difference seems more strategic in Michael Skey's sense of furthering her own instrumental goals (fitting in and belonging in Parisian society) rather than any progressive aims or values (241). Marshall, meanwhile, is deeply engaged in a progressive agenda to preserve the integrity of real food, to ensure it is produced in clean, sustainable ways and in fair conditions for growers, and to guarantee accessible prices for consumers. Her encounters with cultural differences in Italy spur her to become politically mobilized at local and global levels by embracing the culture of slow food. In Marshall's case, what begins as a maternal concern for feeding and nurturing her own family with healthy, local, seasonal food expands into a political commitment to safeguard traditional food practices through alignment with a social movement.

The cross-cultural confrontation with food culture afforded by transnational relocation presents Druckerman and Marshall with opportunities to rethink their role as nurturers in relation to local food habits in family life abroad. This in turn elicits a broader reflection on the social construction of motherhood as they examine precepts and practices that define the mothering role and childrearing practices in their respective contexts. Their engagement with the ideological constructions of good mothers in France and Italy is central to the identity reformation they undergo through the experience of transnational relocation. Identity reformation, a main theme in contemporary women's travel texts, recognizes that the process of identity making involves continual self-transformation in which alterity plays a pivotal role.[5] Their immersion in everyday life abroad is at once "disorienting and orienting" as old affiliations are displaced and new ones take root, contributing to a multilayered sense of self through the emergence of dialogical identities. By becoming mothers abroad, Druckerman and Marshall develop a cosmopolitan outlook—an openness to difference and greater intercultural awareness.

Endnotes

1 I am drawing here on Edward C. Knox's use of the term "literature of accommodation" in his study of twentieth-century nonfiction by American writers in France who tell the story of their quest to prove themselves worthy or suitable in their new cultural contexts. Knox uses the term "accommodation" instead of adaptation or integration to draw attention to the "nuances of congruence and reconciliation, of allowances made and recognition of a new norm to which to adhere" (95).

2 See, for example, Ruth Margalit in *The New Yorker* (13 Feb. 2012) and Elaine Sciolino in *The New York Times* (24 Feb. 2012).

3 Susan Douglas and Meredith Michaels similarly describe a contemporary culture of "new momism," in which women are pressured to conform to a motherhood paradigm that presents women with a model of near impossible standards based on three tenets: first, motherhood completes a woman; second, mothers are the best caretakers for children; and third, mothers must devote themselves fully to their children. Consequently, women feel guilty for their ongoing perceived failures to measure up to this idealized model.

4 Pierre Bourdieu's work on class and food consumption suggests that everyday food practices do not simply express a class identity but also produce and reproduce class identities. Bourdieu describes a "class habitus" as an embodied class-culture in which lifestyle emerges as the result of particular material circumstances and class dispositions. Lifestyle choices, including food habits, are a way of cultivating "distinction"—a social process in which people distinguish themselves from others through the exercise of particular tastes.

5 According to Edward Said, identities are dialogically constructed through difference: one defines oneself based on the recognition of what one is not in relation to others: "the Other" acts as "a source and resource for a better, more critical understanding of the Self" (xi).

Works Cited

Bourdieu, Pierre. *Distinction: A Social Critique of the Judgement of Taste.* Translated by Richard Nice, 2nd ed., Harvard University Press, 1984.

Chodorow, Nancy. *The Reproduction of Mothering: Psychoanalysis and the Sociology of Gender.* 2nd ed., U of CA P, 1999.

Clifford, James. "Traveling Cultures." *Cultural Studies*, edited by Lawrence Grossberg et al., Routledge, 1992, pp. 96-112.

De Solier, Isaebele, and Jean Duruz. "Food Culture: Introduction." *Cultural Studies Review,* vol. 19, no. 1, 2013, pp. 4-8.

Douglas, Susan J., and Meredith W. Michaels. *The Mommy Myth: The Idealization of Motherhood and How It Has Undermined Women.* Free, 2004.

Dow, Dawn Marie. "Integrated Motherhood: Beyond Hegemonic Ideologies of Motherhood." *Journal of Marriage and Family,* vol. 78, no. 1, 2016, pp. 180-96.

Druckerman, Pamela. *Bringing Up Bébé* and *Bébé Day by Day.* Penguin, 2014.

Edwards, Justin, and Rune Grauland. *Mobility at Large: Globalization, Textuality and Innovative Travel Writing.* Liverpool University Press, 2012.

Germann Molz, Jennie. "Eating Difference: The Cosmopolitan Mobilities of Culinary Tourism." *Space and Culture,* vol. 10, no.1, 2007, pp. 77-93.

Hannerz, Ulf. "Cosmopolitans and Locals in World Culture." *Theory, Culture, Society,* vol. 7, 1990, pp. 237-50.

Hays, Sharon. *The Cultural Contradictions of Motherhood.* Yale UP, 1996.

Hulme, Peter. "Travelling to Write: 1940-2000." *The Cambridge Companion to Travel Writing,* edited by Peter Hulme and Tim Youngs, Cambridge University Press, 2002, pp. 87-101.

Knox, Edward C. "A Literature of Accommodation." *French Politics, Culture & Society,* vol. 21, no. 2, 2003, pp. 95-110.

Margalit, Ruth. "The Secret to French Parenting." *The New Yorker.* 14 Feb. 2012,

https://www.newyorker.com/books/page-turner/the-secret-to-french-parenting. Accessed 5 Feb. 2018.

Marshall, Jeannie. *The Lost Art of Feeding Kids: What Italy Taught Me About Why Children Need Real Food.* Beacon, 2013.

Said, Edward W. *Humanism and Democratic Criticism.* Columbia University Press, 2004.

Sceats, Sarah. *Food Consumption and the Body in Contemporary Women's Fiction.* Cambridge University Press, 2003.

Sciolino, Elaine. "Mama Knows Best." *The New York Times,* 24 Feb. 2012, http://www.nytimes.com/2012/02/26/books/review/pamela-druckermans-bringing-up-bebe.html. Accessed 5 Feb. 2018.

Skey, Michael. "What Does it Mean to Be a Cosmopolitan? An Examination of the Varying Meaningfulness and Commensurability of Everyday 'Cosmopolitan' Practices." *Identities,* vol. 20, no. 3, 2013, pp. 235-52.

Sutherland, Jean-Anne. "Mothering, Guilt and Shame." *Sociology Compass,* vol. 4, no. 5, 2010, pp. 310-21.

Swigart, Jane. *The Myth of the Perfect Mother: Parenting Without Guilt.* Contemporary, 1991.

Szerszynski, Bronislaw, and John Urry. "Cultures of Cosmopolitanism." *The Sociological Review,* vol. 50, no. 4, 2002, pp. 461-81

Taylor, Erin N., and Nora E. Wallace. "For Shame: Feminism, Breastfeeding Advocacy, and Maternal Guilt." *Hypatia: A Journal of Feminist Philosophy.* vol. 27, no. 1, 2012, pp. 76-98.

Warner, Judith. *Perfect Madness: Motherhood in the Age of Anxiety.* Riverhead, 2005.

EXIGENCY

Chapter 19

From the Backstreet to Britain: Women and Abortion Travel in Irish History

Cara Delay

"Two women, one procedure, 48 hours away from home."
"Not the first or the last bleeding women about to face a long treck (sic) home

@EndaKennyTD#twowomentravel."

irected to Ireland's *Taoiseach* (Prime Minister) Enda Kenny in August 2016, these above-cited tweets made headlines when the two Irish women in question revealed they were travelling so that one of them could receive a medical abortion in Britain (O'Sullivan). Illegal in Ireland until January 2019[1], abortion in mainland Britain remained relatively accessible for Irish women throughout the late twentieth and early twenty-first centuries. Therefore, Irish women's transnational abortion travel experiences have been ubiquitous for decades, particularly since 1967, when abortion was decriminalized in Britain. Between 1980 and 2000, no less than eighty thousand women left Ireland seeking abortion services in England, Scotland, or Wales. By the year 2000, at least twenty Irish women left home every day to take the "abortion trail" across the Irish Sea (Ruane 7-10).

The advent of social media has helped publicize Irish women's abortion journeys and has brought much-needed attention to a serious healthcare crisis (Berer). Migrations to seek abortion care, however, are nothing new; Irish women's abortion travel experiences predate 1967. Well before the legalization of abortion in most of Britain, dozens of Irish women left their homes seeking to terminate unwanted or unplanned pregnancies, travelling to other parts of Ireland, and usually from rural to urban areas, such as Dublin and Belfast.[2] From 1900 to 1967, many of these women appeared in court either charged with abortion crimes or as witnesses in illegal abortion cases.[3]

Most analyses of Irish abortion travel focus on the experiences of women who have embarked on cross-border voyages since decriminalization in Britain in 1967. This chapter, however, offers a more complex comparative analysis of Irish abortion history by examining both the twentieth and twenty-first centuries as well as by linking the largely domestic journeys of 1900 to 1967 with the transnational trips that have characterized the past fifty years. Based on an analysis of archival materials, memoirs, and first-hand accounts, this chapter sheds light on the migrations—near and far, past and present—that Irish women have undertaken to end unwanted pregnancies across generations. Indeed, although abortion history is often viewed as one with turning points and transformations, for Irish women, the main narrative of abortion is often one of continuity, marked by secrecy, stress, and an encounter with unknown places and spaces. "It was the scariest thing that I have ever done," claimed one woman who travelled to Britain for an abortion in 2015—"going into a place you don't know anything about, the whole travelling aspect of it. I was a nervous wreck" (qtd. in Gentleman). "It's all a blur in my mind now," remembered one woman in the 1990s. "The flight and getting the train and finding the place. I was engulfed in a very lonely space and felt very frightened" (qtd. in Ruane 40).

Abortion voyages, particularly in the Irish context, also complicate concepts of motherhood, domesticity, and national identity. In Irish culture and history since the early twentieth century, mobility and motherhood were depicted as at odds with each other, as women's only contributions to the nation were to remain in the domestic sphere as mothers. This notion of home was essential in the Irish nation-building project. Irish women's politicized roles as mothers, then, depended on their fixity to the domestic sphere—on their lack of mobility. In November 1922, for example, Catholic priest J.S. Sheehy published an article titled "The Influence of Women in Catholic Ireland." He wrote that "a nation is what its women make it" and that this "was especially true in the case of mothers who reigned within the homestead." (*Cork Examiner* November 22, 1922, qtd. in Ryan, *Gender, Identity, and the Irish Press*, 151-2) When thousands of women travelled for abortion care across the twentieth century, not only did they seem to reject or refuse motherhood, they also complicated notions of Irishness by their very movement and mobility.

This chapter recognizes that women who travelled to seek abortion, despite difficult circumstances, displayed tenacity in attempting to control their reproductive health. Even with this resolve, however, Irish women's abortion travels should not be interpreted as liberating or framed as a form of tourism. The words and narratives of women themselves testify that abortion seekers interpreted their voyages, whether domestic or cross-border, as involuntary exiles marked by displacement, dislocation, and a sense that going home again was nearly impossible.

Current scholarly interpretations of abortion travel in Ireland and beyond have complicated the terminology used in the field. First examined within the context of "medical tourism," the term "abortion tourism" has been applied not only to the Irish case but also to other parts of Western Europe and North America. Focusing on the Canadian context, Christabelle Sethna and Marion Doull argue that abortion travel, both international and domestic, must be considered a form of "medical tourism" ("Accidental Tourist" 458). More recently, however, scholars have questioned the utility and appropriateness of "abortion tourism." The word "tourism," of course, signifies "agency, freedom, and mobility" (Sethna and Doull, "Accidental Tourists" 457; Gilmartin and White 276). Certainly, some forms of medical tourism may represent agency and privilege—Americans and Western Europeans seeking fertility treatments abroad come to mind. Abortion tourism, however, is different. In Ireland, abortion travel exists because of a lack of choice or autonomy; abortion travel, therefore, can be interpreted as a temporary but involuntary exile or emigration. In addition, although Irish women technically are legally free to travel to seek abortion, not all are able to do so. Recently, Katherine Side has analyzed the difficulties that Irish migrant women face in accessing cross-border abortion. (Side) Economic realities, age, marital status, and geography all complicate access to travel (Gilmartin and White;

Sethna and Doull, "Spatial Disparities" 56).

Not surprisingly, the interpretation of abortion travel in the Irish context has been overly negative. Tapping into Ireland's traumatic history of emigration, representations of abortion travel feature the loneliness, fear, and isolation of women's experiences. However, a more complicated picture of both women's emigration and abortion travel has emerged recently— one in which scholars are trying to move beyond uniformly negative interpretations and to recognize instead the complex and varied experiences of different women. Women comprised the majority of Irish emigrants in certain decades of the nineteenth and twentieth centuries; by the early twentieth century, most went to Britain. Initially interpreted as an exclusively reluctant, desperate, and forced phenomenon, women's emigration from Ireland has been recast as an attempt, particularly by single women, to reject patriarchy and actively pursue a better life abroad (Meaney, *Reading the Irish Woman* 4). What exactly were these women seeking to escape, and how does this relate to abortion experiences? In the first half of the twentieth century, a unique Church-state coalition in Ireland implemented a "regime of inward-looking repressiveness" that defined women solely as wives and mothers and attempted to contain them within the domestic sphere (Fischer 822). Those women who rejected or attempted to rework this system were deemed "polluted outcasts" (Smith 35). Exiled from Irish society, women who were sexually experienced, became pregnant out of wedlock, committed infanticide, or fell out of favour with authorities often ended up in institutions such as Magdalen asylums and mother-and-baby homes.

This containment scheme helped preserve the moral purity of the nation. "Notably, the moral purity at stake in the project of Irish identity formation," writes Clara Fischer, "was essentially a sexual purity enacted and problematized through women's bodies" (822). The only acceptable Irish woman was one who embraced married motherhood and domesticity. Domestic wives and mothers, in turn, represented the nation and signified the understanding that "Ireland must be reimagined as a gendered space that is essentially pure" (Gerend 36). Although some, notably unwed mothers, were cast out of society and contained in institutions, high levels of female emigration suggest that others sought an escape from the so-called pure nation.

Therefore, although Irish women emigrants from 1900 to 1950 certainly sought better economic circumstances through emigration, some also were looking for independence outside of Ireland, acting to escape the restricted patriarchy that had developed at home (Meaney, *Reading the Irish Woman* 124-125). Within the context of women's emigration, then, mobility could, indeed, represent bodily autonomy and a rejection of restrictions.

Thinking through notions of body, space, and place in more depth can be useful here. Moving from rural to urban space was a common experience for Irish women migrants. Louise Ryan, who examines Irish women emigrants to London in the 1930s, points out that "the press and the Catholic hierarchy, in particular, propagated an image of these vulnerable young women as lost and alone in the big, bad cities of England" (Ryan, "Irish Female Emigration" 271). The migrants themselves, however, demonstrated agency and created opportunity; according to Ryan, they actively navigated and transformed space and, thus, engaged in identity construction. By their very movement, they arguably rejected not only fixity and domesticity but also Irish notions of motherhood. In this way, then, women's emigration resembled abortion voyages. Ryan's work fits well with research that has illuminated how migrations to cities in particular can mark important turning points for women's mobility and agency (Ryan, "Moving Spaces" 69). Abortion migrations, however, require a different reading. They bring to mind women's containment in institutions rather than liberating voyages. Before 1967, most Irish women travelled domestically to seek abortion. Although these voyages did not always cross national borders, they served to keep the nation (idealized as rural at the time) pure by concentrating vice in cities like Dublin and Belfast. At the time, the city was associated with sin and sex; it was thought to be teeming with single women who rejected domesticity and motherhood. Indeed, urban areas often are represented as "spaces of social and sexual liberation" but also danger (Johnston and Longhurst 80). In the first few decades of the twentieth century urban centers such as Dublin and Belfast existed on the edge of Irishness— depicted as "disorderly, uncontrollably complex and chaotic" (Ryan, "Irish Female Emigration" 275)—and often served as cesspools to contain sexual vice and keep it out of the rural heartland. At the same time, family and motherhood were firmly located in rural Ireland.

Prime Minister Éamon DeValera's famous 1943 "dream speech," for example, which laid out his vision for an ideal nation, talked of "a land whose *countryside* would be bright with cosy homesteads, whose *fields* and *villages* would be joyous with the sounds of industry" (my emphasis, "RTÉ Archives").

The purity of the land, home, and Ireland itself was inextricably linked with motherhood and, thus, depended on women receiving abortions far from their villages or towns. Women who left rural areas to receive abortions in cities, then, were also, in some ways, cast out of the pure nation. And since 1967, as most Irish women have left their own nation and headed to the UK for abortion, they have become "polluted outcasts" even more—expelled from the land of Ireland itself and castigated as rejecting both motherhood and Irishness. For abortion travellers, then, moving through space and across borders does not comprise an act of identity construction; rather, it serves to fracture some women's sense of national identity. The Irish abortion traveller, as Ryan writes of the female emigrant, is "in danger of becoming denationalised: cut off from her roots, her culture and ultimately her identity" ("Irish Female Emigration" 278). One woman who travelled to the UK for an abortion in the early 2000s when she was seventeen expresses this notion of feeling ejected from one's nation: "Traveling for the abortion was difficult, I felt like an outcast [sic] and it made me feel so ashamed about the whole experience, like [I] was dirty and should be hidden away" ("Share Your Abortion Story").

Unwanted pregnancies and abortion attempts troubled the purity of the domestic sphere, motherhood, and, by extension, the nation. Women's abortion voyages also, however, trouble the notion of travel as escape or agency. In her research on abortion travel from Ireland to England, anthropologist Alyssa Best asks if embarking on a voyage across the sea to end a pregnancy could be empowering for some women. "The boat or plane ride from Ireland to England," she writes, "could be viewed as navigating a liminal space that creates hope for women who escape the oppression they feel at home in favor of reproductive freedom abroad. And the trip alleviates the feeling of entrapment women may have about their pregnancy" (Best 430). Best's views offer a new perspective on abortion travel by recognizing the movement of women's bodies in space and raising intriguing possible connections between the experiences of abortion travellers and female emigrants. They also challenge the connection between fixity and motherhood, suggesting instead that women's choice to be (or not to be) mothers is concomitant with mobility and travel. Fundamentally, however, Best's claims do not change the fact that the majority of Irish women, past and present, have interpreted abortion travel not as freeing but as forced. As Mary Gilmartin and Allen White write, in the case of abortion, mobility is not liberating, and "'abortion tourism' is a masculinist construction, the result of (rather than resistance to) Irish patriarchy" (279).

Despite the reality that Irish women have been travelling to seek abortion for decades, women's actual experiences of travel remain understudied, especially for the pre-1967 era. How do historical narratives focusing on domestic voyages inform our understandings of the meanings of abortion travel? And how do they compare with the abortion travels and travails of more recent years? Overall, historical cases demonstrate the creative ways in which Irish women seeking to terminate pregnancies navigated space and transgressed boundaries while also affirming the sense of dislocation and displacement felt by these women. The movements of Kathleen O., from Blarney, County Cork, are representative of pre-1967 domestic travel experiences. Kathleen travelled to Dublin in the 1940s to visit professional abortionists Christopher Williams and Mary Moloney.[4] Like dozens of other women, she left her home for Ireland's central metropolis either because she had no options in her own community, wished to preserve her anonymity, and/or had heard rumours that Dublin was the place to secure an abortion. Kathleen later (in her court testimony) described her movements around the city once she arrived in Dublin:

> My sister & I stayed at the Regent Hotel, D'Olier St. that night. On the following morning I went to Rathmines Road with my sister…. The lady that opened the door was Mrs. Robinson, one of the defendants in this case. I asked her if Williams & Moloney lived there. She said no, that they had left but that she would give me their addresses. She gave me their address. She wrote it down for me on the back of a cigarette packet…. The address was 15 B Old Kilmainham … [later] I came down stairs & went for the bus. (qtd. in *Case of Maureen F*)

Kathleen endured several different abortion attempts across several days at the Old Kilmainham address and then waited for miscarriage to occur. After three days, she returned to Moloney asking for lodging while she was "indisposed." Moloney sent Kathleen and her sister back to Mrs. McColgan at the Portobello Hotel at Rathmines Rd., about a twenty-minute walk away. Over the next few days, Kathleen walked or took the bus back to Moloney's chemist shop several times. Frustrated and exhausted, Kathleen eventually told Moloney that "I could not stay on in Dublin indefinitely & I asked her when I should be all right" (qtd. in *Case of Maureen F*).

In just over a week, Kathleen traversed the city repeatedly, walking and taking the bus along what was known at the time as a type of "abortion corridor" in Dublin (McAvoy). Her experiences seeking abortion care were similar to many women at the time, who were strained by their travel experiences and the often lengthy process involved in seeing a termination through to completion. These women had to fabricate excuses for being out of town for several days and in some cases up to a week. They had to secure the finances for both the abortion and the trip, even as they confronted the unknown in new places when they travelled. Noteworthy in the Dublin account above are both the length of time that Kathleen had to be away from home and the logistics involved in making transportation and lodging arrangements. We don't know if this was Kathleen's first trip to Dublin, but even had she been there before, the unique circumstances of this journey contributed to her sense of dislocation. As another Irish woman, Angela, later remarked of her abortion experience in England in the late twentieth century: "I had been in London many times before, had even lived there for a while. But this was like a secret visit" (qtd. in Ruane 22). When travel originated because of an unexpected or unwanted pregnancy, secrecy and stress determined the experience. Leaving home, in these cases, signified not freedom of movement or identity construction; rather, it represented an uncomfortable encounter with the unknown in a strange place.

Abortion narratives reveal how women's movement and autonomy were limited. However, abortion cases, particularly in urban areas, also demonstrate the ways in which Irish women navigated and marked space as they expressed their agency—deciding whether or not to be mothers on their own terms and well outside the idealized scenes of rural domesticity. Whether the destination was Dublin in the 1940s or London in the 1990s, Irish abortion experiences are, as Aideen Quilty argues, "drenched in questions of place, or more appropriately the place of elsewhere ... their stories are always about their bodies in places: the boat, plane, taxi, the clinic" (193). In her recollections of the 1940s, for example, Kathleen grounded her experiences in place and space; she remembered precise addresses and recalled clearly her specific movements around town. This attention to place is not unique in Irish abortion narratives. Another woman who travelled to Britain for an abortion in the 1990s would later write the following: "I kept a diary with all the information I needed, maps, addresses, train and bus times. That diary anchored me during that time. I felt very much at sea, adrift" ("Share Your Abortion Story"). For Kathleen and the anonymous woman who kept a diary in the 1990s, making clear connections to particular places during travel and even recording these places may have mitigated somewhat the sense of being untethered during abortion voyages.

In a 1930s Belfast case, the woman who sought abortion navigated the city on foot; her urban travels were imbued with intrigue and secret communications. The abortion seeker, H., was brought by a friend to Sackville Street, where the abortionist met her in secret around the corner to make arrangements for the procedure. On the day of the abortion, H. went to a particular home, and she saw an old man there: "He gave me certain instructions and I went to the second door round the corner.... Defendant was there and she nodded her head to me to go outside. She came out after me and said to let on I was down for Evelyn as her husband did not know she carried that on. I went round with Evelyn to the house No 30 I had been in on the first occasion" (qtd. in *Case of H.R*). The surreptitious movements of all involved in this case are not surprising; according to an officer who testified in the trial, the area in question in Belfast was a "police protection point" where constables routinely walked the neighbour-hood (qtd. in *Case of H.R*). Although the movements of the abortion seeker, the abortionist, and their acquaintances only spanned a few streets within a particular part of Belfast, they, too, were characterized by fear and secrecy, and they, thus, mirror other abortion narratives featuring more distant travel.

Another example tells us a bit more about women's movements in early twentieth-century Dublin. William Coleman, an electrician who claimed to be a medical professional, had an office at 25 Merrion Square. There, he gave illegal abortions to dozens of women in the 1930s and 40s.[5] Margaret B. would later testify in court that she travelled to Dublin from her home in nearby Dun Laoighaire in 1936 to get an abortion. Margaret did not seek out Coleman immediately; rather, she went first to Roches Chemists on O'Connell Street for abortifacient pills. She took the pills for a week; when nothing happened, she visited Coleman at Merrion Square. Coleman x-rayed her, confirmed that she was pregnant, and told Margaret to come back in two days. She did so, and Coleman then attempted to induce miscarriage. Margaret had to return to Coleman the following day for a follow-up procedure. Each time, she travelled from her lodging in Dun Laoghaire to Dublin. Eventually, back at home, Margaret began to bleed, and three days after that, her employer noticed that she was feeling poorly and called for the doctor. She was taken from Dun Laoghaire back to Dublin and eventually to St. Patrick Dun's hospital, located just a few blocks from Merrion Square. This, of course, reminds us that no matter where abortion attempts began, some ended in hospitals or morgues and later in courtrooms. Margaret's voyages, like the others studied here, involved a significant amount of time as well as complicated travel arrangements and a sense of dislocation in new places, culminating in what must have been a frightening hospital stay.

In the 1990s, fifty years after the ordeals of Kathleen and Margaret, Catherine left Ireland to seek an abortion in Britain. Whereas Kathleen, discussed above, brought her sister to Dublin with her, Catherine asked her best friend to accompany her to London; indeed, many women from 1900 to the present day sought support and assistance from female friends and relatives. Like Kathleen, however, Catherine, too, was concerned about the time that the abortion would take and feared feeling displaced. "We went over and back in the shortest possible time, for all the practical reasons," she later said. "But also because I'd feel like a displaced person if I was there a few days waiting to have an abortion" (qtd. in Ruane 49). In Catherine's recollections, the "abortion trail" to London was similar to a forced migration or exile, and Catherine described herself almost as a refugee.

Approximately twenty years after Catherine's experiences and seventy after Kathleen's and Margaret's, in 2012, the *Irish Times* published several women's first-hand accounts of abortion travel. Again, the continuities are noteworthy. One woman, who visited the UK via train, ferry, and plane, said the following: "Driving home from the airport, I was crying hysterically. It was as if I had been so distracted and stressed out by cancelled flights and rushing for trains that I never really had time to think about what I was actually doing" (qtd. in Sheridan). Another woman claimed that "The whole experience was dreadful; how could it not be? But, undoubtedly, it was made more awful by virtue of the fact I had to travel to London" (qtd. in Sheridan).

In these examples, crossing borders represents not a rejection of patriarchal constrictions but rather strangeness and loss: strangeness because of the need to navigate unfamiliar spaces and people and loss because of a sense that one's connection to Ireland is somehow transgressed or broken during abortion voyages. Tapping into traumatic histories, transnational abortion travel can be likened to an exile—a "desperate migratio[n] across the water" or even an "underground railroad" (Rossiter 121; Sethna and Doull, "Accidental Tourists" 458). One website that publicizes Irish women's cross-border abortion travel experiences is even called the x-ile project. Abortion voyages have been likened to being on the run or to becoming part of "Ireland's hidden Diaspora" (Ruane, 2000). Abortion travel also "might be described as asylum seeking, however temporary, especially if its covert nature, the fear of persecution and the loneliness associated with it are taken into account" (Rossiter and Sexton 5).

As an abortion-seeker in the 1990s later remembered, "they were very supportive at the clinic [in London] but it all seems slightly unreal now. I've no place in my mind to connect it to—just England" (qtd. in Ruane 44). One mother who travelled with her daughter in the 1960s recalled the following: "For all the talk of women travelling to England for abortions, I'd never thought of the actual journey. The travelling somehow compounds everything. Before that it was all mostly a private crisis, now it became public with cover stories and lies. It separated [my husband] and I at the worst time—I'll never forget the sight of Kate going down for the operation and my sense of loneliness in that waiting room in another country" (qtd. in Ruane 55). In these accounts of transnational abortion travel, there is a disconnect not only from the comforts of home but also, and more explicitly, from motherhood and from Mother Ireland itself. Here, England is a foreign place, even if familiar to the traveller. It is not home and, indeed, represents the alien rather than the familiar. Cross-border abortion travel since 1967, however, has performed an important function in that it has allowed Irish society to safeguard the falsehoods of its sexual and national culture. When vice is exported to the former colonizer, "the myth of holy Ireland" is preserved and the "sinful decadence of Britain" is upheld (Ryan, "Irish Female Emigration" 273).

The abortion voyages made by Irish women, past and present, also must be placed within the context of a complex dialogue about home in Ireland—both the home, or domestic sphere, and the nation. Commentary on the home as a site of not only domesticity but also nation building was endemic throughout the first half of the twentieth century; the legacies of which are still felt today. Women's place in the home, substantiated by the glorification of the Catholic wife and mother, was essential to nation building (Meaney, *Gender* 3). Indeed, Ireland itself was gendered female and represented as a mother. In 1976, Irish writer Edna O'Brien, recognizing the way that Ireland was represented as a mother, wrote the following: "Countries are either mothers or fathers, and engender the emotional bristle secretly reserved for either sire. Ireland has always been a woman, a womb, a cave, a cow, a Rosaleen, a sow, a bride, a harlot, and, of course, the gaunt Hag of Beare" (1). Having to leave home for an abortion, therefore, may have signified for some women not just a temporary trip but a rejection of or denial of motherhood and Irishness, a rupture with their sense of home and nation. As one woman recounted to the *Irish Times* in 2012: "I deeply resent those, my husband included, who demand my silence, and I wish people realised how 'going to England' damages one's sense of worth" (qtd. in Sheridan).

Cross-border abortion travel experiences also cause many women to feel resentment toward "the country [they call] home" (qtd. in Gentleman). "I was mortified," recalled one woman who traveled to the UK in 1998, "that my own country had made me feel like I was doing something wrong" ("Share Your Abortion Story"). Forcibly exiled to seek what many view as routine healthcare, punished and isolated based on historical notions of gender, nation, and motherhood, how then can Irish abortion seekers comfortably return home after terminating pregnancies? "Because women's source of identity was located in the home place" writes Ryan, "women who left home risked losing their true, authentic identity." (Ryan, "Irish Female Emigration" 276)

If Irish women do indeed experience some sort of loss of identity through abortion travel, then the notion of home itself is fundamentally transformed. This reality, of course, distinguishes abortion travel from emigration: for abortion seekers, the voyage is temporary, and the sense of dislocation involved in travelling must be reconciled with a return to Ireland. The latter frequently involves pretending things are normal and maintaining secrecy—most Irish women likely do not tell others about their abortion travel experiences. "I returned home with no follow up and no counselling. I unraveled," wrote one woman ("Share Your Abortion Story"). And many claim that after their abortion, familiar places and spaces associated with home or Ireland became uncomfortable or even sinister. "Just imagine them at school/college/work muttering 'baby killer' under their breath," thought one woman after she returned home (qtd. in Rossiter and Sexton 6). Another wrote: "I returned home and I don't remember what happened. My parents were extremely supportive, and took me out of school for two weeks because rumours were starting in my school" ("Share Your Abortion Story"). The grief and sadness that some women experience after their ordeal is not centred on themselves but on Ireland. It is an Ireland that they have become alienated from and an Ireland that, because they chose abortion over the national ideal of motherhood, they have a fractured relationship with:

> In the years which have passed I have not felt an instant of regret about my choice, but I feel sad for Ireland, my home. Ireland does not allow itself to be an informed society, instead hanging on to strange beliefs, ruled by patriarchal institutions, misogyny and scaremongering. Ireland does not take care of its own living daughters in their time of need. ("Share Your Abortion Story")
> Here, the nation itself is the primary loss.

In this chapter, I build on the arguments of scholars such as Aideen Quilty, Sinéad Kennedy, and Catherine Conlon, who claim that abortion should be placed within a framework of continuity in Irish history, as part and parcel of a long-term, systematic "regulation of women's fertile bodies" (23). Just like Irish women today, women in earlier decades who could not access abortion close to their homes had to grapple with not only the stress of an unwanted pregnancy but also the burdens of coming up with a travel plan, making bookings, finding the money necessary for the journey, embarking on the actual travel, finding, paying for lodging, and, of course, as Ann Rossiter argues for a later period, "adopting a strategy of silence and subterfuge" (34). The same travails that Irish women go through today were shared by the women of their mothers' and grandmothers' generation, albeit usually within the island rather than across the Irish Sea. By foot, bus, train, boat, and plane, the secret journeys of women with unwanted pregnancies remind us of the sometimes frightening continuities in Irish women's lives. From the 1910s to the 2010s, Irish women struggled with the pressures of interacting with Mother Ireland and actively tried to determine for themselves if, when, and under what circumstances they would become mothers. Abortion journeys also remind us that we require much more investigation into the connections between mobility, space, and identity; the Irish reproductive body and the nation; and the ordinary experiences and voices of women who travel in search of abortion.

Acknowledgment

This research was completed as a result of a Fulbright Faculty Award to Ireland. I am grateful to the Ireland Fulbright Commission and to the University College Dublin Humanities Institute for their continuous support of this research. Funding was also received from the School of Humanities and Social Sciences and the History Department at the College of Charleston. I also thank the archivists and staff at the National Archives of Ireland, Dublin, and the Public Record Office of Northern Ireland, Belfast, for their invaluable assistance.

Endnotes

1   Abortion in the Republic of Ireland remained illegal until January 2019. In a May 2018 referendum, Ireland's people voted to decriminalize abortion in certain circumstances; legislation allowing for this came into effect in January 2019. The new legislation does not affect Northern Ireland, where abortion, in most cases, is still prohibited.

2 Scholars have argued that some Irish women travelled to mainland Britain to seek abortions well before the 1967 act but that these voyages were rare and difficult, especially during the Second World War (McAvoy 238; Rose 121-123).

3 My analyses of these court cases in this chapter are based on archival research conducted at the National Archives of Ireland, Dublin, and the Public Record Office of Northern Ireland, Belfast, as well as newspaper accounts of the criminal cases. I thank all of those who assisted in my research there.

4 For an in-depth discussion of the cases of Williams and Moloney, see McAvoy.

5 William Coleman, brought to trial in Dublin in 1944, was an electrician who provided abortions at his offices in Merrion Square. Coleman Case, Court of Criminal Appeal, 1945, file CCA 1945/18, National Archives of Ireland, Dublin.

Works Cited

Berer, Marge. "Termination of Pregnancy as Emergency Obstetric Care: The Interpretation of Catholic Health Policy and the Consequences for Pregnant Women: An Analysis of the Death of Savita Halappanavar in Ireland and Similar Cases." *Reproductive Health Matters*, vol. 21 no. 41, 2013, pp. 9-17.

Best, Alyssa. "Abortion Rights along the Irish-English Border and the Liminality of Women's Experiences." *Dialectical Anthropology*, vol.29 no.3/4, 2005, p.423. Print.

Case of H.R. 1937. Belfast Petty Sessions. File BELF/1/2/2/47/96, Public Record Office of Northern Ireland, Belfast.

Case of Maureen F. 1943. Central Criminal Court Dublin. National Archives of Ireland, Dublin.

Case of William Coleman. 1945. Court of Criminal Appeal, file CCA 1945/18, National Archives of Ireland, Dublin.

Fischer, Clara. "Gender, Nation, and the Politics of Shame: Magdalen Laundries and the Institutionalization of Feminine Transgression in Modern Ireland." *Signs*, vol. 41, no. 4, 2016, pp. 821-843.

Gentleman, Amelia. "'It Was the Scariest Thing I've Ever Done': The Irish Women Forced to Travel for Abortions." *The Guardian* 31 Oct. 2015. *The Guardian*. https://www.theguardian.com/world/2015/oct/31/abortion-ireland-northern-ireland-women-travel-england-amelia-gentleman. Accessed 27 Jan. 2019.

Gerend, Sarah. "'Magdalene Versus the Nation': Ireland as a Space of Compulsory Motherhood in Edna O'Brien's Down by the River." *Motherhood and Space: Configurations of the Maternal Through Politics, Home, and the Body*, edited by Sarah Hardy and Caroline Wiedmer, Palgrave Macmillan, 2005, pp.35-53.

Gilmartin, Mary, and Allen White. "Interrogating Medical Tourism: Ireland, Abortion, and Mobility Rights." *Signs*, vol. 36, no. 2, 2011, pp. 275-280.

Johnston, Lynda, and Robyn Longhurst. *Space, Place, and Sex: Geographies of Sexualities*. Rowman & Littlefield Publishers, 2010.

McAvoy, Sandra. *Aspects of the State and Female Sexuality in the Irish Free State, 1922-1949*. Dissertation, National University of Ireland Cork, 2011.

McCormick, Leanne. "'No Sense of Wrongdoing': Abortion in Belfast 1917-1967." *Journal of Social History*, vol. 49, no. 1, 2015, pp. 1-24.

Meaney, Gerardine. *Gender, Ireland, and Cultural Change: Race, Sex, and Nation*. New York: Routledge, 2010.

Meaney, Gerardine. *Reading the Irish Woman : Studies in Cultural Encounter and Exchange, 1714-1960*. Liverpool University Press, 2013.

O'Brien, Edna. *Mother Ireland*. Plume, 1999.

O'Sullivan, Donie. "Irish Women Live-Tweet Journey to Great Britain for Abortion." *CNN*, 21 Aug. 2016, https://edition.cnn.com/2016/08/21/world/irish-women-live-tweet-abortion-journey/index.html. Accessed 27 Jan. 2019.

Quilty, Aideen. "Water, Water Everywhere...Exploring Education Geographies of Abortion." *The Abortion Papers Ireland: Volume 2*, edited by Aideen Quilty et al., Attic Press, 2015, pp.189-202.

Quilty, Aideen et al. "Editors' Introduction." *The Abortion Papers Ireland: Volume 2*, edited by Aideen Quilty et al., Attic Press, 2015, pp. 12-23.

Rose, R.S. *An Outline of Fertility Control, Focusing on the Element of Abortion, in the Republic of Ireland to 1976.* Dissertation. University of Stockholm, 1976.

Rossiter, Ann. *Ireland's Hidden Diaspora: The Abortion Trail and the Making of a London-Irish Underground, 1980-2000.* Irish Abortion Solidarity Campaign, 2009.

Rossiter, Ann, and Mary Sexton. *The Other Irish Journey: A Survey Update of Northern Irish Women Attending British Abortion Clinics, 2000/2001.* Marie Stopes International, 2001.

"RTÉ Archives | Politics | Address by Mr de Valera." *RTÉ Archives,* 29 June 2017, https://www.rte.ie/archives/exhibitions/eamon-de-valera/719124-address-by-mr-de-valera/. Accessed 27 Jan. 2019.

Ruane, Medb. *The Irish Journey: Women's Stories of Abortion.* Irish Family Planning Association, 2000.

Ryan, Louise. *Gender, Identity, and the Irish Press, 1922-1937: Embodying the Nation.* Edwin Mellen Press, 2002.

Ryan, Louise. "Irish Female Emigration in the 1930s: Transgressing Space and Culture." *Gender, Place & Culture,* vol. 8 no. 3, 2001, pp. 271-282.

Ryan, Louise. "Moving Spaces and Changing Places: Irish Women's Memories of Emigration to Britain in the 1930s." *Journal of Ethnic & Migration Studies,* vol. 29, no. 1, 2003, pp. 67-82.

Sethna, Christabelle, and Marion Doull. "Accidental Tourists: Canadian Women, Abortion Tourism, and Travel." *Women's Studies,* vol. 41, no.4, 2012, pp.457-475.

Sethna, Christabelle, and Marion Doull. "Spatial Disparities and Travel to Freestanding Abortion Clinics in Canada." *Women's Studies International Forum,* 2013, p.52. *EBSCOhost.* Web.

"Share Your Abortion Story." *Share Your Abortion Story,* http://shareyourabortionstory.tumblr.com. Accessed 1 May 2017.

Sheehy, J.S. "The Influence of Women in Catholic Ireland." *Cork Examiner.* 22 Nov. 1922.

Sheridan, Kathy. "Stories of Abortion: By People Who Have Been Through It." *Irish Times* 24 Mar. 2012, https://www.irishtimes.com/news/stories-of-abortion-by-people-who-have-been-through-it-1.488183. Accessed 27 Jan. 2019.

Side, Katherine. "A Geopolitics of Migrant Women, Mobility and Abortion Access in the Republic of Ireland." *Gender, Place & Culture*, vol. 23, no. 12, 2016, pp.1788–1799.

Smith, James M. *Ireland's Magdalen Laundries and the Nation's Architecture of Containment.* University of Notre Dame Press, 2007.

X-Ile Project. 2018, http://www.x-ileproject.com/. Accessed 27 Jan. 2019.

Chapter 20

Sins of Omission: Unpacking the Rhetoric of Sexuality within Nineteenth-Century American Mothers' Travel Diaries

Monica Reyes

> It strikes me as I think of it now that Mothers on the road had to
> undergo more trial and suffering than anybody else—Martha Ann
> Morrison, Overland Trail Traveller, 1844 (qtd. in Schlissel 35)

Although the journeys could be challenging, painful, and tragic, the United States experienced one of the greatest times of movement during the nineteenth century. Perhaps the most massive recorded selective relocation was the Great Westward Migration, which began in 1843. Even with the dangers of nineteenth century wagon travel—such as warlike confrontations with Native Americans, sickness, wagon accidents, stampedes, or even erroneously-charted trails—scores of families risked and sacrificed much to settle in the American West, and at the heart of these families was usually a mother, who recorded the journey in her travel diary.

Over the past four years, I have explored women's travel writing of the American frontier from the long nineteenth century through edited collections and primary sources in archives. As I study and write about the lived experience of these females, I am reminded of the fair and sobering warning from the faithful Sancho Panza within the journey of *Don Quixote*: "those who turn other people's lives into texts hold real power" (paraphrased in Newkirk 14). When I sit with their words on my lap, I remember how I often carry an overwhelming responsibility to "shape-re-member-[an alternative] rhetorical presence" (Glenn 8),[1] in the work of marginalized voices, such as women and—perhaps even more neglected—mothers. My work with these first-person narratives motivates me to ask valuable questions about the complex power structures surrounding female rhetoric in the nineteenth century.

My curiosity about these works has grown out of my personal desire to think, speak, and travel on my own terms. I grew up in a small town within a patriarchal family structure on the Mexican-American border. My desire to journey outside my community to learn about or even discuss issues that would empower women to make independent choices was culturally shamed and denied. As a young woman, I found strength in stories I read and the female characters that artfully created ways to voice their opinions in silently subversive ways; reading and writing became outlets for my own suppositions, musings, and secrets that my community would not allow or desire to hear. As a scholar, I began poring over nineteenth-century women's travel diaries, and I discovered that these women also travelled, read and wrote according to the permission of their brothers, fathers, and husbands. Although I identified with the authors' loyalties to their culture, communities, and families, I also wondered if, like me, they had used their seemingly innocuous and tame writing as an outlet. And if so, what messages were they attempting to convey? In time, my work has led me to agree with scholars Suzanne Bunkers and Lillian Schlissel: although women writers of the American frontier often kept the focus of their writing on their socially accepted realm of domesticity, they found clever and meaningful ways to subtly express their own unique points of view on a variety of issues.

In the sections that follow, I offer first a thorough theoretical framework that informs my thinking on the rhetorical affordances of mother-diarists of the American West. This section aims to contextualize the unique characteristics of travel diaries during the nineteenth century as well as provide insight on the diary as a literary construct.

Next, I briefly examine two texts by mother-diarists—the diary of Amelia Stewart Knight (which describes her 1853 trek from Iowa to Oregon) and Susan Shelby Magoffin's *Down the Santa Fe Trail and into Mexico* (the author's edited and published 1846 travel diary while journeying the title's namesake route)—to suggest how and why mother-diarists are able to creatively communicate on matters concerning sexuality.[2] Ultimately, I posit that travel, and the varied geographical contexts that travel affords, perpetuated American mother-diarists' use of omission and encoding, such as pathetic fallacy, to both construct a discreet sexual self within their travel diaries and to powerfully comment, albeit indirectly, on the sexual life of the American travelling mother.

Mothers and Travel Diaries in the American West

The call to travel West often came at the most emotionally and physically strenuous time for women and mothers. Schlissel affirms how "neither pregnancy nor the care of very young infants were judged by emigrant families as sufficient cause to defer travel…. The decision to make the journey rested with the men, and farm men of the early nineteenth-century were not inclined to excuse women from their daily responsibilities to prepare for the occasion of childbirth"(35).

After all, "free" land in the West was the worthy reward for a journey that could take as long as a year to complete. Pregnancy and caring for children was as common on the trail as at home; in fact, one in five women was pregnant at some time during the journey to the West, and "virtually every married woman travelled with small children" (Schlissel 14); unfortunately, infant death was also a high possibility on the plains. Despite the fear of losing a child or a mother's own life due to childbirth, birth control was at best painful and at worst life threatening. Diaphragms were not available for purchase until 1880s, so women travelling during Magoffin and Knight's time period were left to their own, often ineffective, devices. Although there was much to be said about the demanding journeys, many mother-diarists could not communicate their pains or pleasures in the manner that twenty-first-century diarists would recognize.

Less than one percent of the half-million sojourners who travelled to the American West during the 1800s are represented in self-writing that exists today, either through published pieces, archival material, or within family collections (Faragher 11). These works, mostly describing life on the Overland Trail, usually ending in California or Oregon, are largely written by women, many of whom were mothers; however, these mothers, unsurprisingly, are hardly allowed within larger discussions of nineteenth-century American life, mobility, culture, or identity. Instead, male literature of the frontier has often taken the role of the stereotypical American experience of solitary adventure and dominance over land and marginalized Native peoples. But the truth is that daily life on the Overland Trail—cooking, healing, washing, and nurturing—was essential for survival, and this was the context in which mother-diarists usually lived and wrote.

Consequently, women and mothers who left their homes relied on the practical advice of those who left before them, often other diarists within their family or published travel writers. For example, *Hints to Lady Travellers*, published in 1889, by Lillian Campbell Davidson provides practical insight and advice to women while in transit, such as "how to walk in soaking wet skirts" or "how best to keep cool in high temperatures" (Foster and Mills, "Introduction" 8-9). However, other crucial advice about how to travel while handling menstruation, childbirth, and sexual intimacy is glaringly missing. It is not my goal in this discussion to undermine contributions like Davidson's; the ethical considerations of my research with diaries of marginalized people, such as women, demand respect and appreciation for what women were afforded to discuss (and even read) at the time they wrote. I also agree with Shirley Foster and Sara Mills who understand how "the narrator's femininity, however, had to be guaranteed in order for her work to be appropriately authenticated in gender terms. Indeed, most women travel writers themselves were acutely aware of the textual constraints imposed on them by gender appropriateness" ("Introduction" 10). The omission of details pertaining to sexuality in nineteenth-century travel writing indicates the challenges women had writing about issues that breached a certain standard of femininity; for example, emigrant mothers rarely write about the care of infant children because "the realm of children" was "consigned to the oral tradition along with information about menstruation, marriage, and pregnancy and childbirth" (Schlissel 82), which made even the care of offspring a, sometimes, taboo writing subject for many women.

Indeed, even travel life was suspect, and "women had to apologize for their public presence as they travelled because in the 'domestic sphere' they "were considered sexually 'safe'" (Foster and Mills, "Women & Space"). To add to this, mother-diarists perpetuated the taboo by "contriv[ing] to hide their fears and anxieties" (Schlissel 111) within their entries so that in many ways those who seriously study the life on the frontier and the diaries of such lives wonder about the silences and the missing information that modern writers would divulge, such as pregnancy, birth, and miscarriage. According to Foster and Mills, women travel writers navigated the travel diary platform as skillfully as they could and "had to try to position themselves somewhere in relation to these discourses of aesthetics, science and imperialism and find a voice for themselves amid these authoritative statements of surveying, analysing, assessing and evaluating" ("Women & Space" 172).

"Finding a voice for themselves" within a nineteenth-century journey often sprang from the advantageous opportunity to write in travel diaries, a unique genre with rhetorical possibilities unlike most women had encountered. Travel diaries are particular in that they are a hybrid of discourse—both an autobiographical and a travel account of a particular experience of exploration and movement. Within my discussion of how mother-diarists can communicate in subversive ways through their travel diaries, it is important to briefly expound on the affordances of diary and travel writing.

Such diary scholars as Margo Culley, Francine Prose, and Elizabeth Hampsten define diaries as literature because "this periodic life-writing springs from the same source as the art created for a public audience: the urge to give shape and meaning to life with words, and to endow this meaning-making with a permanence that transcends time" (Culley xi). Additionally, many personal narratives may also exhibit powerful rhetorical devices, which further establish them as literature. As diarists reread their diaries, they often edit their work in an effort to create a literary piece; a complex protagonist, a setting, and subplots all exist within diaries, and these edits and rhetorical choices are motivated by audience (Prose). Culley explains how "the importance of the audience, real or implied, conscious or unconscious, of what is usually thought of as a private genre cannot be overstated ... [Audience] has a crucial influence over what is said and how it is said ...

and determines more than anything else the kind of self-construction the diarist represents" (12).

Culley's scholarship points out how the role of the diary author as both creator and literary character perpetuates the diary's hybridity of fiction and truth in a type of paradox: "Even in some of the earliest American women's diaries we can see this kind of 'double conscious-ness,' as the self stands apart to view the self" (10). Culley's and Prose's perspectives are rare and insightful: diaries are literary constructs, not simply historical artifacts. In other words, these mother-diarists do not write in a vacuum, and their writing is artfully crafted. Although diaries, such as those written by women, are appealing to feminist historians and/or postcolonial critics for their varying perspectives, I agree with Culley that diaries are first literature and are valuable as such: "The process of selection and arrangement of detail in the text raises an array of concerns appropriately 'literary,' including questions of audience (real or implied), narrative, shape and structure, persona, voice, imagistic and thematic repetition" (Culley 10). Reading a diary, viewing the edits and the second thoughts, shows that self-writing is a tool for perpetually creating and recreating the self.

Adding the context of travel—movement across varied geographical spaces—to diary writing afforded even more opportunities for mother-diarists to express themselves in unconventional ways, as the travel experience often became a metaphor for the psychological journey they recorded within their diaries and journals, a journey "more subtle and more inward" (Thompson 96). Because of the overlapping movements of Romanticism and American westward migration, mother-diarists would have had access to the tools of fiction to create a type of hybrid of observational journaling of the passing panorama and a thoughtful, creative autobiography. Maureen Mulligan comments on this synchronicity at play: "Travel writing works on two levels, simultaneously. In literary terms, travel writers employ a diverse range of rhetorical stylistic devices, paradoxically often used in fiction writing ... but alongside the literary enjoyment, we can sometimes get a glimpse of the truly remarkable reality of human possibility" (184). The literary conventions already at play within diary writing—such as poetry, suspense, characterization, and symbolism—are amplified within a substantive motif of journey already existing in the traveller's life. In this way, mother-diarists of the American West are able to use the travel experience, namely the unfamiliar and varying geography of the trip, to discuss socially or morally prohibited topics. For example, at times mother-diarists compare their life experiences and emotions with the land they trek and the nature that surrounds it, a technique known as pathetic fallacy.[3] As Culley explains, autobiographical authors recreate themselves through metaphor; for instance, whether conscious or not, "a record of the weather may tell us much about the diarist who chose to record it" (19). In other words, "Romantic travellers ... do not simply observe, they also react to the scenes around them, and record those reactions, and their reflections, on them, in their accounts" (Thompson 117). For instance, during her first Sabbath on the prairie, Magoffin views wilderness as an extension of her own worship to God:

> Everything has been perfectly still and quiet, scarcely a breath of air, or the flitting of a feathered warbler has appeared to disturb the solemn stillness. Ever and anon the sharp whistle of a partridge, the chirp of a lark, or the croaking of a raven in the distant woods, were heard. Save these and the unusually gentle noise made by the waggoners [sic], no other sound conspired to mar the solemn stillness of a Sabbath on the Prairies. (9)

Magoffin's creative interpretation of nature's silence as reverence and worship allows her to effectively communicate her own faith through the passing panorama of her travels and possibly to rationalize her inability to attend a formal service as she is accustomed.

Similarly, Mary Clearman Blew's foreword of Schlissel's *Women's Diaries of the Westward Journey* remarks how an entry by Amelia Stewart Knight reveals the literariness of her writing:

> Amelia Knight remarks, as her train crosses the Cascade Mountains on September 8, 1853, "Many of the trees are 300 feet high and so dense to almost exclude the light of heaven, and for my own part I dare not look to the top of them for fear of breaking my neck" ... we know to ask whether her inability to look at the tops of trees had to do only with her discomfort in her eighth month of pregnancy. ("Traveled 14 miles [today] over the worst road that was ever made, up and down, very steep, rough and rocky hills, through mud holes, twisting and winding round

stumps, logs and fallen trees") … or whether it also had to do with fear of losing sight of "heaven," which is to say, losing her assurance of order in her world and her place in it. (xi)

Here, Knight is inspired by her surroundings to find a voice for her fears and doubts, and the physical trek is no doubt working as a metaphor for a much larger, personal journey. Knight is able to skillfully develop the narrative of her own perpetually unstable and taxing journey as a mother who lives day to day fixated on earthly, hand-to-mouth cares by referencing her very real experience of the jarring westward journey obscuring her view of the sky, "heaven," and eternity.

While appreciating the art of these mother-diarists' work is meaningful in itself, it is valuable to uncover how nineteenth-century mother-diarists were most likely motivated to write about taboo subjects with great creativity to communicate in concealed ways. Suzanne Bunkers has written about how "the central strategy of the women who wrote these diaries and journals was the selective use of speech and silence. What remained unsaid was every bit as important as—and, in some cases, more important than—what was said" (191). Bunkers explains that the reader must respect the author's use of "self-editing [and] "self-censoring as a means of encoding messages and maintaining a perceived sense of self in her text" (193). "Encoding," according to Bunkers, can take many forms, such as "indirection, contradiction, deviation and silences," but in general, it is when an author communicates indirectly, even through omission. It is paramount to understand that women of the nineteenth century were expected to be "asexual" (Murphy 193); in other words, their thoughts and feelings about sex, and all that it entails, were assumed neutral—neither with pleasure nor with particular disdain—and a casual reading of their writings may erroneously confirm those assumptions. Yet similar to Foucault's theories on the interconnected structures of rhetoric, sexuality, and power most notable in *The History of Sexuality*, Bunkers claims that when a woman chooses not to write (or speak) regarding taboo subjects, she is exercising her power and "finding avenues in which to speak … about what has previously remained unspoken" (194). While there is some scholarship regarding the rhetoric of female diaries and sexuality, there is little evidence that scholars have realized the effects travel had on mother-diarists and their writing concerning sexuality. By observing the entries of Magoffin and Knight, this chapter aims to reveal how the act of travel provided mother-diarists opportunities a new discourse in which to safely contextualize and discuss their sexuality.

Emilia Stewart Knight and Susan Shelby Magoffin: Sexuality Creatively Coded

At the start of her journey in June 1846, Magoffin was eighteen years old and had been married just eight months to a prosperous merchant, Samuel, who was twenty-seven years her senior. She was also pregnant with her first child when her journal begins. As an extended honeymoon and trading expedition, the Magoffins followed the Santa Fe Trail for fifteen months, and their trek is full of calamity—including the violence of the Mexican-American War, wagon accidents, fire, theft, sickness (Susan herself contracts malaria and yellow fever), and death.[4]

Less than a decade after Magoffin set off on her journey, Amelia Stewart Knight left her home in Iowa in 1853, caring for seven children and pregnant with her eighth. In addition to her children, she is accompanied by her husband, whom she mentions frequently. The Knight family finally does reach Oregon and settle in a log cabin after a tumultuous journey of sickness, loss, injury. and birth.

Both of these mother-diarists are highly aware that their writing is not private, even among extended family; Howard R. Lamar warns about Magoffin's own editing in the foreword to *Down the Santa Fe Trail and into Mexico*: "It is also apparent that while Magoffin did not contemplate publication, she did write with certain self-consciousness that her words might one day be read aloud to her family" (xvii). Mother-diarists like Magoffin tend to be conspicuously silent about their pregnancies or use metaphors to communicate about their state. Like many of the Overland female diarists, Magoffin cannot fully disclose the happy feelings of discovering she is pregnant, and, later, she only leaves clues about her experience with the pains of miscarriage (66). Almost a week after her loss, Magoffin finally confesses the tragedy of losing her child (67-68). Curiously, she reports of her "abortion" (68) while focusing more on the loss of many American soldiers at the fort in which she is staying, describing the place as "desolate" (69). Magoffin most likely conceals her pregnancy because of the taboo of documenting anything which would link to sexual activity and the likelihood of infant death in transit, which is common in female frontier diaries. Similarly, Knight's concluding entries of her travel diary mention the worst roads en route to Oregon; she carries her youngest child across mountainous terrain and over many toppled trees in rain and mud. One week of entries later, she mentions in passing that her eighth child has been born healthy, but she never alludes to her pregnancy all throughout her travel account. For twenty-first-century social media over-sharers, it is difficult to imagine Knight carrying a toddler across such dangerous landscapes, managing six other children, and being nine months pregnant without making mention of her pregnancy in her journal—but this type of concealment in writing was normal. Similarly, Magoffin refuses to mention her second pregnancy on the trail a few months later as well, mentioning only "my head and stomach are somewhat delicate of late" (228) when she was most likely already three months pregnant.

Magoffin also tragically experiences the initial pains of miscarriage due to a wagon crash (41, 47), and although she is most likely unaware of the effects of the crash that day, she describes how nature corresponds with her fears of losing her child: "Oh how gloomy the Plains have been to me today! I am sick, rather sad feelings and everything around corresponds with them. We have never had such a perfectly dead level before us now. The little hillocks which formerly broke the perfectly even view have entirely disappeared" (47).

Magoffin interprets her possibly losing a child with the imagery of the nature before her—"dead" and without the curving lines of small hills, which resemble the pregnant form. In the same entry she writes that the weather and scenery of late are "the most disagreeable ... the Prairie ever gave birth to" (47), which shows how her elucidation of the weather corresponds with her gloomy thoughts of an eminent miscarriage, especially seen in her choice of the word "birth."

Although Knight's children, and their illnesses, are frequently mentioned, her diary exemplifies how she is able to skillfully code a possibly sexual encounter with her husband:

Wednesday, July 27th [1853]: Came 15 miles today, and have camped at the boiling springs, a great curiosity. They bubble up out of the earth boiling hot. I have only to pour water on my tea and it is made. There is no cold water in this part. (Husband and myself wandered far down this branch, as far as we dare, to find it cool enough to bathe in. It was still very hot, and I believe I never spent such an uneasy sleepless night in my life. I felt as if I was in the bad place. I still believe it was not very far off.) I was glad when morning came and we left. (Knight qtd. in Schlissel 211)

This particular entry from Knight about the hot springs showcases her rhetorical savvy to subversively communicate about, and simultaneously deviate from, privately bathing with her husband on the frontier. The "curiosity" of the springs is seemingly a new sight for Knight and her family, and I suggest that Knight, because of travel, is afforded the rhetorical opportunity to comment on a private, intimate experience she shares with her husband. She first makes mention of the usefulness of the spring to brew her tea, a moot point in this context and most likely a distraction from the bath. Knight's use of parentheses to separate her description of the bath is expected as she uses parenthesis often to communicate private matters, as when she is ill, out of money, frightened, or overcome with grief. And although those ideas are important in a diary entry, Knight often equates her emotions with extraneous information. Within this parenthesis, the act of bathing with her husband is seemingly whispered.

It is unclear why Knight decided to mention that she and her husband shared this brief and vulnerable experience in the first place, but her descriptions showcase her possibly negative feelings about the sexually tense experience of bathing with her husband through employing pathetic fallacy and focusing on the spring itself. Knight likens the spring and its heat to "the bad place," possibly her interpretation of biblical hell. Her classification with her "dar[ing]" bath to the penalty of sin allows her readers, and herself, to understand that Knight desires no guilt or shame in her experience. Ultimately, she admits to being "uneasy" and "glad" to leave. Still it is curious that Knight decides to record this information, and there is a likelihood that her travel experience provides her the freedom to share it at all.

Conclusion

What makes writing by travelling mothers like Knight and Magoffin so meaningful, even over a century later, is that their focus on domesticity while moving to the West now has a larger context. As Casey Blanton explains:

> What travel books are 'about' is the interplay between observer and observed, between a traveler's own philosophical biases and preconceptions and the tests those idea and prejudices endure as a result of the journey. The reverberations between observer and observed, between self and world, allow the writer to celebrate the local while contemplating the universal. (qtd. in Saunders 4)

Or put another way, travel writing is a means to encourage exploration, curiosity, tolerance, and freedom; ultimately, travel is a tool for travellers to perceive their own culture more clearly (Mark Cocker qtd. in Thompson 6). In this way, the travelling experience allowed mother-diarists to confront their fears and preconceived notions about faith, family, and culture in ways that most likely influenced their own parenting.

It is simultaneously exciting and overwhelming to consider the archival research that is yet to be done with the work of mother-diarists of the frontier, especially considering how "archives are now viewed as primary sources for creating knowledge rather than mere storehouses for finding what is already known" (Gaillet 39). In other words, as we ask varied questions about the rhetoric of travel diaries, it is necessary to approach these life stories with respect, appreciation, and awareness so that our curiosity about mother-diarists travel writing allows their work to speak more clearly, perhaps in unexpected ways, about issues that were worthy of telling—sex, children, loss, and birth.

Endnotes

1   In her pivotal work, "Sex, Lies and Manuscript: Refiguring Aspasia in the History of Rhetoric," Cheryl Glenn discusses the importance feminist scholars to reexamine the role of women whose "texts, lives and manuscripts have been annexed by men" (181). By using the example of Aspasia of Miletus, who lived, worked, and spoke in Athens during the fifteh century, Glenn invites scholars to

reconsider, through archival research, how women were able to have significant rhetorical influence in societies of patriarchy.

2 For the purposes of this chapter, "sexuality" refers to acts or states of being which, in the nineteenth century, would indicate a female's bodily rhythm, such as menstruation, ovulation, birth, or miscarriage, or it would connote sexual desire or activity.

3 I posit that within their own travel diaries, early American female diarists use the geographical space of the frontier as a fitting analogy for their own femaleness, as both are considered objects of domination.

4 Although Magoffin does not travel with children, she is pregnant twice throughout her travel diary, and she discusses her pregnancies and miscarriages subtly and, at times, openly, making her story valid within this discussion.

Works Cited

Armitage, Susan and Elizabeth Jameson, editors. *The Women's West*. University of Oklahoma Press, 1987.

Blew, Mary Clearman. Foreword. *Women's Diaries of the Westward Journey*. Schlissel, 1982.

Bunkers, Suzanne L. "Midwestern Diaries and Journals: What Women Were (Not) Saying in the Late 1800s." *Studies in Autobiography*, edited by James Olney, Oxford University Press, 1988, pp. 190-210.

Campbell, Mary Baine. "Travel Writing and its Theory." *The Cambridge Companion to Travel Writing*, edited by Peter Hulme and Tim Youngs, Cambridge University Press, 2006. Kindle Edition.

Culley, Margo. "Introduction." *A Day at a Time: The Diary Literature of American Women from 1764 to the Present*, edited by Margo Culley, The Feminist Press, 1985, pp. 3-26.

Foster, Shirley, and Sara Mills. "Introduction." *An Anthology of Women's Travel Writing*, edited by Shirley Foster and Sara Mills, Manchester University Press, 2002, pp. 1-12.

Foster, Shirley, and Sara Mills. "Women & Space". *An Anthology of Women's Travel Writing*, edited by Shirley Foster and Sara Mills. Manchester University Press, 2002, pp. 171-180.

Foucault, Michel. *The History of Sexuality: An Introduction.* Vintage Books, 1976.

Gaillet, Lynée Lewis. "(Per)Forming Archival Research Methodologies." *College Composition and Communication,* vol. 64, no. 1, 2012, pp. 35-58.

Glenn, Cheryl. *Rhetoric Retold: Regendering The Tradition From Antiquity Through The Renaissance.* Southern Illinois University Press, 1997. Kindle Edition.

Hampsten, Elizabeth. "Lena Olmstead and Oscar Phillips: On Love and Marriage." *The Women's West,* edited by Susan H. Armitage and Elizabeth Jameson, University of Oklahoma Press, 1987, pp.127-142.

Knight, Amelia Stewart. "Amelia Stewart Knight." *Women's Diaries of the Westward Journey,* edited by Lillian Schlissel, Schocken, 1982, pp. ix-xii.

Lisle, Debbie. *The Global Politics of Contemporary Travel Writing.* Cambridge University Press, 2006.

Magoffin, Susan Shelby. *Down the Santa Fe Trail and into Mexico,* edited by Stella M. Drumm. Bison, 1962.

Mulligan, Maureen. "Women Travel Writers and the Question of Veracity." *Women, Travel Writing, and Truth,* edited by Clare Broome Saunders. Taylor & Francis, 2014.

Murphy, Mary. "The Private Lives of Public Women: Prostitution in Butte, Montana, 1878-1917." *The Women's West,* edited by Susan Armitage and Elizabeth Jameson, University of Oklahoma Press, 1987, pp. 193-206.

Newkirk, Thomas. "Seduction and Betrayal in Qualitative Research." *Ethics and Representation in Qualitative Research Studies,* edited by Peter Mortensen and Gesa E. Kirsch, NCTE, 1996, pp. 3-16.

Prose, Francine. "Reclaiming Anne Frank's Diary as Literature." *YouTube,* 23 Apr. 2012, https://www.youtube.com/watch?v=t0VY WndMWTs. Accessed 27 Jan. 2019.

Schlissel, Lillian, editor. *Women's Diaries of the Westward Journey.* Schocken, 1982.

Chapter 21

When Monsters Move the Mother in You

Janet MacLennan

Letting go of all I've held on to
I'm standing here until you make me move—
"Hanging by a Moment," Lifehouse

P arrots squawk from the tree outside my third-floor window as I compose this story. We are lucky that the tree still stands. Its leaves grew back eventually; its branches may. The parrots have been visiting daily in recent months—more regularly and more often than I ever remember. Maybe their movements have been altered by the same monster storm that is making me move.

Growing up in Canada, I was used to movement. We moved from the country to a town to a city to a smaller town. For a four-year span I was never in the same school two years in a row; the movement included two different provinces and two different languages. Moving meant we were always moving on down the road—to stay with grandparents, to spend time with old friends, to visit aunts and uncles and cousins who also lived in far-flung locales. Friends and family were on the move, too, so our home hosted people passing through on their travels.

Movement I was used to, but that's not the same as travelling. It wasn't until graduate school that I was bitten by the travel bug, not through the experience of leaving Canada to study in the United States but rather through my interactions and relationships with other international students that opened my heart, mind, and being to the world awaiting. I began to say yes to travel any chance I got, even if during graduate school these trips were brief and basic.

My travel pursuits were solo, even when they were social. I might have shared these journeys with friends or fellow students or family members, but I experienced them in a solitary way. I stared at scenery flashing by, stole moments to walk alone down strange streets, sat quietly with my thoughts in new places, and touched and smelled and tasted sensory experiences that stirred and strengthened my spirit even as I watched myself change in response.

One year, when I had finished my master's and was already into course work for my doctorate, I travelled home for the summer, thirsty, so thirsty, for just such a change through travel. And one day, on a set of train tracks far into the woods of New Brunswick, I almost died. The reason I'm here to write this now is because someone with better reflexes snatched me from certain death. The only thing that died that day, though, was the chance that I would follow a predictable path from then on. My studies continued because my passion for the discipline of human communication stayed the same but most everything else changed for me. After graduation, I wanted to live not in Canada or the United States but somewhere else. Anywhere else. Several somewhere elses. And I wanted to start in the Caribbean.

You see, I was born on an island, one of heart-breaking beauty. In all of the places I lived growing up in the Maritime Provinces, I moved to the rhythms of the tides—the wild Atlantic Ocean, the highest tides of the Bay of Fundy, the warm gentle waters of the Northumberland. Living in Ohio throughout graduate school had felt wrong; it was not right for me to live so far from the ocean, a fact that struck me every day of my years there. So I was seeking a new island to explore, with waters to surround me, and a slow rhythm, which I considered would be a reward after the fast pace of completing three university degrees in seven years.

What is better than travelling to exotic locations? Living in one. I got a job in my field in Puerto Rico. Contemplating the location of the tiny nation on the globe, I traced my finger from the huge land mass of Canada all the way down, all the way across to the gathering of specks that promised warm breezes, warmer waters, and colourful, lively living.

I live where you vacation. What an amazing thing to get what you wish for! What a wonderful experience to encounter this new-to-me culture and language. What a gift as an educator to practice what you preach and teach about intercultural communication. I arrived to Puerto Rico not sure how long I would stay, but I never left. I kept travelling, both to other destinations and to every delight the island had to offer. And people travelled to me, letting me show off my new island home. Half of my life I have lived here now, whereas previously I had never lived in one place longer than six years.

Yet it felt like a brand-new place when I gave birth to my son. The kinds and depths of relationships you develop, the way you spend time on the streets and parks of your neighbourhood, the chance to see the island through the eyes of a child encountering absolutely everything for the first time. Mothering my son made me feel like I was travelling without ever leaving home.

That doesn't mean I stopped travelling to other places once I became a mother. No, I felt profoundly that if I was going to be a mother, I was going to be a travelling mother. Whether it was this intention or simply serendipity, I have a kid who is a great travel companion and has been since he received his first passport stamp at seven months old. He is now almost seven years old, and we have travelled to many provinces of Canada and states of the United States. We have crossed the Atlantic Ocean twice en route to Europe and have dipped our bodies in the Pacific Ocean on a trip to Central America. Seas, rivers, lakes, mountains, volcanos, forests, jungles—we have explored them together as mother and son. My greatest joy each year is planning the trips we will take to spend time with loved ones here and there as well as the trips to a country where we have never been.

My days of being a solo traveller are behind me in both practical and emotional ways. Travelling as a mother, I no longer feel nor seek solitude, but rather experience journeys as a joint encounter. Familiar places are made new, and new places are understood through his reactions as much as my own. Perhaps this reality of myself as a connected rather than solo traveller is the reason that I now must move away from Puerto Rico.

In September 2017, two monster storms in the span of two weeks bore down on the islands of the Caribbean; one of these hurricanes devastated Puerto Rico to a magnitude not seen in modern times. In one fateful day, my whole life swirled up into the air, and when it slammed back down to ground, it wasn't in one piece anymore, and it wasn't something I recognized. Surviving a natural disaster of this magnitude, you at first feel glee, then relief. You feel deeply what is important and are grateful you still have it with you. Yet you don't know what is coming. You don't know that the leaders elected to protect will instead profit. While disaster capitalism flourishes, livelihoods (and lives) and healing and peace float out to sea.

All the kids I know have handled the trauma of this disaster better than all of the adults I know. If I had to move through an experience like this, I'm grateful to have gone through it with my son to keep me connected to good. Maybe you think that as a mother I should feel mother guilt for not having protected him from the experience of a natural disaster, but I don't. So many mothers in this world cannot, through no fault of their own, protect their children from disasters, such as famine, floods, drought, earthquakes, and war. Privilege has meant that my child may never have to experience any of these, yet I feel profoundly that we no longer live in a world where privilege will— or should—protect. And that children should be raised in the world that exists so that they can care about it, change it, and perhaps transform it.

I don't feel guilt. I do feel anger. Not the randomness of a natural disaster, but the deliberateness of an unnatural disaster left in its wake is making me move. I will have to leave our home, our neighbourhood, our friends, our island, and my dream for our future. It is not me who will be moving away; it is the mother in me. If it was just me, I would find a way to stay. Instead, I as a mother, son at my side, will be moving on. I don't know what kind of birds will be singing to me while I work wherever we go. But it won't be parrots.

Notes on the Contributors

Holly Anderson (1955-2017) was a poet, artist, lyricist, Minnesota native, and frequent collaborator in a variety of creative disciplines. An active participant in downtown New York City experimental scenes starting in the early 80s, Anderson created interdisciplinary works with many other artists: she wrote texts for choreographers Bebe Miller, Kinematic and Wally Cardona, theater companies Dear Knows and Music Theater Group, and her lyrics were recorded by musicians including post-rock pioneers Mission of Burma and Consonant.

She also shared her creative practice as an Artist-in-Residence at Smith College, Colorado College, Bates College, the University of Illinois at Urbana-Champaign, the Catskill Center's Platte Clove Preserve, and NYU's Steinhardt School.

Anderson's limited edition books *Lily Lou* (Purgatory Pie Press) and *Sheherezade* (Pyramid Atlantic) are in library collections including MOMA, The Metropolitan Museum of Art, The Victoria & Albert Museum, The Brooklyn Museum, The Bennett Avant Writing Collection at Ohio State University, The Harry Ransom Center at UT, Austin and The Downtown Collection at Fales Library, NYU.

Her work has been anthologized in numerous publications, including *Up is Up, But So Is Down: New York's Downtown Literary Scene* (NYU Press), *Wreckage of Reason Il* (Spuyten(Duyvil), *The Unbearables* (Autonomedia), and *First Person Intense* (Bandana Press).

Anderson's most recent book is *The Night She Slept With A Bear* (Publication Studio).

Charlotte Beyer is a Senior Lecturer in English studies at the University of Gloucestershire, UK. She has published widely on crime fiction and contemporary literature. Her edited monograph *Teaching Crime Fiction* was published by Palgrave in 2018 as part of the Teaching the New English series. Her edited volume *Mothers Without Their Children* (with Andrea Robertson, Demeter Press) was published in

2019. Charlotte is currently editing the 2019 issue on feminism and motherhood in the twenty-first century for the journal *Feminist Encounters*, and is co-editing *Mothers Who Kill/Infanticide* with Josephine Savarese for Demeter Press. She is on the editorial boards for the journals *Feminist Encounters*, *The New Americanist*, and *American, British and Canadian Studies*. In 2016-17, she was a co-investigator on the AHRC/ESRC-funded PaCCS Interdisciplinary Innovation Award research project "Representation of transnational human trafficking in present-day news media, true crime, and fiction."

Angela Castañeda is Edward Myers Dolan Professor of Anthropology at DePauw University. Her current research interests include the cultural politics of reproduction, birth, and motherhood. Dr. Castañeda's most recent publication is *Doulas and Intimate Labour: Boundaries, Bodies and Birth* (Demeter Press, 2015). She is a practicing birth and postpartum doula, and she volunteers as a Spanish childbirth educator in Bloomington, Indiana.

C.M. Clark's poetry has appeared in the *Metonym Literary Journal*, *The Lindenwood Review*, *Dogwood Journal*, *Painted Bride Quarterly*, the *South Florida Poetry Journal*, and *Gulf Stream* magazine, A chapbook of her latest work—*The Five Snouts*—has been published by Finishing Line Press, following her full-length collection, *Dragonfly*. Clark was runner-up for the Slate Roof Press/Elyse Wolf Prize, and she was a finalist for the Rane Arroyo Chapbook Competition. She was inaugural poet-in-residence at the Deering Estate Artists Village in Miami, resulting in the collection, *Charles Deering Forecasts the Weather & Other Poems*. Clark is a freelance writer currently living in South Florida.

Cara Delay holds degrees from Boston College and Brandeis University. Her research analyzes women, gender, and culture in nineteenth- and twentieth-century Ireland, with a particular focus on the history of reproduction, pregnancy, and childbirth. She has published in *The Journal of British Studies*, *Lilith: A Feminist History Journal*, *Feminist Studies*, *Études Irlandaises*, *New Hibernia Review*, and *Éire-Ireland*, and has written blogs for *Nursing Clio* and *broadsheet.ie*. Her co-edited volume *Women, Reform, and Resistance in Ireland, 1850-1950*, was published with Palgrave Macmillan in 2015. At the College of Charleston, she teaches courses on the history of birth and bodies.

Melanie Duckworth teaches British and postcolonial literature at Østfold University College, Halden, Norway. She has a PhD from the University of Leeds, in which she examined representations of the European Middle Ages in twentieth-century Australian literature, particularly poetry. Her publications include "Grievous Music: Randolph Stow's Middle Ages" (*Australian Literary Studies*, 2011), and "'Travelling North Together'—the North, Whales, and Intercultural Communication in Kathleen Jamie's Essays and Poems," in *Travel and Intercultural Communication: Going North,* edited by Eva Lambertsson Björk and Jutta Eschenbach (2017). Her current research interests include contemporary poetry and the environment, temporality, and animals.

Laura Foley is the author of six poetry collections, including *WTF, Joy Street*, *Syringa*, and *Night Ringing*. Her poem "Gratitude List" won the Common Good Books poetry contest judged by Garrison Keillor; "Nine Ways of Looking at Light" won the Joe Gouveia Outermost Poetry Contest, judged by Marge Piercy. A palliative care volunteer and a mother of three grown children and two granddaughters, she lives with her wife and two dogs among the hills of Vermont. Please visit her at: laurafoley.net.

Jane Frank is a poet from southeast Queensland, Australia, and she teaches in humanities at Griffith University. Her chapbook *Milky Way of Words* was published by Ginninderra Press in 2016, and *Flotsam*—a collaborative work with Scottish poet Hugh McMillan—is forthcoming with Flarestack. Her poems have recently appeared in *Poetry Salzburg Review, The Frogmore Papers, London Grip, Popshot Magazine*, and *Pressure Gauge*. She likes her poetry to evoke forgotten histories, and here poems are often inspired by literal and figurative travel, the fantastic, or the odd angles of the everyday.

Anne Hamilton lives in Edinburgh, Scotland, with her young son. She is a writer, tutor, and editor of fiction and creative nonfiction, and the editor of online magazine, *Lothian Life*. Anne also has a PhD in creative writing. She has travelled extensively, and her travelogue *A Blonde Bengali Wife* supports the charity Bhola's Children. Anne is published in a number of journals and anthologies and has read at the Edinburgh International Book Festival. She is currently working on her second novel.

Vanessa Couto Johnson's third chapbook, *speech rinse*, won Slope Editions' 2016 Chapbook Contest. Her second chapbook is *rotoscoping collage in Cork City* (dancing girl press, 2016), and her first chapbook, *Life of Francis*, won Gambling the Aisle's 2014 Chapbook Contest. "Try the yen relish," a sixteen-page prose poem sequence, is forthcoming in a BoxSet from Oxidant | Engine. Her poems have appeared in *Softblow, Thrush, Field, Blackbird Qwerty, Cream City Review*, and other journals. A Brazilian born in Texas (dual citizen), she is currently a lecturer at Texas State University, where she earned her MFA.

May Joseph is the founder of Harmattan Theater, Inc., an environmental performance company in New York City. Joseph is the author of *Fluid New York: Cosmopolitan Urbanism and the Green Imagination* (Duke University Press 2013); *Nomadic Identities: The Performance of Citizenship* (Minnesota 1999), and co-editor of *Performing Hybridity* (Minnesota, 1999). Joseph's theater work explores islands and archipelagoes. Through performance, Joseph investigates the junctures between coastal communities and oceanic landscapes. Joseph teaches at the Pratt Institute. www.mayjoseph.com.

Maria Lombard is an assistant professor in residence at Northwestern University in Qatar. She teaches first year writing and travel literature. Her research focuses on the field of writing studies, with particular interests in second-language writing pedagogy, student motivation to write, minority and gendered voices, and travel writing. She also has a passion for teaching children's literature. She received her PhD from Purdue University in English, and she has a MA in literature and a BS in language arts education.

Li Miao Lovett stopped being a good Chinese daughter in her twenties. Nowadays, she's trying to be a good enough mom to her eleven-year-old. Her novel, *In the Lap of the Gods*, is a tale of love and loss set in China amid the rising waters of the Three Gorges dam. She has written about science and environmental issues for *KQED, San Francisco Chronicle*, and *PRI*. In fiction and nonfiction, Li's work has won awards or finalist standing from *Stanford Magazine, Glimmer Train, Writer's Digest*, Soul-Making Keats, Room of Her Own Foundation, and the James Jones First Novel Fellowship.

Katharyn Howd Machan, author of thirty-seven collections of poetry (most recently her *Selected Poems* from FutureCycle Press), has lived in Ithaca, New York, since 1975 and, now as a full professor, has taught writing at Ithaca College since 1977. After many years of coordinating the Ithaca Community Poets and directing the Feminist Women's Writing Workshops, Inc., she was selected to be Tompkins County's first poet laureate. Her poems have appeared in numerous magazines, anthologies, and textbooks, and she has edited three thematic anthologies.

Janet MacLennan, born on an island in the Atlantic, has made her way to an island of quite different climes—from Canada to the Caribbean—to make her home as a professor of communication, narrative researcher, and travellin' mama to a travellin' boy. Currently a full professor in the Linguistics and Communication Program of the Department of English at the University of Puerto Rico Río Piedras in San Juan, she graduated with her doctorate from Ohio University. This is the second book she is co-editing with Demeter Press.

Lynn Mastellotto is a transplanted Canadian who studied in the UK, lives in northern Italy, and is raising a son with transcultural tastes. She is an assistant professor of English language and translation in the Faculty of Education, University of Bolzano, where she does research on multilingualism, multiculturalism, and intercultural communication. She is interested in the way complex identities emerge when people and ideas cross national, cultural, linguistic, and disciplinary boundaries.

Dena Moes is a Hollywood-born, Yale-educated midwife. She found her husband Adam under a tree in a California forest in 1996, and they have been together ever since. Adam and Dena share two daughters, two businesses, and a love of adventure. Dena ran a homebirth midwifery service in Chico, California, for years. Her family left town each summer to travel but always came home before school started. Then in 2014, they shuttered their house and backpacked through India and Nepal for a year, preteen daughters in tow. Information about Dena's memoir The Buddha Sat Right Here can be found at www.denamoes.com

Monica Reyes is a wife, mother, educator, and scholar. She currently lectures in the Writing and Language Studies Department at The University of Texas, Rio Grande Valley. She is also a PhD student with Old Dominion University's English Studies program in Norfolk, VA. Her research interests include literary and cultural rhetorics of travel, postcolonialism, refugee studies, and geopolitics. Her work on travel writing has been featured in *Watchung Review* (2017), *Coldnoon: Travel Poetics* (2015), and *The Journal of South Texas English Studies* (2013).

Karem Roitman holds a DPhil in development studies from Oxford University, and has lectured on politics, gender, race, development and Latin America in Oxford University, Regents University, and the Open University. She has also worked as a development consultant with clients, including DFID and the UN. Karem lives in the UK with her husband and children. She was born in Ecuador, immigrated with her parents to the USA, and is the granddaughter of a refugee.

Dorsía Smith Silva is an associate professor of English at the University of Puerto Rico, Río Piedras in the Faculty of General Studies. She is the co-editor of *Caribbean without Borders: Caribbean Literature, Language, and Culture* (2008), *Critical Perspectives on Caribbean Literature and Culture* (2010), *Critical and Feminist Perspectives on Caribbean Mothering* (2013), *Mothers and Daughters* (2017), and *Mothers, Mothering, and Globalization* (2017), and she is editor of *Latina/Chicana Mothering* (2011). She is currently co-editing *Mothering, Community, and Friendship*. In addition, her poetry has appeared in *Adanna*, *POUI*, and *Nourish*.

Marjorie Tesser is the author of two poetry chapbooks *THE IMPORTANT THING IS* (Firewheel Award Winner) and *The Magic Feather*. Her poems and short fiction have appeared in *Drunken Boat*, Akashic Press' *Thursdaze*, *Earth's Daughter*, *The Saturday Evening Post*, and others. She co-edited the anthologies *Bowery Women: Poems*, and *Estamos Aqui: Poems of Migrant Farmworkers* for Bowery Books, and she is the editor-in-chief of *Mom Egg Review*.

Nicola Waldron is a native of England and graduate of Cambridge University and the Bennington Writing Seminars. Her work has been featured in *Agni*, *Sonora Review*, *The Common*, and *Los Angeles Review of Books*, among many others. She is the recipient of Britain's Bridport Prize for poetry and the Broad River Prize for prose, and is author of *Girl at the Watershed*, a poetry chapbook. Nicola currently teaches at the

University of South Carolina in Columbia, where she lives in a state between presence and perpetual longing, halfway between the mountains and the sea.

Kimmika Williams-Witherspoon, PhD (cultural anthropology), MA (anthropology), MFA (theatre), graduate certificate (women's studies), BA (journalism), is an associate professor of urban theatre and community engagement in the theatre department at Temple University. The author of *Through Smiles and Tears: The History of African American Theater (From Kemet to the Americas)* (Lambert Academic Publishing 2011) and *The Secret Messages in African American Theater: Hidden Meaning Embedded in Public Discourse* (Edwin Mellen Publishing 2006), Williams-Witherspoon has had over twenty-nine plays produced, and she has performed poetry in over ninety-three national and international venues.

Deepest appreciation to
Demeter's monthly Donors

DEMETER

Daughters
Muna Saleh
Rebecca Bromwich
Summer Cunningham
Tatjana Takseva
Kerri Kearney
Debbie Byrd
Laurie Kruk
Fionna Green
Tanya Cassidy
Vicki Noble

Sisters
Kirsten Goa
Amber Kinser
Nicole Willey
Regina Edwards